DATE DU

Diego Garcia

Diego Garcia

Creation of the Indian Ocean Base

Vytautas B. Bandjunis

Writer's Showcase
San Jose New York Lincoln Shanghai

Diego Garcia
Creation of the Indian Ocean Base

Writer's Showcase
an imprint of iUniverse.com, Inc.

For information address:
iUniverse.com, Inc.
5220 S 16th, Ste. 200
Lincoln, NE 68512
www.iuniverse.com

ISBN: 0-595-14406-3

Printed in the United States of America

Diego Garcia

Creation of the Indian Ocean Base

Vytautas B. Bandjunis

Writer's Showcase
San Jose New York Lincoln Shanghai

Diego Garcia
Creation of the Indian Ocean Base

Writer's Showcase
an imprint of iUniverse.com, Inc.

For information address:
iUniverse.com, Inc.
5220 S 16th, Ste. 200
Lincoln, NE 68512
www.iuniverse.com

ISBN: 0-595-14406-3

Printed in the United States of America

Dedication

There were so many people who fought for and against the establishment of a United States military presence in the Indian Ocean Area that a list would be endless. This history is dedicated to both sides.

Contents

List of Illustrations

Figure

List of Tables

Foreword

The early 1970s were a time of change in the waters and littorals of the Indian Ocean. British presence East of Suez was being withdrawn; India was leading efforts to establish a Zone of Peace; former colonies such as Mauritius were gaining status as independent nations; and the U.S. was caught in a dilemma of presence, dependence on Middle East oil, and a reluctance to expand naval commitments into a new area of interest. Strategically located almost at the center of the Indian Ocean, the remote atoll of Diego Garcia became a focal point of U.S. efforts to establish a needed presence effectively and unobtrusively.

My first direct contact with Diego Garcia was in the summer of 1975, as commander of a surface force task group making one of a series of periodic swings through the Indian Ocean to show building U.S. interest in the area. Leaving Singapore, our flagship, a cruiser, suffered a bearing casualty, disabling one shaft at the beginning of a tightly scheduled six weeks of operations and port visits. With no spare on board, we were faced with a decision to return to Singapore for repairs or to proceed, repairing the shaft after taking delivery of a new bearing at the first possible stop. Our initial destination was a visit to Mauritius, about 3,000 miles across the Indian Ocean. The decision was made to continue our plan, but divert enroute Mauritius to the vicinity of Latitude 7° 12' South, Longitude 72° 27' East, to receive the replacement bearing. No mention was made in our messages that we were to lie offshore from Diego Garcia for delivery of a bearing that had been flown in to the airstrip recently constructed there by the U.S. Navy. The part was delivered by boat, repairs made, and our operations completed on schedule. The reasons for the anonymity of our pit stop are a story of sensitive diplomatic and Congressional negotiations so well covered in Van Bandjunis' book.

To tens of thousands of sailors, Seabees, airmen and merchant mariners, Diego Garcia has become a modern embodiment, on a less grand scale, of forward bases such as Ulithi in World War II; it can even relate to the island plantation (though now abandoned) romanticized by James Michener in *Tales of the South Pacific.* Our activity on the island began in the 1970s with the communications station and an airstrip and expanded greatly through the 1980s to the point that Diego Garcia was a major contributing factor to success in Desert Shield/Desert Storm. The airfield and harbor facilities were built up to stage the lengthy supply line from the Pacific to our task forces in the Arabian Sea and Persian Gulf. Repair ships anchored in the lagoon provide maintenance to ships of all types in the harbor and support to facilities and aircraft ashore. The original Near Term Prepostioning Force performed as planned in rapidly delivering war equipment and supplies to the Desert Shield buildup and has become the model for Maritime Preposition Squadrons now ready in the Atlantic, Pacific and Mediterranean as well as the Indian Ocean. During Desert Storm, B-52s flew bombing sorties from Diego Garcia into the heart of Iraq.

Our support facility and operations at Diego Garcia are a testimony to the "Can Do" tradition of the Seabees and to the dedication of the men and women who serve today a year's unaccompanied tour on the isolated "Footprint of Freedom." *Diego Garcia* is the underlying story of foreign policy, diplomacy, military strategy, requirements development, planning, budgeting and Congressional action that made it possible. The book serves as a clear example of

the sometimes years of complex efforts needed to move from strategic concept to operational reality.

Donald P. Roane
Rear Admiral, Retired
U.S. Navy

Preface

When I went to work for the Bureau of Yards and Docks in July 1964, in their temporary World War II building next to the Arlington National Cemetery, I assigned as the Navy project manager for construction of a new naval base in the middle of the Indian Ocean. I followed the development of the base even after I left the Bureau of Yards and Docks, renamed the Naval Facilities Engineering Command in 1966, in 1968 to accept a position in the Office of Secretary of Defense, overseeing military construction programs. I had a unique opportunity interacting with many action officers involved in planning and programming the new naval base, and watched most of the events unfold that lead inexorably to development and construction of the base.

A Navy base on Diego Garcia was a military objective that appeared to pit those planners in the United States Navy who believed the United States should have a naval presence in the Indian Ocean against initial opposition within the Navy itself by those who feared the additional mission would dilute the already stretched naval resources, and also opposition in the Office of the Secretary of Defense, the National Security Council, the White House, and in Congress, and in littoral countries bordering the Indian Ocean, who had declared the Indian Ocean a Zone of Peace.

The Indian Ocean advocates within Navy persevered. Event after event had unfolded, each served to strengthen the need for Diego Garcia. First there was a communications gap in the middle of the Indian Ocean, then the need to counter Chinese Communists and later

Russian Communists interest in the area, then the military and political power vacuum created by the withdrawal of the British east of Suez, always a concern about freedom of the seas, the ever present dependence on the unimpeded flow of oil by Western nations, the fall of the Shah of Iran that caused the United States to change its strategy because Iran could no longer provide the security buffer sought by the United States, the Soviet invasion of Afghanistan, the possibility of Soviet invasion of Iran, and a series of regional conflicts and unrest in Southeast and Southwest Asia.

The establishment of a logistics base in the Indian Ocean precipitated considerable national and international debates regarding United States interests and policies in this vital region of the world. How Diego Garcia became a linchpin of United States strategy in the Indian Ocean illustrates the complexities and difficulties that a democracy faces whenever it addresses national security issues.

Acknowledgments

This history could not have been done without the generous contributions by people intimately involved in developing a Naval Base at Diego Garcia. Special thanks to Stuart Barber, Admiral Moorer, and Ambassador Komer who provided the background and reasons for developing a naval presence in the Indian Ocean. Thanks to Frank McGuire, who helped shaped the facilities needed, and for sharing his personal experiences during the 1964 Joint survey of Diego Garcia. I need to thank Peter Wrike, a friend and historian, who encouraged me to pick up a rough manuscript and shape it into a presentable document.

1

How Diego Garcia Began

United States Navy operational commanders long viewed the Indian Ocean as an important, but neglected region between the Atlantic and Pacific Oceans. An increased American naval presence in the Indian Ocean was advocated by several senior naval officers including the commanders of the Pacific and Atlantic fleets in the 1950's. Shifting their naval assets through one of five major chock points in the Indian Ocean and between the two major fleet commands entailed long logistic lines and uncertain communications. Once, the nuclear carrier *Enterprise* (CVAN-65) and two nuclear cruisers suffered a total communications blackout for eight to 12 hours while transiting across the Indian Ocean. These communication blackouts in the Indian Ocean and South China Sea were common and troubling. As the British slowly reduced their naval presence in the Indian Ocean area, American warships traversing the area had increased difficulty finding British refueling tankers.

In early 1954, Chief of Naval Operations Admiral Robert B. Carney established an ad hoc committee to study and develop a long range shipbuilding program. This committee after, a period of study, recommended among other things that the Navy establish a permanent group for long range analysis of not only ship building, but other Navy future needs, such as aircraft, research and development, and bases. The Long

Range Objectives Group, designated within Navy as OP-93, was established in the 1955 to early 1956 period. The group was initially headed by Admiral C.D. Griffin and staffed with five or six naval officers and one civilian, Stuart B. Barber, who would provide continuity as membership of the group changed by normal military rotation. In the summer of 1957, Admiral Jerauld Wright, the Navy's Commander in Chief of the Atlantic Forces and Atlantic Fleet, was flown by Marine pilot David Rickabaugh to the British airfield at Trincomalee, Ceylon, where Admiral Wright boarded a United States Navy vessel, and departed from there to Diego Garcia to inspect the island for future use.

Admiral Roy L. Johnson, who followed Admiral Griffin as Director of the Long Range Objectives Group, credited Stuart Barber as the first person to come up with ideas about Diego Garcia.[1] Barber's basic idea was that the United States, in anticipation of the independence of colonial territories, should acquire base rights in certain strategically located islands, mostly in the southern hemisphere, and stockpile them for future use as potential refueling stations, air patrol bases, and communication sites. Those remote colonial islands with small populations would be the easiest to acquire, and would entail the least political headaches. Barber searched atlases and charts, and began building a list of possible candidates including the Chagos Archipelago, Desroches, Cocos, Phuket, and Masirah in the Indian Ocean area; and many in other oceans. His prime candidate was Diego Garcia, in the Chagos Archipelago.

In May 1960, Director of the Long Range Objectives Group Admiral Horacio Rivero proposed that the British be asked to detach Diego Garcia and other islands from Mauritius, before Mauritius became independent, as a British strategic territory, and that the United States secure rights to use the islands for future naval facilities. Admiral Arleigh A. Burke, the Chief of Naval Operations liked the idea and informally explored the concept with his British counterpart. There was some interest in the proposal, but also some reluctance. Until the United States made a formal proposal, little more could be done. Within the United States Navy, Strategic Plans (OP-60) did not certify any Navy requirements in the Indian Ocean while the British had available bases in the region. While Navy civil engineers were directed to start base development studies for 50 to 60 strategic islands as future refueling and replenishment, and staging bases, the "Strategic Island" concept languished within the Navy.

Admiral Thomas H. Moorer followed Admiral Rivero as Director of the Long Range Objectives Group in 1961. During this period Moorer was often diverted from long range planning to responding to issues originating from the systems analysis team that came to the Pentagon when Robert McNamara became Secretary of Defense. The survey of strategic islands was completed in 1961, and Moorer saw the merit of stock piling base rights and the immediate need for an advanced navy facility in the Indian Ocean. Admiral Burke approved Moorer's proposal to move ahead with the Diego Garcia part of the Strategic Island concept.

Moorer took the plan to the Joint Chiefs in 1962 and got their approval over initial Air Force reluctance, and then went to see Paul H. Nitze, the Assistant Secretary of Defense for International Security Affairs. Secretary Nitze concurred in proceeding with the concept, and initiated formal diplomatic discussions through his liaison officer in the State Department, Jeffrey C. Kitchen, Assistant Secretary of State for Political-Military Affairs, toward the establishment of a British Indian Ocean territory that would include United States base rights in all the Chagos Archipelago, which included Diego Garcia and Salomon, Aldabra that could be developed into an air staging base, Farquhar that the RAF had shown some interest, and Desroches. The Diego Garcia idea became one of the most valuable contributions made by the Long Range Objectives Group, and many of its directors, Admirals Johnson,

Rivero and Moorer kept the Indian Ocean base idea alive as they moved up in the Navy's command structure.

In October 1962, because of worldwide communications inadequacies brought to light during the Cuban missile crisis, President John F. Kennedy established a special subcommittee on communications, chaired by Mr. William H. Orrick, Jr., then Deputy Under Secretary of State for Administration, to provide an urgent solution to the critical national communication system problems worldwide. One of the significant results of the Orrick Committee deliberations was the affirmation of the need for an Indian Ocean gateway station to fill the communications gap in the area south and east of Suez for maritime operations. In the Defense Communication Agency Mid-Range Plan of 1962, the Navy was tasked to provide such a station. Project "KATHY" was the code name given to establishment of a communications station on Diego Garcia that would remedy the communication blackout problem. Other communication base locations studied were Turkey, Greece, Asmara; all under code names using girls' names, like KATHY, and JUDY.

Robert W. Komer, the White House Middle East and South Asia Planner on the National Security Staff, on 19 June 1963, recommended in a short and independently drafted memorandum to President Kennedy that because the United States had growing interests in the Indian Ocean area, and would grow bigger since the British were planning to pull out of their bases east of the Suez, the United States should propose to the British that if they acquire an appropriate island in the Indian Ocean, the United States would build on it a base that would be for joint use. President Kennedy thought the proposal sounded good, approved the proposal, and instructed Komer to tell Secretary of Defense McNamara to carry out the plan. McNamara sent Komer to discuss the President's approved plan with the Navy, who had been interested in the Indian Ocean area for a long time. Komer met with

Claude Ricketts, the Vice Chief of Naval Operations to set the President's plan into action.

Late in 1963, President Kennedy conceived a plan to extend the operations of the Pacific Seventh Fleet into the Indian Ocean to serve as a deterrent to any expansionist moves by Communist China. A naval base in the Indian Ocean would be needed to support the fleet operations. A joint United States and United Kingdom survey team was sent in July 1964 to inspect islands in the Indian Ocean that could be potential operating bases. The Americans were more interested in naval communications facilities, while the British were looking for air staging bases, similar to those at Aden and Gan.

Diego Garcia

Diego Garcia, named after the Portuguese explorer who discovered the island, is a flat coral atoll located within the Chagos Archipelago in the center of the Indian Ocean. The heavily vegetated island consists of 6,700 acres with average elevation of three to 7 feet, some of which is low and swampy. The highest elevation is only 22 feet above sea level. The island, shaped like a wishbone, is about 40 miles in perimeter. Three islets are located at the northern opened end; West Island, Middle Island, and East Island. Between the islets are two channels that allow entry into the lagoon. The enclosed lagoon is five and one-half miles wide by thirteen miles long with average depths of 30 to 100 feet. The width of the island surrounding the lagoon varies between 300 and 7,200 feet. Around the ocean side of the island is a coral-sand berm.

Diego Garcia lies 7 degrees south of the equator, and is outside the cyclone belt. Incessant winds and high average temperature of 85 degrees Fahrenheit, high average humidity of 75 to 90 percent, and 104 inches of rainfall per year combines with salt spray and coral dust to produce harsh living conditions.

In the 1780s, a French company began extracting coconut oil from the palms, and the population, including slaves and a small leper colony, numbered 275. With the defeat of Napoleon, Diego Garcia passed from French to British sovereignty in 1814. By the turn of the century, Diego Garcia boasted three flourishing copra factories, a less successful coaling station for ships on the Australia run, a church, a hospital, a jail, a light railway, some handsome French colonial style houses, and more than 500 inhabitants.

During World War II the Royal Air Force used Diego Garcia as a radio station, a PBY Catalina flying boat base, and by the Royal Navy as an anchorage. A garrison of Indian troops was also established. They manned huge guns located on the northern side of the island. Diego Garcia attracted few visitors. A boat occasionally called from Mauritius with supplies. A weather station reported by radio to Port Louis, the islanders' only contact with the outside world. The main source of income for the islanders was copra oil. There was little meat on the island, but there was an abundance of fish in the lagoon and the deep waters beyond the reef. Justice was administered by family councils, but a magistrate called from Mauritius once a year.

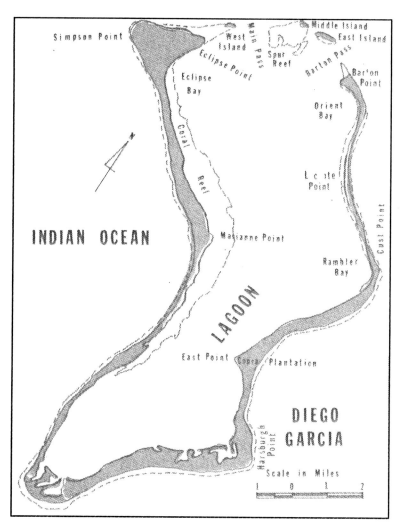

FIGURE 1 Map of Diego Garcia

Animal life on the island is limited to lizards, chameleons, and insects. There is only one bird species, a brilliant scarlet-chested cardinal. On some parts of the island there is an infestation of land crabs, a foot or more across with long, hairy legs and eyes on the ends of stalks. The wild but protected donkeys, as well as domesticated chickens and cats on the island are descended from the animals brought in by plantation owners.

The population of the three inhabitable islands in the Chagos Archipelago, Diego Garcia, Peros Banhos, and Solomon, was approximately 1,000 in 1964. About 640 were considered Mauritian and some 360 Seychellois. On all three islands, the sole economic activity was the production of copra and other coconut products at plantations owned since 1962 by the Chagos Agalega Company, headed by Paul Moulinie of Mahe, in the Seychelles. On Diego Garcia, out of a population of 483, all but seven persons were engaged in work on the coconut plantations, or were dependents. The exceptions were six officials of the Mauritius Government meteorological station, and one unemployed.

The 204 male workers on the plantations were under contract for two years at a time, if married, and for eighteen months, if they were bachelors, for which they were paid $3 to $4 a month, plus housing and rations. On Peros Banhos and Solomon, the entire population of 291 and 219 were dependent on coconut plantations, except for two unemployed persons on Peros Banhos. In 1964, perhaps 42 men and 38 women, with 154 children, out of the total population of Diego Garcia might be considered to be Ilois (French for native born islanders) of whom, no more than three men and seventeen women could be regarded as having their permanent homes on the island.

Navy Seeks Role in Indian Ocean

The United States Government sounded out the Indian Government on the possibility of extending the operational jurisdiction of the United States Seventh Fleet from the China Sea to the Indian Ocean. The purpose of the plan, which was said to have been conceived by President Kennedy, was to serve as a deterrent force against any expansionist moves by Communist China. President Kennedy did not live to see his plan carried out because of his assassination on 22 November 1963. General Maxwell D. Taylor, Chairman of the United States Joint Chiefs of Staff, visited the area and met with Prime Minister Jawaharlal Nehru, Defense Minister Y.B. Chavan and other military leaders.[2]

Nitze Suggests Bases

Paul H. Nitze left his position as Assistant Secretary of Defense to become Secretary of the Navy in November 1963. Secretary of the Navy said on 9 January 1964 there was a "power vacuum" in the Indian Ocean area, and suggested that the Navy might seek bases in that part of the world. "Today we have the challenge of determining whether it is feasible and possible to acquire base rights to support permanent or temporary deployment in that area," Secretary Nitze said in a speech to naval and marine officers stationed in the Washington area. General Maxwell D. Taylor had discussed the base prospects with representatives of India and Pakistan in December, but he received a cool reception. The United States, nevertheless, sent a small task group, an aircraft carrier, two or three destroyers and a tanker into the Indian Ocean during April 1964.

First Communications Project

The fiscal year 1964 Military Construction Bill submitted to Congress in early 1963 included a classified communications project at an estimated cost of $5,000,000. The project consisted of procurement and erection of prefabricated buildings on concrete footings and slabs, concrete hardstands for communication vans, concrete foundations for antennas and guy anchors and utilities including communication lines and security features. The justification for the project was to fill a requirement for reliable, high capacity, secure communications established by the Defense Communication Agency for the Indian Ocean

Area based on a determination by the President's Committee on National Communications to be essential for improvement to the Defense Communications System.

According to former State Department intelligence officer John Marks, the Central Intelligence Agency was an enthusiastic supporter in the mid-1960s of a permanent United States presence somewhere in the Indian Ocean since it was assumed that when China tested an Intercontinental Ballistic Missile, it would do so in that area.[3]

The project was disapproved by Congress.[4] The Chairman of the Senate Armed Services Committee, Senator Richard B. Russell, made the reduction because the committee did not feel planning was sufficiently advanced to allow construction of the project in the near future.

Secret Talks Revealed

Unpublicized high-level discussions were going on, mostly in London, between State Department and Pentagon representatives, and the British Ministry of Defense and Colonial and Commonwealth Offices in 1963. In spite of tight security arrangements, the nature of the talks leaked out in London in August 1964.[5] The Diego Garcia story, which the United States and Britain were jointly exploring the possibility of a series of island bases in the Indian Ocean to reinforce security in South and Southeast Asia, was on the front page of Washington's major newspaper, but the story went largely unnoticed. Robert McCloskey for the United States State Department said on 31 August 1964 that the proposed radio station would "provide improved circuitry between the Middle East, Southeast Asia, and the Far East."

In the fall of 1964, the United States was deeply involved in the Vietnam War. On 4 August 1964, the United States destroyer, the *U.S. Maddox*, was reported as being attacked. This action lead to the Tonkin Gulf Resolution. President Lyndon B. Johnson was also planning to run for the Presidency of the United States in his own right in November. Senator Hubert H. Humphrey was selected as Johnson's running mate. Senator Barry Goldwater was the Republican candidate for the Presidency. The election on 4 November 1964 was a record landslide for Johnson. He won 62 percent of the popular vote. The Navy's planning for the Indian Ocean bases was ignored and forgotten by the Congress.

The discussions between the Americans and British included the construction of an American naval communications facility on Diego Garcia, which was then a dependency of the self governing Colony of Mauritius; and a British airstrip in the Aldabra Islands, which were then a dependency of the Seychelles. Other islands in the Indian Ocean were considered as potential air and sea bases and as staging areas for the air-lift of troops. Island bases, without native populations, had long been a planning objective of some United States Navy strategists because of the political turmoil affecting base rights. Building on uninhabited islands would involve fewer political liabilities. The State Department had strongly supported American presence in the Indian Ocean as a political stabilizer. Secretary of Defense Robert S. McNamara supported a small scale undertaking, but was reluctant to enter any arrangement that might be used as an argument for an American Indian Ocean Fleet or detract from the primary British responsibility in the area.

1964 Site Survey

The 1964 site survey on Diego Garcia, a joint British-United States effort, was made in July and August. The survey team's departure was delayed for about two weeks because of the sudden death of Vice Chief of Naval Operations Admiral Claude V. Ricketts. Admiral Ricketts had been a strong advocate of a multilateral nuclear strike force in the Atlantic Alliance, and an advocate for a naval facility on Diego Garcia.

The American team left Andrews Air Force Base on 13 July 1964 headed to Mildenhall on an Air Force Hercules C-130 cargo aircraft, loaded with supplies and camping gear. The team included Commander Harry S. Hart, head of the American contingent and from the Office of the Chief of Naval Operations; Lieutenant Oreland R. Carden, Civil Engineer Corps; Major Herbert J. Gall, USAF; Communications Petty Officers Richard M. Young, ETCM, and M.J. Mesiji, RMC; Mr. Vance Vaughan, a communications systems command representative from the Navy's Communication Annex on Nebraska Avenue in Washington, Mr. R.L. Clinkenbeard, a civilian communications engineer in the Yards and Docks Chesapeake Division; and Mr. Francis D. McGuire, from the Bureau of Yards and Docks Planning Division.

The American survey team switched to a Navy Hercules C-130 cargo aircraft at Mildenhall, and added more members of the survey team. They were joined on 16 July by Commander David M. Feinman, Civil Engineer Corps, from the Commander in Chief, United States European Naval Forces Headquarters Command in London; Mr. W.P. Dayton and Mr. G.N. Marks, both contract civilian engineers from the GEEIA Air Force unit in Germany; Mr. A. Kravis, a British communications technician from Marconi; Mr. M. Pollock, a British fuel storage technician; and Mr. R. Newton, the liaison officer, from the British Colonial Office. (See Figure 4)

The joint survey team flew to Naples, and then to Aden. At Aden the team switched to a Britannia RAF transport, and flew to the British base at Gan. At Gan, the team switched their gear and provisions, and boarded the British hydrographic ship *H.M.S. Dampier* for the final leg of the trip to Diego Garcia.

The survey team found a couple of mementoes of World War II on Diego Garcia. A coast artillery gun was set up to drive away the German raiders that attacked merchant ships in the Indian Ocean. The massive concrete foundation laid hidden in heavy growth on

Eclipse Point. Disguised as commercial ships, the German raiders had concealed guns behind fake sides. Australians visited Diego Garcia in PBYs during World War II. One of the flying boats developed engine trouble, and was abandoned on East Point, where it was seen by the American and British survey team. During World War II, the United States Army Corps of Engineers surveyed Diego Garcia, and even planned to build a 4,000-foot runway on Eclipse Point. The field was never built. The Russian were more recent visitors to the island, and left some Russian beer cans and bottles. The oldest structure the survey team found was the foundation of an abandoned church on Marianne Point dated 1868.

One of the first things done by the survey group was to test communications from Diego Garcia. Lieutenant Carden, and Petty Officers Young and Mesiji set up a 25 watt skid mounted generator, and using a 20-foot dipole antenna began sending out the code name WOLF WOMAN to any American ships that could pick up the signal. The Navy had assigned the code name and disseminated the code to all its ships. They were to respond to its transmission. A Navy ship in the Philippine Sea picked up the call signals, and belatedly responded, "Oh yeah!" The test confirmed the Navy's expectation of good communications, and was considered a success. Additional communications transmission, receiving and interference tests were conducted along with ground conductivity determinations.

Because the triangulation points set in the early 1900s could not be found, the surveyors on the *H.M.S. Dampier* reset the points so that picture points for a later aerial photographic survey of the entire island could be made. The *H.M.S. Dampier* also made additional sounding in the planned harbor area. The survey team also located the best source of aggregate for future construction in a large coral outcropping offshore on the west side of the island.

After completing the Diego Garcia survey, the team returned to Gan on the *H.M.S. Dampier*. Communications experts, Lieutenant Oreland

R. Carden, and Mr. Vance Vaughan left the ship to return to Washington. The survey team picked up two more members at Gan; Mr. Alex McLaren, a British airfield planning and construction expert; and RAF Wing Commander Graves. The *H.M.S.Dampier* departed Gan, and began a survey of other potential staging bases. They visited the Agalega Islands, Coetivy, Desroches, Farquhar, refueled in Diego-Suarez (Antsiranana) on the northern tip of Madagascar, back to Port Victoria in Mahe, and finally back to Gan. The team boarded a Comet IV C for its return flight, passing by and avoiding Nasser's Corner, and stopping at El Adem, Libya, and back to London.

After the survey team returned to Washington, the Air Force became interested in Diego Garcia. They wanted to use the base for B-52 operations, but because of the additional length, width, and thickness of the runways, the Navy did not want to absorb the increased costs. Besides the additional cost was a political problem and perception that B-52 bombers brought nuclear capabilities. India's strong opposition could not be ignored. No one in the White House wanted to be the first to introduce nuclear weapons into the region.

In the fall of 1964, when the Department of Navy submitted its Program Change Proposal for the fiscal year 1965 budget, the communications project at Diego Garcia was deleted by the Secretary of Defense Robert S. McNamara because of gold flow considerations.

After the survey team returned to Washington, Francis McGuire briefed Vice Chief of Naval Operations Admiral Rivero about the trip, and particularly about plans for Diego Garcia. Some members of the Chief of Naval Operations staff at the briefing were not enamored with Diego Garcia, but Admiral Rivero was. He said, "I want this island!", and he turned to one of his staff and told them to write a letter to the British, using whatever words or justification that were necessary.

British Indian Ocean Territory

Because of the British Commonwealth's island colonies trend toward independence, the demands for closure of the Aden Base, and Britain's intended withdrawal from Singapore, the United States urged Britain to think of new locations for British bases. In April 1965, the Colonial Secretary, Anthony Greenwood, traveled to Mauritius for independence talks at which the hiving off of some smaller islands, especially the Chagos group, was discussed. At the constitutional convention on Mauritius in London, in September 1965, it was agreed that defense talks should be held between the British Government and the Mauritius Government led by Sir Seewoosagur Ramgoolam. The British offered three million pounds, about $8.4 million, for Diego Garcia for a future American communications base and a British fueling facility. The Mauritian Cabinet split over the offer, and stated the offer was inadequate. "We will not accept an Anglo-American Base if America and Britain are not ready to buy all our sugar at a preferential price and accept Mauritian immigrants." But in March 1966, the three million pound payment to the Government of Mauritius as compensation for the taking certain islands that formed the British Indian Ocean Territory was laid before Parliament.

The Government of Mauritius informed the non-Seychellois workers on the Chagos islands in 1965, that with detachment of those islands from Mauritius to form the British Indian Ocean Territory, the workers there should seek employment elsewhere. A number of workers on the islands recruited on Mauritius consequently decided against renewing their contracts. Those working in the Chagos islands declined from more than 1,000 in 1964 to 839 by 1971.

In November 1965, the British Government announced the establishment of a new colony, the British Indian Ocean Territory, which was to be available for British and United States defense purposes.

Negotiations for the purchase of the British Indian Ocean Territory real estate from Mauritius, and the Seychelles were in progress early 1967.[6] The total population of 1,500 was mostly Creoles of Mauritian and Seychelles extraction.

Mauritius leased the Chagos Archipelago for $7,200,000. The deal was part of the terms for Mauritian independence. Aldabra, Farquhar and Desroches, dependencies of the Seychelles received $2,400,000, and a step forward to independence. The territory was administrated from the Seychelles by Commissioner Sir Bruce Greatbach, who was also Governor of the Seychelles.

Fiscal Year 1967 Project Deferred

The Indian Ocean project at Diego Garcia was estimated to cost $17,800,000 for construction and consisted of an airfield strip, aircraft support facilities, troop landing ship ramps, and other general support, plus a communications complex. Since submission in March 1965, the Navy recommended elimination of all but the communications complex at an estimated cost of $5,000,000 for military construction and asked that the project be included in the fiscal year 1967 budget. During the budget review, the Defense Communications Agency recommended the following three alternatives be presented to the Secretary of Defense:

1. Approve at original estimate for Fiscal Year 1967 budget.
2. Approve at reduced level for Fiscal Year 1967.
3. Approve at reduced level but defer to Fiscal Year 1968.

The Deputy Assistant Secretary of Defense for Installations and Logistics Telecommunications Policy Review Panel recommended that the Secretary of Defense McNamara approve the third alternative because "diplomatic negotiations have not been concluded." The Secretary of Defense decided to defer the project to a subsequent fiscal year.

In 1966, the Navy dropped the code name "KATHY" for the austere communications station at Diego Garcia, and began using the code name "REST STOP" when the mission evolved into a significant naval support facility. Project "REST STOP" began with an urgent telephone call from the Shore Facilities Programming Division in the Chief of Naval Operations Office in the winter of 1965. The Navy base planners in the Bureau of Yards and Docks were given one day to price out a complete naval facility at Diego Garcia. Two of the planners, Francis McGuire and Charles Laedlein, came up with a $50,000,000 estimate, which was slightly modified by Navy programmers, and then forwarded to Secretary of Navy Nitze.

On 4 February 1966, the Secretary of the Navy Nitze, forwarded a memorandum to Secretary of Defense, Robert S. McNamara, describing a proposed $45,000,000 Fleet Support Activity for Diego Garcia. The Secretary of the Navy Nitze estimated that engineering planning would cost approximately $1,000,000, which he proposed to obtain from the fiscal year 1967 Military Construction Appropriation. The Secretary of the Navy also proposed including the first increment of construction in the fiscal year 1968 program, and requested approval of the overall concept.

To support the request, the Navy reasoned that their commitments in the Western Pacific required movement of carriers and support forces through the Indian Ocean, and that political factors were restricting access to the littoral countries for bunkering. The Navy cited communications problems in the mid Indian Ocean area that were not covered by the existing communications facilities at Asmera, Ethiopia, or the Philippines station. Finally, the Navy noted the United Kingdom's review of its role east of Suez, and that it was therefore evident that the United States will have to increase its military presence in the Indian

Ocean littoral to maintain stability and to compensate for reduction of British power in the area.

The Navy proposed the island of Diego Garcia as the site of the fleet support activity. The United Kingdom had recently grouped the Chagos Archipelago and several other islands into the British Indian Ocean Territory to reserve them for future, joint United States-United Kingdom defense use, which would be invulnerable to political attack. The Navy was negotiating with the United Kingdom on terms of access and use of the islands. As part of the agreement, the United Kingdom would undertake to compensate and move the population of those island areas where construction of defense facilities was to take place. For Diego Garcia, this involved about 400 people, mostly contracted nonresident personnel working the coconut plantations.

The proposed naval support facility would include a POL (Petroleum, Oil, Lubricant) storage capacity of 655,000 barrels, mostly NSFO; a deep water anchorage for one attack carrier task group, an air strip for logistics support, an austere communications facility, and a base to support approximately 250 men. The Navy estimate of $45,000,000 was based on an area cost factor of 2.5, as compared to 1.0 for the Washington, D.C. area. The facility could be operational in three years, but would take four years to complete all construction.

The Assistant Secretary of Defense for International Security Affairs, John T. McNaughton met with the Secretary of the Navy Nitze a week after receipt of the 4 February memorandum, and on 19 February 1966, sent the Department of Defense response to the Secretary of the Navy Nitze. McNaughton's memorandum confirmed that "it appeared prudent and necessary to continue in-house studies toward development of engineering plans for construction of logistic support facilities to serve United States interests in the Indian Ocean area." Advance planning would be timely in the sense that current United States-United Kingdom discussions on the United Kingdom Defense Review are expected to raise questions on future plans for development and use of British Indian Ocean Island Territory.

United States and United Kingdom interests in the Indian Ocean Islands were also affected by the planned United Kingdom's withdrawal from Aden by 1968, and the British estimated that Singapore will become untenable once the Indonesian/Malaysian confrontation has ended. United States Navy studies were to be done on a no foreign disclosure/sensitive basis since negotiations toward obtaining a British commitment to maintain United Kingdom presence in the area, and to maintain and operate the Indian Ocean facilities would be prejudiced if the British got the impression that the United States was willing to expand its military role and influence in the area.

On 23 February 1966, Britain announced that it would reduce overseas forces by a third in the next four years, but would continue to play a military role east of Suez. The Aden base, the last remaining large British military presence in the Middle East was to be abandoned in 1968. British Defense Secretary Denis Healey said the reason for pulling out of the 150 million pounds base at Aden is that it is "an area where our presence is liable to be more of an irritant than a stabilizing influence." But Britain would stay at Singapore as long as that government welcomed the British base on acceptable terms. The decision was seen as a symbolic sunset for the days of imperial power. Britain's military commitments now exceeded limited resources.

British Staging Base

The Royal Air Force considered that the island of Aldabra would make a good staging post for its VC 10 and Belvedere aircraft. They proposed to build a 3,000-yard runway, buildings to house a permanent garrison of about 300 men, have transit accommodations for hundreds more, and fuel and ammunition depots. The strategic arguments for the staging base arose from the Royal Air Force's wish to preserve sovereign routes to the Far East, so that aircraft could fly from London to Singapore without having to land at foreign airfields. There also were other arguments concerned with the possible future need to have an air base situated close to Africa. In July 1966, the British proposed the construction of a joint United States-United Kingdom air base costing $50,000,000 on Aldabra.

There was controversy regarding the British staging base. Retired British Vice Admiral Peter Gretton said an airstrip on Aldabra would be, "astronomically expensive," and that an airstrip at Diego Garcia might be awash during tropical storms. There were alternative islands considered, such as Gan and the Cocos. British and Australian air staffs had a common aim to set up a chain of forward bases suitable for F-111A operations. Gan would cost less because the Royal Air Force already had a thriving base there.

Aldabra and Diego Garcia

The Assistant Secretary of Defense for International Security Affairs, Mr. John T. McNaughton, on 2 August 1966 forwarded two important Indian Ocean base recommendations to the Secretary of Defense Robert S. McNamara.

1. That the Secretary of Defense accept in principle the British proposal, of 14 July 1966, for a jointly financed facility on Aldabra costing $50,000,000 and authorize the Air Force to participate in detailed planning with British authorities, join in the September surveys, and include funding of the United States share in its fiscal year 1968 program.

2. That the Secretary of Defense inform the British that the Department of Defense is examining the feasibility and utility of austere naval support facilities including an air strip on

Diego Garcia, and seek early arrangements with the British for a joint engineering survey. The Department of Defense would make clear to the British that they have made no final decisions to build, and would seek to stimulate some degree of British participation in the project should it materialize.

McNaughton's recommendations were approved by the Secretary of Defense Robert S. McNamara on 4 August 1966.

Secretary of Navy Nitze told his Navy base planners to restructure planning for Diego Garcia so that the United States share would cost about $26,100,000. Apparently, the balance of the base cost was based on the hope of British financing. The $26,100,000 figure became sacrosanct within the Navy budget. One of the first things Navy did to reduce costs was to delete the lagoon dredging at Diego Garcia.

The revised estimate for Project REST STOP was sent back to the Secretary of Defense on 9 August 1966 for budget approval. The Navy stipulated that access to and use of the island was to be obtained by agreement with the United Kingdom, that the United Kingdom would make use of the facilities, and that the British would be asked to share in the cost of construction and maintenance. Furthermore, early arrangements were to be made with the British for a joint engineering survey to assure the economic feasibility of constructing the facility. The programmed construction cost was $26,100,000, which was to be funded in the fiscal year 1968 and 1969 programs for $13,100,000 and $13,000,000, respectively.

On 12 November 1966, the Deputy Secretary of Defense, Cyrus Vance, agreed to the Navy's proposal to establish a jointly financed naval activity on the island of Diego Garcia. The evaluation of the Navy's proposal within the Office of the Secretary of Defense concluded that:

    1. **Military Benefits.** The facility had both a present application, and a future defense potential. It would support United States operating forces transiting the Atlantic Fleet and the Far East and Southeast Asia by providing a bunkering facility,

and reliable communications support. The facility would provide a nucleus to support contingency operations and mobilization plans. From the standpoint of strategic mobility, there was no clearly demonstrated advantage.

2. **Political.** Provides a defense facility in an area where United States tenure can be assured with minimum political vulnerability, and provides the opportunity to obtain United Kingdom participation, thus assuring the continued presence of the British in the Indian Ocean.

The Secretary's decision also required, following discussions with the British, that a negotiated proposal for a jointly financed austere facility be presented to the Secretary of Defense.

FIGURE 2 RADM Thomas H. Moorer presents an award to Stewart B. Barber in 1961. U.S. Navy Photo

FIGURE. 3 Abandoned 1868 church at Point Marianne

FIGURE 4 July 1964, Joint Survey Team leaves Mildenhall. Left to right: Mr. R. Newton, Major Herbert J. Gall, Mr. A. Kravis, CDR Harry S. Hart, Mr. W. P. Dayton, Mr. M. Pollock, Mr. R. L. Clinkenbeard, CPO M. J. Mesiji, CPO Richard M. Young, LT Oreland R. Carden, CDR David M. Feinman and Mr. Vance Vaughan. U.S. Navy Photo

FIGURE 5 Project Reindeer temporary mess hall of Amphibious Battalion 2 in May 1971 U.S. Navy Photo

Detailed Plans Shelved

The Navy wanted to hire a civilian architect-engineer firm to prepare construction plans and specifications, and detailed cost estimates. The Bureau of Yard and Docks estimated that architect-engineering services would cost $200,000 for preliminary engineering, and $385,000 for preparation of final plans and specifications. By law, notification to the Armed Services Committees of the House and Senate was required before the award of an architectural-engineering contract exceeding

$150,000. On 13 October 1966, the Assistant Secretary of the Navy for Installations and Logistics, Graeme C. Bannerman, requested Department of Defense approval so that the Armed Services Committees of the House and Senate could be notified about the proposed architect-engineer contract for the advanced planning the classified facility called "Project REST STOP." Up to this point, the Congressional committees were not aware of the status of base planning for Diego Garcia. Congressional opposition was expected. The Navy's request was put aside, pending the outcome of the ongoing budget review. After Deputy Secretary Vance's decision of 12 November 1966, the proposed notification was sent back to the Navy on 7 December 1966, and temporarily shelved.

1966 BIOT Agreement

On 30 December 1966, the United States and the United Kingdom formally reached an agreement whereby the United Kingdom would detach the islands now comprising the British Indian Ocean Territory from Mauritius and the Seychelles to make them available for possible joint defense purposes for 50 years. The Agreement was signed by a junior minister in the Foreign Office, Lord Chalfont, and by the United States Ambassador David Bruce. In a classified note to the agreement, the United States agreed to provide up to half of the total British detachment costs, but not to exceed $14,000,000. Compensation was required for such matters as loss of sovereignty by Mauritius and the Seychelles, purchase of privately owned property or land, and resettlement of inhabitants.

The United States share of detachment costs was to be provided through a waiver of the 5 percent research and development surcharge imposed on procurements under the 6 April 1963, Polaris Sales Agreement between the United States and the United Kingdom. This surcharge was expected to reach $17,000,000 by mid 1972, but at 30 November 1966, it was about $4,300,000. Secretary of Defense Robert S. McNamara made the decision to forego the surcharges until the amount that would have otherwise been payable by the British, reached $14,000,000. When this amount was reached, the surcharge was to be reimposed on subsequent sales.

However, to give the British earlier budgetary relief, as it would have taken several years to make the contribution through the research and development surcharge accrual alone, the United States provided the entire $14,000,000 to Britain after entering into the 1966 agreement by:

1. Applying toward the current procurement charges the amounts already paid into the Polaris Trust Fund by the British for research and development surcharges and overhead and facilities charges. (The overhead and facility charges were fixed amounts to be paid over a 24 quarter period.)
2. Waiving British payments in December 1966 and March 1967 for then-current Polaris procurement charges (reflecting the application of funds as above), overhead charges, and facility use charges while allowing the British to restart overhead and facilities charges on an accelerated basis to repay the Trust Fund within the original payment schedule.

Thus, in effect, the United States loaned the British the $14,000,000 from the Polaris Trust Fund that was subsequently repaid except the research and development surcharge that had been waived. The detachment of the Indian Ocean Islands had to be accomplished quickly because a British withdrawal from the area was feared. Accordingly, the Polaris financing arrangement was deemed the best solution by Defense, as the regular appropriations route via Congress would be subject to considerable delay.

A 12 November 1965 Defense memorandum for the State's Deputy Legal Advisor described the legal basis for the Polaris offset technique. A subsequent investigation by the General Accounting Office was unable to say these financial arrangements violated United States law. But they believed the method of financing—a technique that masked real plans and costs—was clearly a circumvention of the congressional oversight role.

By 1967, the British Government completed purchase of the lease holds of the Chagos Agalega copra plantations, and entrusted the management of Diego Garcia to Marcel Moulinie, whose family had owned a third of Chagos Agalega Ltd. The rundown of the plantations started in 1968 with workers who went on holidays or visits to other islands by simply not being allowed passages to return. Work on the plantations stopped in 1971. An agreement was also reached on the use of the island of Mahe in the Seychelles for tracking and telemetry facilities in April 1967.

1967 Site Survey

The 1967 site survey of Diego Garcia was conducted from 7 June to 31 July, and was sponsored by the Naval Facilities Engineering Command. Francis McGuire, who had been a member of the 1964 survey team went from the Naval Facilities Engineering Command to Davisville, Rhode Island to brief Lieutenant Robinson, Civil Engineer Corps, the leader of the new survey team. The survey party included a team of Seabees, representatives of Grad-Wall, the Navy's consultant architect and engineer firm, and representatives of the United States Naval Oceanographic Office, and Dr. H.A. Fehlmann and Mr. C.F. Rhyne from the Smithsonian Institution, who studied the island's ecology.

The survey provided engineering data on quality of material for concrete aggregate, data on which later aerial photography and topographic maps were based, and subsurface exploration, both on land and in the harbor area. Additional detailed hydrographic soundings were taken in the entire lagoon. Transportation was furnished by Royal British Navy Hydrographic Survey Ship, H.M.S. *Vidal,* under the command of Captain C.R.K. Roe, D.S.C., Royal Navy. The British team included Dr. D.R. Stoddart, Department of Geography, Cambridge University, and Mr. J.D. Taylor, Department of Palaeontology, British Museum. After Diego Garcia, the scientists went to Aldabra, under the auspices of the Royal Society.

The British later flew many aerial photographic missions over Diego Garcia due to dense clouds over the island before they could get complete coverage of the island. The United States Hydrographic Office took the British aerial photographs, and in October 1967, transformed them into a detailed map of Diego Garcia, including ground contours.

The information gained from the survey enabled the architect-engineer to prepare final designs for a communications facility. Buildings were planned to be single story slabs on grade, with poured in place columns, beams and roofs. Aggregate for concrete came from the ocean reefs.

Tortoises and Rails

An alliance between the Royal Society, the Smithsonian Institution, and the United States National Academy of Science, had other plans for Aldabra. The scientists believed that the planned base threatened the rare plant and animal life on the island. They wanted to preserve the unique scientific environment, and establish a permanent research station of their own. Aldabra was the home of the giant land tortoises, and the only breeding place for the Flightless Rails and Frigate birds. On 29

May 1967, Secretary of State for Defense Healey replied to the Royal Society's recommendations. He said that no decision had been made on the staging base, but his object was to make sure that changes to the ecosystem be kept to a minimum.[7] The scientists from the United States and United Kingdom continued active opposition to the construction of an air base on Aldabra.

By the fall of 1967, the Defence Ministry agreed on the need to build a Royal Air Force staging base on Aldabra. But a firm decision could not be taken until the views of the Pentagon had been recorded and the Cabinet weighed political disadvantages against strategic. A series of deep British defense cuts resolved the issue. On 22 November 1967, Prime Minister Harold Wilson told the Commons that the government decided not to build the staging post on Aldabra, and they could do without Aldabra for most contingencies. Official estimates had put the cost of the Aldabra base at 20 million pounds. The United States had been interested in sharing facilities with the British, but were not prepared to go ahead unilaterally.

British White Paper

On 19 July 1967, Britain announced its plan to withdraw troops from Singapore and Malaysia by the middle 1970s, ending its military role East of Suez. President Lyndon Johnson and Defense Secretary McNamara had hoped the British would have left the long term policy open. This was the third major policy statement since February 1966. The British White Paper announced a new long term reduction in British military expenditures by one-seventh and of military manpower by 75,000. There was still a possibility of using facilities in Australia, and of making a new staging airfield in the British Indian Ocean Territory.

On 27 October 1967, Secretary of Defense McNamara deferred approval of a recommendation by the Joint Chiefs of Staff to construct a naval facility on Diego Garcia, however, the memorandum contained a provision for reconsideration of the proposal after a firm understanding had been reached with the British on Aldabra.

Architect-Engineer Report

A complete Preliminary Cost Estimate, utilizing data developed during the site survey in June and July 1967, was completed by the architect-engineer firm of Wall-Grad in November 1967. The consultant's total budget cost for contractor accomplishment was $27,300,000. Construction schedules were prepared based on funding in two equal increments. A planning report was also prepared for construction of the facilities by Naval Construction Forces. The completed report was forwarded to the Chief of Naval Operations to support programming actions.

British Withdrawal Announced

The American Embassy, London, on 16 January 1968, reported Prime Minister Wilson's announcement to withdraw United Kingdom forces from the Far East and Persian Gulf by the end of 1971.

In March 1968, two months after the British announcement, four warships of the Soviet Union from Vladivostok entered the Indian Ocean from the west and called at ports on the Indian Ocean Subcontinent, the Persian Gulf, and the coast of East Africa. After 1969, Soviet naval units were regularly deployed to the ocean.

On 10 April 1968, the Joint Chiefs of Staff proposed a $44,000,000 joint United Kingdom-United States military facility on Diego Garcia. The Joint Chiefs of Staff had reexamined the political situation and strategic requirements in the Indian Ocean area against the background of events evolving from the Arab/Israeli War and the United Kingdom decision to accelerate withdrawal from east of Suez. In July 1967, when the Joint Chiefs of Staff had recommended funding the first increment of construction of $13,000,000 in the fiscal year 1969 Budget, the prospects for a limited but effective British presence in the Indian Ocean appeared excellent. Now, the British financial condition and the attendant retrenchment offered little probability of future United Kingdom participation in the development or manning of any joint United States-United Kingdom facility.

The Joint Chiefs of Staff believed that the British withdrawal would create a power vacuum, which would generate situations inimical to United States national interests and long-range security. Predominance over the natural resources of the Indian Ocean or dominating influence over the governments of the surrounding land areas by the USSR could have a serious impact on the economic and strategic positions of the United States and its allies.

On 15 June 1968, the former Secretary of the Navy and now the deputy to Secretary of Defense Clark Clifford, Paul H. Nitze, responded to the 10 April 1968 Joint Chief of Staff proposal. Deputy Secretary of Defense Nitze concluded that no justification existed at that time for the establishment of a major support facility, however he did believe that justification existed for the construction of a modest facility at Diego Garcia. This facility—including ship to shore communications, telemetry, scientific, and intelligence monitoring capabilities, and attendant support installations would provide the United States increased future flexibility at moderate cost. It could provide a potential backup site in the event that Middle East Force cannot be based at Bahrain, where we have been since 1949, after the United Kingdom withdrawal. In addition, some of our activities at Kagnew Station, Ethiopia, could be transferred to Diego Garcia should the security situation in Ethiopia warrant a reduction in our military presence there. The establishment of the facility would also demonstrate to concerned leaders that we are not totally uninterested in the area.

Should further study reveal that Polaris submarine operations in the Indian Ocean are both feasible and desirable, Diego Garcia could serve as a useful site for replenishment and support. No additional construction or maintenance costs would be incurred in providing such since the necessary anchorage work would have been accomplished. Moreover, the United States could in the future move quickly to Indian Ocean basing for Polaris should the Soviet ABM capability or anti-submarine warfare threat change suddenly.

Deputy Secretary approved in principle the concept of a modest facility, and the development of a plan for its construction to include austere communications, POL storage, an 8,000 foot runway, and anchorage dredging, at a cost of approximately $26,000,000. This plan, including engineering specifications and Program Change Requests, was to be submitted in coordination with the Joint Chiefs of Staff, in time for development of the fiscal year 1970 budget. The Assistant Secretary of Defense for International Security Affairs was to coordinate with the Department of State to make an early approach to the British to obtain agreement to fly a British flag over the facility and to obtain whatever financial and manning participation may be possible. These negotiations were to be undertaken with the clear understanding that implementation of any agreement is subject to final approval and release of funds by the United States Government.

Responding to the Deputy Secretary of Defense Nitze's memorandum of 15 June 1968, the Navy submitted its plan on 4 October 1968 as a Program Change Request. The construction was estimated to cost $26,000,000 based on a United States contractor utilizing United States supervisory personnel, foreign national skilled and unskilled labor, materials and equipment from the United States and foreign sources and United States commercial shipping. However, the Chief of Naval Operations considered that barring any unforeseen military circumstances or other considerations, Naval Construction Forces would be available and would be used for construction.

British Approval

Alan Brooke Turner, in the Foreign Office, on 3 September 1968, confirmed Her Majesty's Government acceptance of the United States proposed project for Diego Garcia, on the understanding that:

- Normal British participation will be provision of one or more liaison officers, and United Kingdom flag flying over the facility.
- British naval ships and military aircraft shall have full rights of access to the facility at all times under arrangements to be mutually agreed.
- Administrative details of project will need to be subject of detailed negotiations before construction is to begin.
- Most difficult question likely to be how and when to make project public knowledge, prefer no public announcement before end of coming session of General Assembly.

Alan Brooke Turner also provided copy of draft report by Dr. D.R. Stoddart, Department of Geography, Cambridge, on conservation at Diego Garcia.

RAND Corporation Study

The RAND Corporation completed a study in September 1968 entitled "Survey of Basing Potentials for the Islands in the Indian Ocean." This study was supported by the Department of Defense under a contract monitored by the staff of the Assistant Secretary of Defense for International Security Affairs. The study was concerned with the evaluation of the islands in the Indian Ocean as potential bases that could support military operations in Asia.

1970 Defense Approval

The Program Change Request had been submitted after the Navy had submitted its fiscal year 1970 budget, and therefor the customary Program Change Decision procedure was not used. The Program Change Request was to be considered as part of the Navy's submitted fiscal year 1970 budget.

After reviewing the Navy's Program Change Request for the fiscal year 1970 program, the Assistant Secretary of Defense for Systems Analysis, Alain Enthoven, on 23 October 1968 made his recommendation. He recommended to the Secretary of Defense's Comptroller, who was responsible for conducting the budget review, that the project be deferred, at least until fiscal year 1971. Also he recommended that the Navy be required to justify or reprogram the additional $8,000,000 for communications and other equipment. The Deputy Secretary of Defense's memorandum of 15 June 1968 had stipulated a total cost of $26,000,000. System Analysis in effect questioned the urgency of the project, and categorized it as "nice to have" but construction could well be deferred.

But review of the Navy's Program Change Request by the staff of the Assistant Secretary of Defense for International Security Affairs resulted in a recommendation for approval. They noted that the Diego Garcia facility was important as a tangible manifestation of United States national interest in the Indian Ocean during a critical period, and for its potential future use. In addition, the Department of State just concluded negotiations with the United Kingdom that resulted in British approval in principle for including the presence of a United Kingdom liaison officer there. Accordingly, International Security Affairs believed that delay or deferral of the project to fiscal year 1971 would raise serious doubts as to United States intentions, and could well result in withdrawal of the present British consent for the establishment of the facility.

The military construction program managers within the office of the Assistant Secretary of Defense for Installations and Logistics on 5 November 1968, recommended to the Comptroller that a separate Program Budget Decision document be prepared for the Indian Ocean project. This would give Secretary of Defense McNamara the opportunity to focus on the merits of the Diego Garcia project, and would allow the Secretary to either approve or defer the project to a future year. For budgeting purposes, the Installations and Logistics staff priced the cost of the project based on accomplishment by construction contracts. The pricing alternative for construction by Naval Construction Forces was deleted because that decision would be dependent on the availability of Naval Construction Forces.

On 27 November 1968, the Deputy Secretary of Defense approved the Navy's request to include $9,556,000 in the fiscal year 1970 budget for Military Construction. The Armed Services Committees were notified on 6 December 1968 that the Navy proposed to award an architect-engineer contract for a project estimated to cost $9,556,000, with a design fee of about $840,000.

1969 Congressional Actions

The Navy's project justification to the Congress read, "An austere logistic support activity has become necessary to insure Navy readiness in the South Atlantic, Indian and Western Pacific Oceans. Access to ports for bunkering and resupply has diminished...Communications in the Indian Ocean are tenuous without satisfactory coverage of the Mid-Indian Ocean area. Lack of fueling facilities and immediately responsive communications, while not prohibiting naval operations, limits operational flexibility. No military facilities of any nature exist in this area and a new facility is required for ship refueling, limited aviation, and communications."

In the Congressional review of the fiscal year 1970 Military Construction Request, authorization for the project was approved by the House Armed Services Committee, disapproved by the Senate Armed Services Committee in August 1969, restored in conference in November 1969, and eventually the $9,556,000 authorization for construction was included in Public Law 91-142 of 5 December 1969. Gaining approval for the appropriations needed for construction proved more difficult.

The House Appropriations Committee in November 1969 approved funding of the project; the Senate Appropriations Committee in December 1969 disapproved funding. Funding for the project was not restored in conference. It was a difficult decision. The Conferees met four times before they could agree that this project would be eliminated from the fiscal year 1970 appropriations program for military construction. The Senate Conferees, under the leadership of Senator Mike Mansfield, were adamant that this project represented another needless entanglement of our nation and appeared in contradiction to our attempt to withdraw from Vietnam and other areas. On 18 December 1969, the House Appropriations Committee receded from its position, and funding for the first increment of Diego Garcia was not to be included in the fiscal year 1970 Appropriations Act.

An oral agreement was reached in which the Navy was instructed to come back in fiscal year 1971 for a new appropriation that would support only a communications station. The rationale at the time for the communications station was that the United States would probably have to withdraw from the main continent of Africa the large communications facility (Kagnew Station) that the United States maintained at Asmera, Ethiopia.

Relocation of Workers

In 1969, the British made tentative plans for moving the plantation workers and their families from Diego Garcia to make way for the joint communications facility that was being considered by the United States Congress. Several alternative relocation sites were considered, including the islands of Peros Banhos and Salomon in the Chagos group. However, the plantations on these two islands were deteriorating, and could not be maintained without considerable investment that was not feasible unless the islands could be exempted from military use for at least twenty years. In any event, such a commitment was not possible, and the British made arrangements to move the plantation workers from Diego Garcia, and later from Peros Banhos and Salomon. The workers recruited from the Seychelles were returned there. The others either went direct to Mauritius or, in some cases to Peros Banhos and Salomon in the first instance and subsequently to Mauritius.

The physical relocation of the workers, which the closure of the Chagos plantations necessitated, was carried out by the Chagos Agalega Company that was responsible for the movement of its workers. Two ships were used for clearances, the *Nordvaer*, owned by the British Indian Ocean Territory, and another vessel, the *Isle of Farquhar*. At first, the islanders were given a choice; either to be taken to Mauritius or to the neighboring islands in the archipelago.

Communications Only

Before Congress completed its action on the fiscal year 1970 legislative program, the Navy submitted the second increment in the fiscal year 1971 budget to the Office of the Secretary of Defense. The Secretary of Defense was Melvin R. Laird in the Nixon Administration. On the assumption that the first increment would be approved by

Congress, the Navy requested $13,100,000 for fiscal year 1971, which was approved by the Deputy Secretary of Defense David Packard on 5 December 1969. Because Naval Construction Battalion Forces were designated to accomplish the construction at Diego Garcia, the estimated construction cost decreased from $26,000,000 to $22,700,000.

Within the Office of the Secretary of Defense, representatives of the Assistant Secretary for International Security Affairs, for Installations and Logistics, and State Department met to discuss future plans for the facility because of the strong opposition in the Senate to the establishment of an American naval base in the Indian Ocean. The representatives agreed that the Secretary of the Navy should present the Navy's rationale directly to the Secretary of Defense Laird, if approval to include this project in the fiscal year 1971 program was still considered urgent and vital, within a week's time. The Assistant Secretary of the Navy for Installations and Logistics was advised on 14 January 1970 that Secretary of Defense Laird desired that the project support only communications, with everything else subsidiary.

Diego Garcia Decision Holds Up 1971 Legislation

Work on the entire Department of Defense Military Construction Authorization Draft Bill was completed, except for the Navy's portion relating to Diego Garcia, and submission of the draft legislation to the Office of Management and Budget for legislative clearance had to be held in abeyance. By law, the Department of Defense was required to submit the legislation to Congress within 10 days after the budget was sent to Congress.

The Secretary of the Navy, John H. Chafee, responded on January 31 to the Secretary of Defense Laird's request to reorient project now called "REINDEER" to a communications facility. The Navy proposed an austere communications facility estimated to cost a total of

$17,800,000. The cost of the first increment that was proposed for the fiscal year 1971 Military Construction Budget was $5,400,000. Construction of the second and third increments came to $8,200,000 and $4,200,000, respectively. The Assistant Secretary of Defense for Systems Analysis still questioned the need of a communications facility, and asked the Navy to respond to several questions including:

- What statistical data was available to justify the stated communications deficiency?
- What provision was made in the new concept for satellite communications filling the communications gap?
- Was a mobile communications ship considered as an alternative?

Deputy Secretary of Defense Packard, was briefed by the Assistant Secretary of Defense for Systems Analysis, Dr. G. Tucker, on the weakness of the communication justification on 10 February 1970. Mr. Packard agreed with the Systems Analysis point of view, and then discussed the problem with the Chief of Naval Operations, Admiral Thomas Moorer. The Department of Defense, by law, could not any longer hold off on the fiscal year 1971 authorization legislation, and decided not to request any new authorization for Diego Garcia since there was the unfunded authorization of $9,556,000 left over from the fiscal year 1970 enacted authorization. However, $5,400,000 would remain in the appropriation request, while the Navy developed a more convincing argument for the new facility.

About 19 February 1970, Dr. Tucker presented the Systems Analysis recommendations to Deputy Secretary of Defense Packard, which was to construct only those waterfront facilities, such as a pier and harbor dredging, which would make access to and facilitate construction of a facility when needed. Secretary of the Navy Chafee, was furnished a copy of the Systems Analysis approach, and was requested to provide a rationale why we should proceed with project "REINDEER" now and what construction should proceed. Resolution of the concept and cost became extremely pressing as the Navy was scheduled to testify before the House Appropriations Military Construction Subcommittee on 9 March 1970.

On 27 February 1970, Defense Secretary Laird presented his Posture Statement before the House Committee on Appropriations. In response to a question from Mr. Talcott, Defense Secretary Laird stated that the new base in the Indian Ocean was limited to electronic activities, relating to intelligence gathering. Mr. Robert Sikes commented, "The House is roughly sold on the importance of the base. We were last year." On the same day, the Assistant Secretary of the Navy for Research and Development, Dr. Robert A. Frosch, forwarded a memorandum to the Deputy Secretary of Defense Packard that offered supporting documentation for the utilization of the Diego Garcia facility in an intelligence collection role in addition to the communications functions planned for "REINDEER" station.

The following day, 28 February 1970, the Assistant Secretary of Defense for International Security Affairs, Mr. G. Warren Nutter, met with Defense Secretary Laird to discuss project "REINDEER." Secretary of Defense Laird reaffirmed his belief that the only justification the House of Representatives would accept was a communications facility plus a capacity for intelligence gathering.

With the Sikes Subcommittee hearing still scheduled for 9 March 1970, time was running out to resolve the conflict within the Office of the Secretary of Defense between Systems Analysis and International Security Affairs. On 6 March 1970, Mr. Laird met with the Under Secretary of the Navy, Mr. Warner, and the Assistant Secretary of the Navy for Installations and Logistics, Mr. Frank Sanders, to resolve the concept for the Diego Garcia facility. Secretary of Defense Laird approved the Navy's concept for an austere communications facility with only those minimum facilities necessary to make the new base self-sustaining, and the $5,400,000 first increment in the fiscal year 1971 funding program.

A few days later, Assistant Secretary of the Navy for Installations and Logistics, Frank Sanders, met with Mr. Edward Sheridan on 12 March 1970, and briefed the Deputy Assistant Secretary about the 6 March meeting with Secretary of Defense Laird. Project justification sheets for "REINDEER" were delivered, as previously agreed with Secretary of Defense Melvin R. Laird. The draft legislation was hand carried to the Office of Management and Budget for clearance, and the Navy started printing the budget books that contained military construction project descriptions and justifications.

Russia Seeking Bases

There was a fear that the Soviets would turn the Indian Ocean into a "Red sea" when the British pulled their forces out of the Far East in 1971. The Soviet fleet in the Indian Ocean was supplied by a "sea train." Warships were supplied at sea by auxiliary ships and oilers, making a land base unnecessary. The big problem for them was that their ships had to return to Black Sea ports via the African cape, thousands of miles away or to the Siberian naval base at Vladivostok for repairs and maintenance. The Soviets were looking for a base on the Indian subcontinent. Their biggest target so far was Mauritius, an island off the African Coast.[8]

Conservative Election Victory

After the Conservative election victory of June 1970, Admiral Elmo Zumwalt, Chief of Naval Operations, wrote a personal letter to the new Foreign Secretary, Sir Alex Douglas-Home, to congratulate him, and to look forward to close cooperation in the Indian Ocean. In December, the two governments agreed in principle to build "a naval communications facility." But the United States Navy seemed to have wider hopes for the use of Diego Garcia—closer to those of its War College, which in October 1970, recommended "a highly visible multilateral military presence, preferably naval, in the area."

Public Affairs Plan

On 17 November 1970, Rear Admiral L. R. Geis, Chief of Information, United States Navy, proposed a Public Affairs Plan for Project REINDEER STATION. No public affairs action concerning the project was to be taken until Congressional action was completed and funds apportioned by the Department of Defense. In addition, the proposed public affairs action was to be low-key and consisted of a brief joint United States-United Kingdom announcement to be made simultaneously in Washington and London, followed by local announcements in the home ports of the departure of the Seabee Units that would construct the facility. It was expected that by late November 1970, Congress would approve and provide funds, and that the public announcement would be made in mid January 1971. The plan and the annexes thereto (Joint United States-United Kingdom News Releases and list of anticipated questions and approved answers) would become unclassified after the joint United States-United Kingdom announcement was authorized.

Also the same day, Barry J. Shillito, the Assistant Secretary of Defense for Installations and Logistics was briefed by Captain Moffit, U.S.N., assigned to the Navy Intelligence Command, regarding the need for approximately 50 additional personnel attributable to "Project Charlie" requirements.

First Public Disclosure

The *Washington Post* newspaper article "Indian Ocean Base Is Sought by U.S."[9] was the first public news that announced that the Nixon administration had asked Congress for military construction funds to build a communications facility on British islands in the Indian Ocean.

The article noted that this would be the first American "base" in the ocean area between Africa and Australia. Virtually no American warships are assigned to duty there, but Soviet fleet strength has been increasing rapidly—21 ships at one point this year—and the Soviets have several "anchorages" on the coastal periphery.

The article also said that the White House has asked a delay in its consideration by Congress pending a full-scale review by the National Security Council of United States strategic aims in the area. The White House was apparently concerned that such a facility could be a first step toward a significant and costly new American presence.

The article noted that Government of India has already protested to Britain and the United States against plans to build any military facility on the islands. India wanted the waters of the Indian Ocean to remain free of big power contests. The Soviet Navy, the article reported, has anchorage buoys off the Seychelles. Through aid to harbor developments, it has access to ports and dockyards in Somalia, Yemen, Aden, and India, and trawler facilities in Mauritius. The Soviet Navy was also reported to be building a military facility on southern Yemen's island of Socotra at the mouth of the Gulf of Aden.

Deputy Secretary of Defense David Packard, on 28 November 1970, approved $8,950,000, for the second increment of the Diego Garcia project, for inclusion in the fiscal year 1972 military construction program. A third increment, estimated at $4,956,000, for dredging was programmed for fiscal year 1973, if that step were subsequently approved. The revised total construction cost was now $19,300,000, and with the exception of the harbor dredging, the work was to be done by Seabees (Naval Construction Battalion Forces or CBs). The revised estimate included an increase of $1,500,000 over the fiscal year 1971 estimate of $17,800,000, which was attributed to higher construction costs and an increase in total personnel from 194 to 274.

Nixon Administration Announcement

On 15 December 1970, the Nixon Administration announced that it intended to build a joint military base on the British-owned island of Diego Garcia. The announcement said that the purpose of the facility was to fill a gap in the system of worldwide United States naval communications. At the same time, the base would provide support for American and British ships and planes in the Indian Ocean.[10] The *Washington Post* newspaper article noted also that British Prime Minister Edward Heath was to visit Washington, and could use the American announcement as backing for his contention that the Soviet presence in the Indian Ocean should be viewed with concern, and that the offer of military cooperation from Mauritius and some East African countries has diminished the formerly overriding need to supply South Africa with arms to help contain Communist expansion along the southern hemisphere's sea lanes.

Previously, the Nixon Administration has declined to be drawn into the argument. On the other hand, India and Ceylon were the moving forces behind the adoption by the third summit conference of non-aligned nations of a motion calling for the Indian Ocean to be made a military-free zone. The conference was held in Zambia in September. In December 1971 the United Nations Resolution 2832 (XXVI) declared the Indian Ocean as a Zone of Peace, and stated that "the Indian Ocean, within the limits to be determined, together with the air space above and the ocean floor subjacent thereto, is hereby designated for all time as a zone of peace."

Resettlement

A joint State-Defense message sent to the American Embassy in London on 17 December 1970, responded to a prior Embassy message regarding British planning for relocation of the approximately 400 copra workers now on Diego Garcia. Resettlement to Seychelles of 230 Seychellois workers was proposed, remaining, including 125 Ilois (French for islanders) born on Diego Garcia, to Agalega, Peros Banhos and Salomon. The message said "We recognize the British problem in returning to Mauritius those Ilois and Mauritian workers now on Diego Garcia, and possibility of resultant financial cost to Her Majesty's Government. That however, was clearly envisioned as United Kingdom's responsibility in 1966 agreements, under which United States is sharing such costs by foregoing up to $14,000,000 in Polaris Research and Development charges (over $10,000,000 has been so credited to Her Majesty's Government to date, and full $14,000,000 was expected to be reached by 1977.)

When the Chagos Agalega Company moved the plantation workers on Diego Garcia to Mauritius in 1971, the total number persons there was 359. A small number of workers were moved to the islands of Peros Banhos and Salomon. A ship breakdown in 1971 delayed the move, and caused food supplies on Diego Garcia to run low, a shortage that was remedied by the American Seabee contingent. When the coconut plantations were closed, there were no further means of livelihood on the island, and the workers reluctantly left. There was also a security consideration for removing the workers.

The United States Navy preferred not to have third-country nationals left on the island. The Navy was also concerned about social problems since they planned to have unaccompanied servicemen on the island. While some workers could have been hired to work on the construction, the Navy decided to do all the work with the Seabee detachments. Some deported islanders had family roots, and had lived on Diego Garcia for up to five generations. There was a church, and a school on the island.

National Security Council

The *Washington Post*[11] reported that the National Security Council staff issued two secret Study Memoranda, one on 9 November and the other on 22 December 1970, highly critical of plans for expansion into the Indian Ocean. The memoranda concluded that the United States had minimal strategic interests in the area, and that those limited interests were not amenable to protection by military intervention. The memoranda encouraged cooperation with the Soviets to limit American and Soviet naval deployments in the area.

Construction Begins

Resembling an amphibious landing during World War II, Seabees landed on Diego Garcia in March 1971 to begin construction of a communications station. The tank landing ship *Vernon County* (LST-1161) was steaming in early March 1971 from Singapore and was scheduled to arrive in Diego Garcia on 9 March 1971. She had embarked approximately 57 personnel from Navy Mobile Construction Battalion 40 and Under Water Demolition Team 12 who comprised an advance landing party to mark a channel and prepare the beach for the subsequent arrival of an advance party on 20 March 1971.

The attack cargo ship *Charleston* (LKA-113) was in route for Monrovia, Liberia, to rendezvous with approximately 150 personnel comprising the advance party at Mauritius on March 15. The *Charleston* would proceed to Diego Garcia and arrive on 20 March 1971. The advance party included personnel from Navy Mobile Construction Battalion 40, a medical team, and a communication unit. These later would augment the battalion capacity and provide interim medical and communications services at this remote site.

The dock landing ship *Monticello* (LSD-35) was in route from Sidney to Perth, Australia, carrying equipment and materials for the Seabee camp. She was scheduled to leave Perth on 11 March and would also arrive at Diego Garcia on 20 March 1971.

The dock landing ship *Anchorage* (LSD-36), was in route to Sidney, Australia, carrying additional Seabee camp equipment and materials. She would make port visits in Sidney and Perth before arrival on Diego Garcia on 4 April 1971.

Without fanfare, the United States Navy on 20 March 1971 started building a communications station and an 8,000-foot airstrip on the remote British Island of Diego Garcia. The facility was being built by a force of 230 Seabees.

A Military Sealift Command Charter vessel *American Champion* was scheduled to load construction materials from Construction Battalion Center Davisville, Rhode Island, on 20 March 1971. A second Military Sealift Command charter vessel was scheduled for loadout from Construction Battalion Center Davisville on 17 April 1971. The vessels were scheduled to arrive at Diego Garcia on 19 April and 19 May 1971.

The main body of Navy Mobile Construction Battalion 40 was scheduled to deploy two contingents to Diego Garcia, one arriving approximately 17 April 1971, and the other arriving approximately 19 May 1971. Upon arrival of these two contingents, the island population would be approximately 820 personnel.

Logistics personnel were being provided as a Logistics Support Component to augment the Naval Mobile Construction Battalion. Some of the personnel comprising this Logistics Support Component

would deploy with the advance party and the main body of the Navy Mobile Construction Battalion with the remainder arriving 19 June 1971 and 18 July 1971.

An industrial site was established that included a rock crusher and a concrete block plant. To feed the crusher and block plant, a tide haul and crescent scraper operation began on the ocean reef. The reef was drilled and packed with explosives at low tide, and then blasted.

An interim C-130 Hercules cargo aircraft capable airfield was scheduled for completion by 18 July 1971. This would provide a 3,500-foot airstrip, built from compacted coral, for minimal air service during the construction period. The runway and apron were completed in March 1973, marking the beginning of weekly C-141 Starlifter cargo jet planes from Utapao, Thailand.

The first British Political Resident, who was supposed to impose the rule of British law upon the Americans on Diego Garcia was Lieutenant Commander P.J.M. Carter. The tour of duty for Americans stationed on Diego Garcia was one year. The Seabee battalions doing the construction work were on a cycle of eight months on-island and six months back at home port.

Christmas Show

On Christmas day 1972, the first Starlifter cargo jet landed on 6,000 feet of completed runway. The jet brought the Bob Hope Christmas Show Troupe, including Dolores Hope and Redd Foxx. Bob Hope was completing his ninth consecutive Christmas appearance in Vietnam, and his twenty-fifth visit to overseas American service personnel. (See Figure 7) Before landing at Diego Garcia, the show had been at Tan Son Nhut Air Base and at Utapao.

United States officials are convinced that when the Middle East conflict is settled and the Suez Canal is reopened the Soviet thrust into the Indian Ocean will intensify and the Russians will establish a naval base. Russian trawlers equipped with electronic-espionage gear now operate out of Mauritius, formerly a British possession and now an independent nation.

Second Communications Construction Increment

Congress appropriated $5,400,000 for the first increment communications facility at Diego Garcia in the fiscal year 1971 Appropriations Act. For fiscal year 1972, the Department of Defense requested $8,950,000 for the second increment. The Department of Defense also requested additional authorization of $4,794,000, which together with the $9,556,000 authorized in fiscal year 1970 totaled $14,350,000, and would make both authorization and appropriation totals identical. The second increment included additional unaccompanied housing for 24 officers and 100 enlisted men, 50,000 barrels of fuel storage tankage, completion of the 8,000 foot runway, and additional utilities to support the new construction.

Congressman Robert L.F. Sikes, Chairman of the Subcommittee on Military Construction of the House Committee on Appropriations, asked Secretary of State William P. Rogers for State's assessment of United States interests in the Indian Ocean and the relationship of the planned facility at Diego Garcia to those interests. David M. Abshire, the Assistant Secretary of State for Congressional Relations sent a letter to Congressman Sikes on 19 March 1971 that responded to the congressman's questions. Of primary concern was the Gulf oil transported through the Indian Ocean, followed by the need to maintain diplomatic relations with States of the region. United States security interests were limited and primarily involved Iran, Ethiopia, and Saudi Arabia. Much of the concern revolved around questions of free access and transit into and across the region. Finally, the United States was concerned about Soviet and Chinese Communist influence in the area.

As to Diego Garcia, State said that the communications facility had been under consideration since 1963, and therefore was not directly related to recent increases in Soviet presence in the Indian Ocean. The facility was designed to close a gap in worldwide communications.

The fiscal year 1972 Defense Request was subsequently approved by Congress, and the second increment of construction for the communications facility at Diego Garcia was enacted into law.

Russian Diplomatic Overtures

Ambassador Dobrynin on 26 March 1971 asked Secretary Rogers informally whether the United States would be interested in a declaration keeping the Indian Ocean free of major power competition. On July 28, Ambassador Beam informed Secretary Gromyko in Moscow that the United States agreed "In principle with the proposition that it would be in our mutual interest to avoid military competition in the (Indian Ocean) area and that it would be useful for us to know what the Soviet side had in mind."

In a possibly related development, on June 11, General Secretary Brezhnev alluded publicly to the possibility of negotiating limits on long-range naval deployments. Three years later, in testifying before the House Foreign Affairs Subcommittee, Director J. Owen Zurhellen, Jr. said, "In spite of an inquiry in Moscow regarding the Indian Ocean question, we have received no further clarification of what the USSR may have had in mind nor any indication that they had an interest in pursuing this subject further. Nevertheless, in the 1971 ANZUS communiqué, we expressed the hope that military competition in the area could be avoided, we have maintained this hope up to the present, and we maintain interested in any ideas that might in the future develop along these lines, perhaps in the form of explicit understandings to avoid competition while safeguarding our respective interests in the Indian Ocean."

Animals Left Behind

The last of the inhabitants to leave Diego Garcia went in September 1971. The Nordvaer, a ship owned by the British Indian Ocean Territory, steamed into East Point, and the islanders discovered that instead of bringing in provisions they expected to replenish their store, it had come to take them off. On 28 September 1971, it was loaded up by the islanders with copra and the plantation machinery that could be salvaged. Late that night, the last 35 islanders were paid off, and allowed to load their own baggage, although their most valuable possessions, their animals, had to be left behind.

The islanders, on the last trip were taken first to the Seychelles so that the ship's cargo could be disembarked. So muddled was the last stage of evacuation that 35 islanders had to spend their first nine days in the Seychelles in prison because no one provided a place for them to stay. Paul Moulinie tried to get them some place to stay, but the only place empty was the prison. The 35, which included women and children, were allowed out of prison by day, but locked up again at nine each night. Nine days later, the islanders were put back aboard ship, and taken 1,000 miles to Mauritius.

The number of workers relocated from Diego Garcia in 1971 was 359. The number of workers moved from the islands of Peros Banhos and Salomon in 1973 was 470, including the small number who had gone to those islands from Diego Garcia in 1971. The total number of persons moved from the Chagos Islands between 1971 and 1973 was 829. Additionally there were some 400 persons who had worked on the islands, who voluntarily settled in Mauritius between 1965 and 1970.

Indo-Pakistan War

Following the Indo-Pakistan War of November 1971, and American alignment with Pakistan, and almost three weeks after the deployment of the U.S.S. *Enterprise* (CVAN-65), the Soviets brought their naval force level up to six surface combatants, six submarines, and nine auxiliaries.

Diego Garcia Draft Agreement

The American Embassy presented a new United States Draft of the Diego Garcia Agreement between 6 December and 8 December 1971. Department of Defense representatives, Mr. Philip Barringer and Mr. Kent, and Captain Hugo from the Office of the Chief of Naval Operations; and a Foreign and Commonwealth Office officer, and a representative of the Minister of Defense, worked together on the draft. The initial reaction of the British to the new United States draft was favorable. The working group said, "We are close to agreement, a number of points will require further refinement, but neither side sees any insuperable obstacle to reaching agreement soon."

Major Strategy Shift

The *Washington Post* reported the presence of the eight ship United States task force lead by the nuclear-powered aircraft carrier *Enterprise*, which had entered the Indian Ocean 14 December 1971, and was still there three weeks after the India-Pakistan War ended.[12] It was reported that the carrier was sent in officially to aid in any rescue of United States citizens from Dacca, but unofficially its mission was to establish the United States presence and possibly to divert Indian naval forces. When the war broke out, the Russians added a guided missile cruiser and a submarine, which brought the Soviet fleet to about 15 ships.

The Pentagon acknowledged that a major shift in the United States strategy was underway, which would send American warships on periodic patrols into the Indian Ocean far more frequently than in the past. The move, which began ahead of schedule when a carrier task force sailed into the Indian Ocean in the midst of the India-Pakistan War, is intended to both offset Soviet naval strength in the area, and to help fill the vacuum left when the British fleet completes its withdrawal from bases there.

Pentagon spokesman Jerry W. Friedheim also announced a plan that gave the Pacific Fleet Commander, Admiral John F. McCain, as of 1 January 1972, responsibility for the Indian Ocean-Persian Gulf, an operating area that previously was split with the Atlantic Fleet Command. Friedheim and State Department spokesman Charles W. Bray also acknowledged that the United States entered into an unpublicized agreement—signed 23 December 1971—to take over the naval base at Bahrain, an island in the Persian Gulf, from the British.

Dredging Project

The Senate Military Construction Subcommittee on Armed Services and the Committee on Appropriations met in joint session in Room 212, in the Old Senate Office Building, to hold hearings on the fiscal year 1973 Military Construction Authorization Request on 25 May 1972. Present were Senators Symington, presiding, Cannon, and Stevens. Navy was represented by Admiral W.M. Enger, Commander, Naval Facilities Engineering Command.

Senator Symington asked Admiral Enger whether the $6,100,000 dredging project was necessary for the communications facility, or whether Navy was planning to establish carriers and submarines at the base. Admiral Enger stated that the dredging was required for provisioning and the depth of dredging based on the 41-foot draft of an AOE ship. Admiral Enger conceded that the channel would be capable of accommodating either carriers or submarines, but that was not the intent of the dredging project. Admiral Enger also testified that the 8,000-foot runway was designed to handle C-141 cargo aircraft, that met current requirements, but there was space available for extension at some time in the future. The Navy planned to dredge 1,360,000 cubic yards of coral pinnacles with a cutterhead dredge. A turning basin, 2,000 feet by 6,000 feet, would be created.

The dredging was accomplished by the Retired Servicemen Engineering Agency of Taiwan, a private contractor. By dredging and use of explosives to blast away coral heads, a three and one half mile long by 750 feet wide channel, with a 2,750 foot by 4,800 foot turning basin at the inboard end was created. The dredging contractor pumped two and one half million cubic yards of coral material fill material next to the shore south of the runway.

1972 Administrative Agreement

On 24 October 1972, the governments of the United States and Great Britain concluded the Administrative Agreement formally providing for the establishment of the joint United States-United Kingdom limited communication facility on the island of Diego Garcia to consist of "transmitting and receiving services, an anchorage, airfield, associated logistic support and supply and personnel accommodations." The agreement was concluded pursuant to the 1966 United States-United Kingdom British Indian Ocean Territory Agreement which provides that facilities such as this one may be constructed on islands in the British Indian Ocean Territory under a mutually satisfactory administrative arrangement.

The administrative agreement, known as the Diego Garcia Agreement 1972, was effected by the exchange of notes. The notes were signed in London on 24 October 1972, and entered into force on that day. Anthony Kershaw, the British Secretary of State for Foreign and Commonwealth Affairs signed the note for the British Government. The American note was signed by Earl D. Sohm, a Foreign Service Officer and Deputy Chief of Mission, the American Charge d'Affairs ad interim. The American Ambassador was absent at the time.

The notes included provisions concerning access and security, conservation of flora and fauna, and future restoration of the three islets at the mouth of the lagoon. The United States agreed to provide meteorological information to the United Kingdom and Mauritius. A plan of Diego Garcia was annexed to the note showing the specific area designated for the communications facility. The communications facility was to be constructed mainly on the western side of Diego Garcia to the 7-degree 24 minute 30-second latitude on the eastern side.

Kagnew Connection

The Navy Facilities Engineering Command forwarded a letter to the Assistant Secretary of Defense for Installations and Logistics that proposed to notify the Armed Services Committee of the House and Senate of the Navy's intent to award an architectural-engineering contract for preliminary engineering concerning a $7,900,000 construction project at the Naval Communication Station, Diego Garcia. In view of Deputy Secretary of Defense, William P. Clements, memorandum to the Navy dated 7 March 1973, which suspended any related action concerning the proposal to relocate to Diego Garcia until a decision has been reached with

FIGURE 6 December 1976, U.S. and British naval personnel hoist their flags in front of the administration building during morning quarters. U.S. Navy Photo

FIGURE 7 Comedian Bob Hope, right, Aerographer's Mate Airman Apprentice Karl Menzer and "Miss World" entertain men assigned on Diego Garcia during Christmas 1972. U.S. Navy Photo

FIGURE 8 Map of Communications Station, Diego Garcia

respect to the feasibility and desirability of withdrawing from Kagnew Station in Ethiopia in 1974. The request was returned to Navy for submission later. While the staff of the Assistant Secretary of Defense for Telecommunications supported the requirement, the Deputy Assistant Secretary of Defense for International Security for Near Eastern, African and South Asian Affairs, James H. Noyes, could not concur with the timing of Navy's proposed notification.

Communication Station Operational

The communication station with about 200 naval personnel went into operation in March 1973. A United States Officer was in charge of the facility, and a British Officer regulated island affairs. Tours of duty for United States military personnel were 12 months unaccompanied by dependents.

The development of the communications station provided the Navy with an austere facility that was logistically self sufficient. The development was authorized by Congress for $20,450,000, but cost over $24,000,000 to construct, and provided:

- A receiver site with a receiver building, a communications operations building and antenna fields.
- A transmitter building and antenna complex.
- Berthing, messing, recreation and administrative facilities for a communications station population of 274 officers and men. Plus 309 additional missions personnel.
- An airfield complex that includes an air operations building, control tower, aircraft parking for two C-141 aircraft, and an 8,000" x 150', C-141 capable runway system.
- A POL causeway and 60,000 barrel storage tank farm.
- Dredging a channel and 303 acre turning basin.

2

Logistics Support Base

Improvement Plan

The Under Secretary of the Navy Frank Sanders forwarded to the Deputy Secretary of Defense Clements, on 31 May 1973, the Navy's Improvement Plan for Diego Garcia. Funding of $7,900,000 construction and $4,800,000 for initial communications equipment was proposed for fiscal year 1974. Additional personnel was estimated at 225 plus 39 transients. Milestones of the plan included completion of plans and specifications by December 1973, starting construction of the additional facilities by February 1974, with communications capability by June 1976, and Navy Construction Force demobilization by September 1978.

Arab-Israel War

After the Arab-Israel War of October 1973, and the resulting cutoff of oil supplies, the United States enlarged its military presence in the Indian Ocean. The Soviets responded to the unanticipated deployment of a United States carrier task group to the Indian Ocean by sending additional naval units into the area—increasing their attack submarine force from one to four.

The Navy found it was very difficult to logistically support those ships with a logistic tail reaching all the way back to Subic Bay. The Navy needed a fueling station somewhere along the way. For lack of a fueling station, the Navy drew down on its logistic assets. The situation was such that had there been another hot spot in the Pacific, the Navy would have been in trouble. Admiral Zumwalt believed that had there been a confrontation in the Mediterranean between the Soviet Fleet and the 6th Fleet during the October War period—the Soviet Fleet would have won. The only base in Europe the United States used to resupply Israel was the Azores. The United States had to fly from aircraft carrier to aircraft carrier. The British did allow the United States to use P-3's for surveillance during the October War, operating out of Diego Garcia.

The Armed Services Committees were notified on 29 October 1973 of the Navy's intent to award an architect-engineer contract for the advanced planning and design for a communications and support facility project at the Naval Communication Station, Diego Garcia. The estimated cost of the architect-engineer contract was $400,000. Construction would include additions to the receiver and transmitter facilities and the associated personnel support, supply, utilities, public works and maintenance facilities. Estimated construction cost was $4,600,000. This project would modify the existing communications facilities and would provide additional capability and coverage required to support the Maritime Forces operating in or transiting through the Indian Ocean and contiguous areas.

Rear Admiral E.K. Snyder, Chief of Naval Legislative Affairs, prepared a letter to the Chairman, House Armed Services Committee, F. Edward Hebert, on 15 November 1973, enclosing a fact sheet and other data concerning Navy's plans for Diego Garcia and Asmera, Ethiopia, which had been requested by the committee's counsel. Similar letters were to be furnished to Senators Stennis and McClellan, and Representative Mahon. The letter had not been cleared by the Office of the Secretary of Defense, and was held up by the Deputy Assistant Secretary of Defense for International Security Affairs.

On 15 November 1973, Jack L. Bowers, the Assistant Secretary of the Navy for Installations and Logistics, forwarded a memorandum to the Assistant Secretary of Defense for Installations and Logistics requesting that Navy be granted the Secretary of Defense's Emergency Authority and funds to construct communications facilities at Diego Garcia. Construction funds were estimated at $4,600,000, and the work was to be accomplished by Naval Construction Battalion Forces whose labor was estimated at $4,168,000. This work was considered vital to the security of the United States "in order to avoid prolonged deficiencies in control communications essential to the support of United States Naval Forces in the Indian Ocean."

Return to Deployments

In his press conference on 1 December 1973, Secretary of Defense James R. Schlesinger announced that the United States was returning to a policy of more frequent deployments of our forces to the Indian Ocean. The carriers *Hancock* (CVA-19) and *Oriskany* (CVA-34) formed the nucleus of Task Groups operating in the Indian Ocean during November and December 1973. The nuclear frigate *Bainbridge* (DLGN-25) and the destroyer escort *Schofield* (FFG-3) were operating in January 1974 in the area.

Resettlement Financing

When the people displaced from the islands comprising the British Indian Ocean Territory first arrived in Mauritius, neither the promised land, nor money for housing was provided. The Mauritius Government had difficulty in buying land, and February's cyclone, Geruaise, left 90,000 people homeless. Mauritius got no further than getting one piece of land in Pointe aux Sables, popularly known as the brothel district of Mauritius, and were negotiating for a second piece of land in Roche Bois, which was known as Port Louis's worst slum.

The Mauritian Government had developed a resettlement plan for the first group of islanders returning from the Chagos Archipelago as early as 1969, but the funds provided by the United kingdom remained largely undisbursed.

In 1972, the Mauritius Government had not yet put into effect its relocation plan for the Chagos workers, partly because it was politically difficult to favor this group over other unemployed and disadvantaged Mauritian citizens. Mauritian unemployment was running close to 20 percent at the time, and British financing was not yet available.

Most of the islanders settled in slums around the Mauritian capital of Port Louis. The islanders claimed that when they were deported, they were promised a piece of land and money for a house when they arrived in Mauritius. They had received neither land, not the house money. The last group of islanders who arrived from Peros Banhos in 1973 refused to leave the boat when they found no help ready for them. They were housed, partly in a complex of dockers flats, and partly in Government housing. After two months in the Government housing, rent demands started.

The United Kingdom reached agreement with the Mauritian Government in 1973 to provide 650,000 pounds sterling, about $1.4 million, to Mauritius for relief and relocation of 1,151 people who had worked or lived in the Chagos Archipelago in 1965 or later, and who subsequently settled in Mauritius. The Mauritius Government acknowledged that the 1973 payment represented a full and final discharge of British obligations in this regard, and accepted complete responsibility for the people involved, most of whom were Mauritian citizens by birth or by virtue of Mauritian nationality provisions. On 1 October 1974, representatives of the resettled islanders petitioned the Mauritian Government to give each family a piece of land, separate housing, and jobs in Mauritius.

Mauritius progress in disbursing funds was slow. By November 1975, the Mauritian Government accepted a British offer of technical advice in setting up a relocation program, and was planning to establish the still unsettled workers on Agalega Island.

Emergency Project Denied

The Navy's request, of 15 November 1973, to use the Secretary of Defense's Emergency authority was denied on 10 December 1973 by Edward J. Sheridan, the Deputy Assistant Secretary of Defense for Installations and Housing. Sheridan suggested that the Navy consider adding this project to the proposed fiscal year 1975 regular military construction program, on the basis that:

- Regular programming would take only six to eight months longer.
- Some degradation of communications was accepted in the closure of Kagnew.
- Satellite will become available in December 1973.
- The project did not meet the criteria that the Secretary of Defense requires to state "national Security."
- Much of the project was for personnel rather than operational requirements.

Rear Admiral F. M. Lalor, Jr., the Director of Shore Facilities Programming Division, under the Deputy Chief of Naval Operations for Logistics, on 13 December 1973, delivered an advance copy of a memorandum to the Secretary of Defense James R. Schlesinger that would upgrade logistic support at Diego Garcia to sustain the Indian Ocean Task Force. The construction proposed included the construction of a 480,000-barrel fuel storage facility with a pier, additional power plant capacity and expanded airfield installations. A military construction contingency project for $19,790,000 was proposed to allow initial construction to begin before 1 July 1974. Additional funding for $9,260,000 was proposed for the fiscal year 1975 budget, and $2,628,000 was proposed for the fiscal year 1976 budget.

The total construction amounted to $31,678,000, and would be accomplished by increasing the Seabee work force of 1.3 to 3.0 Navy Mobile Construction Battalions for about 24 months. The Navy schedule would complete the aircraft parking apron by September 1975, the power plant extension by September 1975, the POL storage by June 1976, and the additional dredging by May 1975. Rear Admiral Lalor briefed Mr. Edward J. Sheridan, the Deputy Assistant Secretary of Defense for Installations and Logistics and Mr. V.B. Bandjunis, his Action Officer; and Mr. Allen D. South and Mr. John N. Gaardsmoe, from the Office of the Assistant Secretary of Defense (Comptroller).

Readiness Supplemental

Allen South advised Mr. Van Bandjunis on 14 December 1973 that Secretary of Defense Schlesinger had indicated to Mr. Fred P. Wacker, Deputy Assistant Secretary of Defense for Program and Budget, that the Diego Garcia project should be included in the Readiness Supplemental. Allen South then advised Rear Admiral F.M. Lalor, Jr.

On 27 and 29 December 1973 the Chairman of the Joint Chiefs of Staff, Admiral Thomas H. Moorer, forwarded memoranda to the Secretary of Defense James R. Schlesinger proposing to secure additional rights at Diego Garcia, and the construction of facilities there which could better support the use of our forces as an instrument of policy in the Indian Ocean. In addition to the operations that could be supported by the Navy's $29,000,000 supplemental request, the Chairman of the Joint Chiefs of Staff recommended additional facilities to support a small maritime surveillance aircraft detachments and periodic Air Force deployments.

On 3 January 1974, Rear Admiral F.M. Lalor, Jr. forwarded a Section 612, Public Law 89-568, Notification to permit the preparation of plans and specifications by architect-engineer contract for the $29,000,000 military construction project for the expansion of facilities at Diego Garcia. The notification was forwarded to the Armed Services Committees on 31 January 1974. The architect-engineer fee was estimated at $1,500,000.

Action Plan

During the period of 11 to 14 January 1974, the staff of the Assistant Secretary of Defense for International Security Affairs was coordinating a memorandum for the Secretary of Defense James R. Schlesinger outlining proposals for expanding facilities at Diego Garcia. The Joint Chiefs of Staff proposals of 27 and 29 December 1973 were included. The action plan called for:

1. Establishing a unified position within the Executive Branch, starting with discussions with State and the National Security Committee staff,
2. Approaching the British,
3. Approaching the Congress, with first priority given to the Armed Services and Appropriations Committees (Senator John C. Stennis, Senator John L. McClellan, Representative F. Edward Hebert, Representative George H. Mahon) and second priority to the Foreign Relations Committees

(Fulbright, Morgan). Informal discussion have taken place between the Secretary of Defense Schlesinger and the Chairmen of the Senate and House Armed Services and Appropriation Committees.

Brigadier General A.P. Hanket, Joint Chiefs of Staff head of Far East/South Asia Division, called a meeting to resolve facility requirements, costs, and funding of the Joint Chiefs of Staff proposal. Representatives at the meeting included Perry J. Fliakas, Deputy Assistant Secretary of Defense for Installations and Housing, his action officer, Van Bandjunis; Jack Gaardsmoe from the Defense Comptroller's office, others on the staff of the Assistant Secretary of Defense for International Security Affairs, staff of the Assistant Secretary of Defense for Telecommunications Policy, Navy, and Air Force.

Additional facilities recommended by the Joint Chiefs of Staff included strengthening and lengthening the runway to accommodate B-52 bombers and increased communications capability, which were initially estimated to cost $5,400,000 and $14,100,000, respectively, above the $29,000,000 Navy facilities.

On 17 January 1974, the Deputy Assistant Secretary of Defense for Security Assistance to the Assistant Secretary of Defense for International Security Affairs, Vice Admiral Ray Peet forwarded a letter to Mr. Seymour Weiss, Director of the Bureau of Politico-Military Affairs in the Department of State. This letter included a detailed explanation of the expansion effort contained in the fiscal year 1974 budget supplemental request; a proposed recommendation on an exchange of notes with the British, and suggesting an agreement, at least in principle, by 25 January 1974; defense views on policy rationale for the Diego Garcia expansion, a detailed Congressional scenario identifying the appropriate key congressional leaders; and contingency statements.

The State Department sent a message to the American Embassy in London on 19 January 1974. The American Embassy was advised that with British approval in principle of the proposal for expansion of Diego Garcia facilities and plans underway for congressional briefings commencing 25 January 1974, the Embassy should discuss with Her Majesty's Government the scenario for confidential notification of interested third countries about the project.

Establishing a Naval Base

The New York Times announced that the Department of Defense is considering establishing an Indian Ocean Naval Base at Diego Garcia.[13] Pentagon officials said that preliminary discussions had been held with the British about expanding the small naval station so it could support naval operations in the Indian Ocean. The mote was planned in view of the expected expansion of Soviet naval power in the area once the Suez Canal is reopened. The original Navy impetus for obtaining rights on the island was to have a permanent air station and base to support operations in the Indian Ocean as the Navy carrier fleet was reduced in size. The Navy is hard-pressed to maintain a carrier force in the Indian Ocean and still meet its commitments in the Mediterranean and western Pacific. The logistics strain on the Navy would be eased if it could rely on a support and refueling base at Diego Garcia. To a certain extent this could also reduce the need for carriers by providing a base for aerial reconnaissance.

The *Washington Post* also published an article announcing the Indian Ocean Base.[14] The *Washington Post* article said that because of concern about Soviet expansion, the Pentagon is asking Congress for about $20 million for air and naval support facilities on Diego Garcia. The article said that a reconnaissance base for long-range P-3 Orion patrol planes might cut down on the need for ship movements, and would also provide a refueling point and potential operating area for Air Force jets.

The Soviet fleet numbers about 30 vessels, more than half of these are auxiliary support and research ships. Opening of the Suez Canal by Egypt, helped by United States Navy minesweeper helicopters and United States and British personnel to train the Egyptians to do the ordnance demolition, means that the Soviet Union can send ships from its Mediterranean or Black Sea fleets to the Indian Ocean 2,200 miles away, rather than make the 11,000 mile trip around Africa or the 9,000-mile trip for the Pacific fleet units based at Vladivostok. The Russians already have some port and airfield use agreements at Umm Qasr in Iraq, and Somalia and South Yemen.

Vice Admiral Peet and General G.S. Brown, Chief of Staff of Air Force met with Secretary Schlesinger on 22 January 1974. Secretary Schlesinger agreed to proceed with the Air Force requirements, and directed his Comptroller to resolve method of funding.

On 23 January 1974, the Navy revised the scope of construction to include an additional 4,000-foot runway extension, making the total runway length of 12,000 feet. The runway would be extended by adding 3,000 foot to the south end, and adding 1,000 foot to the north end. The addition was required to accommodate Air Force K-135 cargo planes and for SR-71 reconnaissance aircraft. Held to a total of $29,000,000, Navy reduced the initial scope by dropping the crash station, aircraft wash rack, and fire station valued at approximately $1,200,000. These reductions would be included in a future military construction program, tentatively in the fiscal year 1976 program.

Nixon Doctrine

The establishment of the logistical support base in the Indian Ocean was perceived by many of the military planners as the end of the "Nixon

Doctrine" which had called for a "low profile" by the United States Government in overseas areas. However, given the geopolitical realities of the Indian Ocean, the United States should seek to lessen dependence on littoral states for logistic support to our naval presence.

Secretary of State Henry A. Kissinger had succeeded in disengagement of Israel and Egyptian armed forces. Negotiations with Israel and Syria continuing. Arab boycott of the United States for petroleum, however, has not been lifted. While rationing has not been carried out in the United States, gasoline and heating fuel oils are in scarce supply with increasing costs to the consumer.

Air Force Construction

Secretary of the Air Force, John L. McLucas, in a memorandum dated 26 January 1974, to the Secretary of Defense Schlesinger formally proposed additional facilities, estimated to cost $4,500,000, beyond the Navy proposals to support Air Force operations. Included were:

- Extension of runway to 12,000 foot to support KC-135 operations costing.
- Additional 25,000 square yards of hardstands costing $1,000,000.
- 160,000 barrel JP-4 storage costing $1,800,000.
- Protective open storage for munitions costing $500,000.

The Secretary of the Air Force McLucas recommended that the Navy fund the additional runway extension as a joint use facility, and that the Air Force include the remainder in the Air Force Budget for fiscal year 1975.

The Air Force operational concepts included F-111/KC-135 team, B-52/KC-135 team, SR-71/KC-135Q/RC-135, and C-141/C-5 airlift.

With refueling capability provided by KC-135 tankers, operations in the Indian Ocean areas would be greatly expanded.

The Navy's fiscal year 1974 Supplemental Request included and absorbed $1,200,000 for the 4,000-foot extension of the runway that the Air Force wanted. The remaining items totaling $3,300,000 that Secretary of the Air Force John L. McLucas recommended on 26 January 1974, was approved for inclusion in the Air Force's Military Construction Request for fiscal year 1975.

TABLE 1—PUBLIC REACTIONS

Country	No Public Comment	No Private Comment	Press Critical	Little or no Press	Officials Critical	Diego Garcia Alignment
Abu Dhabi	X	X				
Australia			X			
Bangladesh			X			
Burma				X		Nonaligne
Ethiopia				X		Pro U.S.
India			X		X	Anti-U.S.
Indonesia			X			Anti-U.S.
Iran			X			Balanced
Kenya			X			Balanced
Kuwait	X	X				
Malagasy			X			
Malaysia			X			
Mauritius			X		X	
Oman	X	X				
Pakistan				X		Balanced
New				X		
PDRY	X	X				Anti-U.S.
Saudi Arabia				X		Pro U.S.
Singapore				X		Balanced
Somalia			X			Pro USSR
South Africa				X		Pro U.S.
Tanzania			X			Pro China
Thailand			X			Nonaligne
Yemen			X	X		Pro U.S.

The Navy's plans for fiscal year 1976 were to pick up projects they were forced to drop from the Supplemental, and additionally to build primarily personnel support projects. Those projects included a corrosion control wash rack, crash fire station, structural fire station, aircraft ready issue refueler, shed storage, fleet recreation pavilion, outdoor recreation, public works shops, flammable Storage, chapel addition, club addition, hobby shop addition, Navy Exchange warehouse, special services issue and office, theater, library addition, education center. Those projects totaled $ 5,232,000.

On 29 January 1974, Secretary of State Henry A. Kissinger sent a message to the American Embassy in London with appropriate questions and answers for use in notifying third countries, congressional hearings, and eventually for contingency press guidance. By 7 February 1974, American Embassies reported reaction of foreign countries upon notification of the Diego Garcia expansion. Some countries viewed the expansion against India's "Zone of Peace Concept," but most did not react or favored the plan. Some countries privately disallowed their public statements to American representatives.

The Armed Services Committees were notified of the Navy's intent to award an architect-engineer contract for the advance planning and design on 29 January 1974, of a project at Diego Garcia estimated to cost $4,600,000, with associated architectural-engineering costs estimated to cost $400,000, according to a legal requirement.[15]

Supplemental Appropriation for FY 1974

The Department of Defense Supplemental Appropriation Authorization Bill, for fiscal year 1974 was referred to the Senate Committee on Armed Services as S. 299 on 8 February 1974. Title III of the bill included $29,000,000 for expanded facilities for Diego Garcia.

Prior to this request, the entire subject of the navy base at Diego Garcia was classified in response to "British sensitivities about the discussion."

The Navy's justification for the $29,000,000 expansion project described the mission and the project. "The Naval Communication Station provides Fleet broadcasts, tactical ship to shore and point to point communications, and is a critical link in the Defense Communications System. A new mission is being assigned to this Station to support periodic presence of an Indian Ocean Task Group. This project provides facilities to improve Diego Garcia for logistically supporting the Task Group."

The Navy project document summarized the requirement as follows: "Recent events in the Middle East, the energy crisis, and the potential for hostilities in an area subject to chronic instability has necessitated a reevaluation of US national interests in the Indian Ocean Area, problems that may affect those interests, and the adequacy of the means now available for their protection. These national interests that could require an occasional increased Navy presence are: (1) free access to and transit in the Indian Ocean, (2) protection of US nationals, and (3) protection of sea lines of communication. These events and interests are the basis of a requirement to provide logistic support facilities to support a task force operating in the Indian Ocean Area. Facilities to be provided are the minimum required to support surface and air operations."

Planning and Design Delayed

The Chairman of the Senate Armed Services Committee, John C. Stennis, sent a letter to the Department of Defense on 11 February 1974 that requested that the awarding of any architect-engineer contract for advanced planning of the expanded facilities at Diego Garcia be held up until the committee has had an opportunity to consider the project. Edward J. Sheridan replied to the Chairman's letter on 19

February 1974. Navy was requested to take no further action to award an architect-engineer contract until the committee's review of the project was completed.

House Foreign Affairs Hearing

The House Foreign Affairs Subcommittee on Near East and South Asia held hearings on the United States Indian Ocean Policy starting on 21 February 1974. The first administration witness was Arms Control and Disarmament Agency Deputy Director J. Owen Zurhellen, Jr. Other witnesses included Politico-Military Director Seymour Weiss and Deputy Assistant Secretary of Defense for International Security Affairs James Noyes, and Chief of Naval Operations Admiral Elmo Zumwalt.

Soviet Naval Build Up

The British sent a letter to Rabetafika, Madagascar, on 22 February 1974, inviting attention to the following facts about the Soviet Naval build up in the Indian Ocean:

1. A Soviet Naval Group was deployed in the Indian Ocean in 1968.
2. This fleet has been progressively increased in quality and quantity and now includes:
    - A modernized SVERDLOV-Class Cruiser,
    - A conventional destroyer,
    - Four escorts,
    - Four submarines, including a long-range missile firer,
    - An amphibious ship, and
    - Over a dozen support ships.
3. The Soviet Naval Forces make regular use of Berbera in Somalia for maintenance and recreation; and they have

shore accommodations and a repair ship there to complement these facilities.

4. The Soviet Naval Forces also make regular unimpeded use of the port of Aden.

5. A Soviet mine sweeping force sent to Bangladesh after the 1971 Indo-Pakistan War was still there.

6. In addition, the Soviets maintained a group of space surveillance ships in the Indian Ocean as well.

Negotiating Teams

The United States and United Kingdom teams in London began hammering out the government to government and service level agreement based on the $29,000,000 expansion plan on 25 February 1974. For the British, the team consisted of Jackson, Head of the Defense Policy Section. The United States team was headed by Jonathan D. Stoddart, the Director ISO, Politico-Military Affairs Bureau in State. Others included William Buell, EUR/NE Director in State; James Michel, Assistant Legal Advisor; Philip E. Barringer, Director, Foreign Military Rights Affairs and Colonel Joseph K. Brown, USAF, both within the Office of the Assistant Secretary of Defense for International Security Affairs; Captain Marjorie H. Mogge, USN, from Navy's Political-Military Policy Division; and Lieutenant Commander Wendell A. Kjos, Naval Judge Advocate General's office. An Ad Referendum was negotiated to replace the 1972 Agreement, and to provide for the construction and operation of the proposed support facility.

Nixon Letter to Sri Lanka

President Nixon replied to a letter from the Prime Minister of Sri Lanka dated 11 February 1974. The President's letter sent on 1 March 1974 stated that the decision to expand facilities at Diego Garcia does not represent any diminution of our strong interest in detente and in the consolidation of world peace. He also said that the maintenance of a general military balance is necessary for the preservation of peace and for the establishment of an environment in which meaningful and balanced force limitations can take place. The President assured the Prime Minister that the expansion of facilities was not directed in any way against the interests of Sri Lanka or other countries in the region.

Seapower Committee

The House Armed Services Subcommittee on Seapower, Chaired by Charles E. Bennett, met in Room 2337, Rayburn House Office Building, in Washington, D.C. on 5 March 1974. The Secretary of the Navy, John W. Warner, and the Chief of Naval Operations, Admiral Elmo R. Zumwalt, discussed the need to expand facilities at Diego Garcia.[16]

U.S. Expects British Approval

State Department officials estimated on 6 March 1974 that the change over in British government from Conservative Party to Labor Party would not block the planned expansion of military facilities at Diego Garcia. On the same day, the United States sent the aircraft carrier Kitty Hawk into the Indian Ocean as part of the Pentagon's plan to operate major fleet units there on a more or less regular basis.

India has protested strongly, and some lesser protests have been heard from Australia, New Zealand, and Sri Lanka. In testimony before the House Foreign Affairs subcommittee on the Near East and South Asia, the State Department's Seymour Weiss said that favorable responses included Pakistan, Iran, Singapore, and the People's Republic of China. Weiss testified that it was Deputy Secretary Clements who made the decision to expand the base.[17]

Readiness Supplemental Hearings

The Senate Armed Services Committee met in the Dirksen Senate Office Building, on 12 March 1974, to receive testimony from Deputy Secretary Clements and the Chairman of the Joint Chiefs of Staff, Admiral Moorer, on S. 299, a bill to authorize supplemental appropriations for fiscal year 1974. Senator Stuart Symington was presiding.

Deputy Secretary Clements said in his opening statement, "Also included as an augmentation is a request for $29,000,000 to finance part of the cost of upgrading the support facilities on Diego Garcia. Since we intend to continue a pattern of regular naval visits to the Indian Ocean on a periodic basis, it is particularly important to have assured support facilities closer than the western Pacific. The island of Diego Garcia is well located to provide useful, if limited support.

We are recommending, therefore, an expansion of the support facilities at Diego Garcia to provide an outpost where ships may perform limited in port upkeep, receive periodic repair services from a tender and receive critical supplies. Diego Garcia will also serve a base for patrol aircraft providing air surveillance support." (See Figure 9.) About 300 manpower spaces would be added to operate the upgraded facility.

Senator Symington asked Mr. Clements, "It is understood that the Air Force will request funds in their fiscal 1975 construction program to provide for fuel storage, parking aprons, and to help defray the cost of lengthening the runway to 12,000 feet in order to accommodate aircraft tankers, B-52 bombers, and other heavy cargo aircraft, is that correct?"

Mr. Clements responded, "Yes, sir.", with Admiral Moorer also indicating agreement. When pressed later by reporters, Admiral Moorer said that he had misunderstood the question. The confusion over the B-52 bombers caused some anxious calls between the State Department and the Pentagon. The State Department's Seymour Weiss had previously told a House committee that no B-52's would use Diego Garcia. The association of B-52's instead of just support forces would create difficult political problems.

In the afternoon session of the hearing, Admiral Moorer clarified the B-52 answer. Admiral Moorer said, "We are not planning to operate B-52's from or station B-52's at this limited support facility. The airfield will be primarily devoted to logistic purposes and perhaps some ASW patrol-type aircraft. The airfield itself, the parking area and support facilities would not accommodate the scope of operations required by the B-52's. In addition to the requirement for about 10 more inches of concrete to increase the strength of the runway, the width of the runway would have to be increased some 50 feet to accommodate the outriggers on the wings of the B-52's."

When asked the reasons why the supplemental included Diego Garcia, Deputy Secretary Clements responded, "Senator Cannon, we feel that the circumstances that prevailed during the October-November situation in the Middle East between Israel and Egypt-Syria are of sufficient importance to have us restudy the entire situation and bring it to your attention. The Suez Canal will be open shortly, the Soviet presence within this area will be enhanced without question, and the lines of supply both to ourselves and our allies in Europe and Japan will certainly be threatened to a degree that they have not been heretofore."

FY 1975 Air Force Construction Request

The Air Force's fiscal year 1975 program for $3,300,000 was for a small addition to the Navy's apron, an additional aircraft operational apron, 160,000 barrels of jet fuel storage, and about 6,000 square yards of open munitions storage, and a handling point for off loading and unloading of munitions that might be staged.

The present apron at Diego Garcia provides only 20,000 square yards of space. The Air Force was requesting an addition of 25,000 square yards, and the Navy 64,750 square yards that would provide a total of 109,750 square yards of apron space. The Air Force space was contingency related, and could be used for westward flights over the Indian Ocean.

TABLE 2

OPERATING RANGE OF AIRCRAFT FROM DIEGO GARCIA

Aircraft Type	Nautical	Aircraft Type	Nautical
KC-133	500-2000	RF-4	500
RC-135	2750	C-141	2150
F-4	675	C-5	2500

The 160,000 barrels of jet fuel would be sufficient to support approximately half a squadron of tactical fighter aircraft on a contingency basis for 30 days, or an airlift effort similar to that staged through Lajes during the recent Yom Kippur War. This fuel could also support KC-135 tankers conducting air-refueling missions.

The 6,024 square yards of open munitions storage would hold 2,800 short tons of munitions, sufficient to accommodate an initial airlift of munitions into Diego Garcia at the outset of a contingency, and compensate for the time-delay inherent in follow-on surface resupply to sustain contingency operations. The Air Force did not plan the storage of nuclear weapons.

The Air Force witness at the House Appropriations Committee hearings on 14 May 1974 was asked why its project was in the classified section. General McGarvey said it was a matter of timing. The classification was based on the fact that the British Government had not yet announced it.

The next week, on 18 March 1974, Congressman Pike asked Deputy Secretary of Defense William P. Clements why he changed the written statement regarding B-52's in oral statement. Deputy Secretary Clements responded, "First Congressman Pike, I changed my statement as it was written because I wanted to make it particularly clear to the committee that in an emergency, a B-52 could land on that strip. However, as Admiral Moorer will elaborate, if fully loaded B-52's were to use that base on a continuing basis, they would break the runway down, because it is not strong enough to handle those heavy aircraft. In addition, when fully loaded with fuel, the outrigger landing gear would extend beyond the width of the runway, thereby preventing a safe takeoff."

Former Pentagon Officers Dissent

The House Foreign Affairs Committee held extended hearings, in March 1974, on the Diego Garcia issue. While this panel could not directly act on the spending request, the committee report could cause other committees to push the request back to the regular 1975 fiscal year defense budget, which was also proceeding through Congress, but more slowly and deliberately.

At these hearings, retired Rear Admiral Gene R. LaRocque, now heading the Center for Defense Information, and former Pentagon systems analyst, Dr. Earl C. Ravenal, recommended against approval of a move that they believed was not necessary militarily and could have serious foreign policy implications. LaRocque argued that the Navy does not need the expanded facilities to counter an expanded Soviet presence in the Indian Ocean, and that the plans are really rooted in a longstanding attempt to establish new reasons for keeping the United States fleet size at a certain level.

Opponents to Supplemental Request

Senator Claiborne Pell appeared before the Senate Armed Services Committee on 19 March 1974 to recommended deleting the $29,000,000 request in the Supplemental Military Authorization Bill. Senator Pell had also joined with Senators Edward M. Kennedy and Alan Cranston in introducing a resolution calling for United States-Soviet talks on naval limitations in the Indian Ocean. He argued that this alternative should be explored thoroughly before the United States goes forward with development of Diego Garcia.

Senator Pell pointed out that the administration, in the recent past considered United States interests marginal in the area and that the Nixon Doctrine, which advocated that the United States seek to replace confrontation with negotiation, applied. He pointed out that less than a year ago, Deputy Assistant Secretary of Defense, James H. Noyes, assured Congress that with reference to Diego Garcia, "there are no plans to transform this facility into something from which forces could be projected, or that would provide a location for basing of ships and aircraft." But on 12 March 1974, before the House Foreign Affairs Subcommittee, Mr. Noyes testified on behalf of the Diego Garcia proposal. In May 1973, Under Secretary of State Joseph Sisco said, "The subcontinent is very far away. I think our interests are marginal. I think the Nixon Doctrine is quite applicable—namely, we ourselves do not want to become involved....In accordance with the Nixon Doctrine, we think the search for stability in South Asia is primarily a task for the nations of that region."

Senator Claiborne Pell also testified that in the early 1960's, Admiral John F. McCain argued for a "four-ocean navy" and summarized the outlook of those seeking a United States presence by saying, "As Malta is to the Mediterranean, Diego Garcia is to the Indian Ocean—equidistant from all points." Admiral McCain further advocated that the United States build a base on Diego Garcia to contest the Russian bid for supremacy.

Readiness Supplemental Hearing

The full House Armed Services Committee met on 18 March 1974 to consider the fiscal year 1974 Readiness Supplemental. F. Edward Herbert presided.[18] The opening statement by Admiral Thomas H. Moorer, Chairman, Joint Chiefs of Staff summarized Soviet activity in the Indian Ocean. Admiral Moorer said, "the Soviet Union, in recent years, has significantly increased its presence in the Indian Ocean. It has increased its ship-days from 4,500 to about 9,000 today. It has acquired access to bases. For instance, the base at Berbera, in Somalia, is used consistently. It has good facilities. The Soviet Union is currently in the progress of expanding an airfield near Berbera, which could be used to operate BEAR-type aircraft for surveillance of the Ocean. It has been visiting frequently other ports, such as Aden, in the south of the Arabian Peninsula, and also in the Persian Gulf at the head of the Persian Gulf at Umm Qasr in Iraq. It has visited ports in India, and in some of the islands here, and along the east coast of Africa, for instance, in Tanzania. It is already established with several places which it can use for refueling and limited logistics support. In addition, its ships frequently anchor here at Socotra Island, which is at the head of the waters leading to the Red Sea. So this request is not a matter of provoking the Soviet Union, since the U.S.S.R. already is well established in the Indian Ocean."

In responding to a question from Congressman William L. Armstrong concerning whether there were other possible facilities in this part of the world that the United States might use, Admiral Thomas Moorer responded, "Yes, sir. As a matter of fact, the first time I studied this particular situation was in 1961. It is obvious from a strategic point of view that its geographical location and a lack of possible conflicts with industry or populations or anything of this kind make Diego Garcia the best possibility for the logistics facility we are seeking." Russian Embassy personnel were present for the hearing.

Congressman Otis Pike asked Deputy Secretary William P. Clements, on the second day of hearings, if people in Australia were unhappy about this because of recent newspaper reports. Secretary Clements responded, "No, sir. But when Secretary Rusk was recently in Australia, there were some people there, both in the Government and outside the government, who discussed this with him at some length. But the Australian Government has not taken any official position whatsoever in this regard." Later in the afternoon Congressman Pike offered an amendment to strike the construction. He noted that, "as recently as about three hours ago, that the only opposition to this was some "nuts" in India, and some ultra-leftists in America who were trying to "gut" American national defense. So I left the committee meeting this morning and walked over to the floor, and have is what was on the wire service today—Canberra, Australia (AP)—Prime Minister Gough Whitlam said today that Australia will oppose plans of the United States to enlarge the base on the British Island of Diego Garcia in the Indian Ocean." Otis Pike's proposed amendment was defeated by a vote count of 26 to eight.

British Labor Party

The British Labor Party's official newspaper[19] carried an article about the Diego Garcia expansion. The article pointed out that;

1. Governments of India, Sri Lanka, Pakistan, Indonesia, and Australia are opposed.
2. Tam Dalyell, Labor Minister of Parliament for West Lothian is leading the opposition, who warned that the project could escalate into a nuclear base for B-52 bombers and Poseidon submarines.
3. The new Labor Government will have to consider and come to a decision, probably by the end of May.

Executive Agent for Diego Garcia

The Joints Chiefs of Staff recommended that the Secretary of the Navy be designated the Executive Agent for the Department of Defense for development of the maritime and air support facility on Diego Garcia. As executive agent, the Navy Secretary would be responsible for the coordination and management of interrelated planning and programming actions of the Military Departments. Arthur I. Mendolia, Assistant Secretary of Defense for Installations and Logistics agreed and formally designated the Navy as Executive Agent on 26 March 1974.

Indian Ocean Fleet

In a March interview with Seapower Magazine, Vice President Gerald R. Ford said, "Now, I think also that we've got to actively explore the desirability of having an Indian Ocean fleet."

Senate Subcommittee Hearing

The Senate Appropriation Subcommittee on Military Construction on 1 April 1974 met in room S-126 of the Capital to hear Admiral Elmo Zumwalt and Major General George Loving discuss the fiscal year 1974 supplemental appropriations requested for Diego Garcia. Senator Mike Mansfield presided.

Senator Mansfield couldn't see the emergency for appropriating money for Diego Garcia out of regular order. Admiral Zumwalt responded that the Navy could save six to eight months by going the supplemental procedure. Additionally Zumwalt said, "The urgency of being able to react to the opening of the Suez, the concern generated by virtue of the fact that we had only one airlift route to Israel and ought to have a second, and even more importantly, the fact that we found we were quite naked with regard to logistics support forces when we peeled off what it took to support from Subic Bay, 4,000 miles, to the Indian Ocean task force."

When asked to provide the cost to American taxpayers, the Navy provided the following information:

TABLE 3
INDIAN OCEAN ANNUAL OPERATING COSTS

ITEM	With Logistics Facility	Without Logistics Facility
DIEGO GARCIA		
Operations	2.53	1.93
Personnel	3.96	3.36
LOGISTICS SUPPORT		
Incremental transitting fuel for logistics	2.46	8.79
Incremental maintenance for logistics	2.95	9.43
Incremental fuel for additional logistic ships deployed	0.42	1.40
Incremental maintenance for additional logistic ships deployed	0.15	6.23
Additional MSC tanker charter	11.90	0.00
TOTAL	25.37	31.14

The operating costs in Table 3 were based on experience to that date given several key assumptions; (1) The Indian Ocean Force consisted of an aircraft carrier with escorts and is provided by the Seventh Fleet. (2) Subic Bay, Philippines was the nearest support base. (3) With a logistic facility at Diego Garcia the task group could sustain operations with the support of one AOE fast combat support ship and three chartered Military Sealift Command tankers, plus three stores/ammo ships. (4) Without a logistic facility at Diego Garcia the task group would require nine logistics supply ships to sustain operations. (5) Tempo of operations was maintained at the level then being experienced by deployed ships.

In responding to Senator Mansfield concerning the "Strategic Island Concept," Admiral Zumwalt said, "…the strategic island concept, as I recall it, was a plan to really retrench and the Pentagon looked at the developing world with the Soviets moving their facilities into populated areas and recognized that it was increasingly less likely that the United States, given its domestic political and foreign policy situation, would be able to hold facilities in the more populated areas, that we ought to aspire to have them in places that are not populated so that we could diminish the friction surrounding them."

Major General George Loving, Air Force Director of Plans, testified Air Force plans for Diego Garcia. General Loving said that Air Force planning for Diego Garcia started toward the end of 1973 and proceeded into January of 1974. Events in the Middle East and the oil embargo caused the Air Force to take a renewed interest in the Indian Ocean Area. At present, the Air Force had been providing six to eight cargo flights per month by C-141 Starlifter cargo aircraft into Diego Garcia.

General Loving pointed out that the runway was 150 feet wide and outriggers on B-52 landing gear were 145 feet apart. The taxiways were only 75 feet wide. These constraints precluded B-52's for the time being. Facilities that were planned there would provide the option to increase transport activity indicated by providing additional ramp space. The ramp space could hold up to a half squadron of tactical aircraft. A tactical squadron could be F-111's. If one wanted to base them temporarily, for example a carrier was not available to deploy in the Indian Ocean and one wanted substitute forces there for a carrier, the United States could employ a half squadron of F-111's and a very modest number of aircraft.

House Passes Appropriations for Supplemental

The House of Representatives voted on 4 April 1974 to provide the $29,000,000 for the Diego Garcia expansion. The action was recommended by the House Appropriations Subcommittee on Military Construction, Chaired by Congressman Robert L.F. Sikes.[20] The subcommittee report, adopted by the full Committee on Appropriations noted that "Early approval of this project should lead to earlier commencement of negotiations. We can be criticized for failing to attempt to negotiate arms limits. On the other hand, the United States cannot properly be criticized for providing facilities for support of our fleet similar to those which the Soviet fleet enjoys or will soon enjoy."

Congressman David R. Obey dissented with these recommendations. He believed that it was not necessary to appropriate money in a supplemental appropriation for Diego Garcia. His principal reasons were:

1. "There was no evidence that the Soviet naval presence "could" expand dramatically, and "could" threaten our supplies of raw materials. "How do two "coulds" make an emergency?"
2. If the expansion will aid the Navy during peacetime, where is the urgency which necessitates supplemental funding?
3. How can we forestall an expansion of war making capability of the super powers by expanding the war making powers of one of the super powers?"

Congressman Obey further questioned, "If the opening of the Suez Canal can have such serious consequences for our security (Soviets will be able to use it to increase its presence in the Indian Ocean), why is this government spending money to help open the canal?" When the Chief of Naval Operations, Admiral Elmo Zumwalt, was questioned about the benefits of negotiations to limit our deployments in the Indian Ocean, thereby saving this country a great deal of money, the Chief of Naval Operations refused to answer.

The Navy later agreed to initiate steps to obtain an answer from the Department of State. In discussing the stability in the region, Congressman Obey noted that the historic tensions were between the littoral countries—examples—India-Pakistan, Iraq-Iran, Iraq-Kuwait, Somalia-Ethiopia, and he questioned, "How can the development of Diego Garcia substantially help stabilize the region?" Also he questioned whether the Indians would continue their resistance to the Soviets for base rights if the United States developed Diego Garcia over the Indian objections. Congressman Obey concluded that the United States didn't know then, if it was to the best interests of the United States to have a permanent base on Diego Garcia.

Senate Armed Services Committee Defers Supplemental

The Senate Armed Services Committee deferred action on the fiscal year 1974 Supplemental Request for $29,000,000 on 9 April 1974.[21] The report stated, "Testimony did not indicate great urgency. It was clearly more than a simple military construction project, and involves United States policy in the Indian Ocean. It is a program that must be examined thoroughly. There is yet no written agreement with the United Kingdom as to the current proposal and future status of the island. Due to the complexity of the issue, the committee deemed it prudent to defer the matter for further consideration in the fiscal year 1975 Military Construction Authorization Bill, which will soon be before the Committee for consideration. This will result in a minimal delay if it is advisable to proceed with the program." The House Armed

Services Committee, however, recommended approval of the request, meaning that a House-Senate conference committee would have to resolve the disagreement.

Appeal to Conferees

Secretary of Defense James R. Schlesinger sent a letter to the Armed Services Committee Conferees on 23 April 1974 recommending restoration of the $29,000,000 project deferred by the Senate from Defense's fiscal year 1974 Supplemental Request. He noted that deferral would result in a six to eight month delay in construction, and that an ad referendum between the United States and United Kingdom was reached in late February 1974. To date, there has been no United Kingdom Ministerial action on the new agreement, but United Kingdom Foreign and Commonwealth Office officials do not perceive any objections to the planned expansion from within either the Foreign and Commonwealth Office or Ministry of Defense. On 6 May 1974, the Senate passed bill excluded the Diego Garcia construction funds.

House Appropriations Subcommittee Hearing

On 23 April 1974, the House Subcommittee heard testimony on Diego Garcia. The $29,000,000 fiscal year request for Diego Garcia was not authorized in the fiscal year 1974 supplemental bill, but was carried over to the fiscal year 1975 program. The British Government said that they delayed a decision on Diego Garcia until such time they complete an overall defense study. Chairman Sikes asked Admiral Moorer about the opening of the Suez Canal.

Admiral Moorer said the effect in peacetime was that the Soviets could draw forces from the Black Sea, through the Dardanelles, into the Mediterranean, and through the Suez to the Indian Ocean, saving them several thousands of miles compared to going around Capetown or from Vladivostok. Likewise, the United States could shift units from the Sixth Fleet. In time of war, the waterway was highly vulnerable. The Egyptian plans for the canal called, over several years, to deepen and widen the canal so that 225,000-ton supertankers could use the canal. When accomplished, United States Navy carriers would be able to transit the canal also.

Captain Giovanetti testified that the Indian Ocean will have no impact on the number of carriers deployed to the Western Pacific region. Periodically, units of the Seventh Fleet would deploy to the Indian Ocean for short periods. However, the Navy also acknowledged that they were requesting a 14-level carrier force level and that it was in the stage of final preparation within Navy and the request had to be for-warded to the Secretary of Defense. The Navy had six aircraft carriers in the Atlantic Fleet, however, the Chief of Naval Operations stated that faced with a reduction to a 12-carrier level, he would have to drop the Atlantic level to five and homeporting one of these in the Mediterranean. Should the 14-carrier level be realized, nine would be stationed in the Pacific, and five in the Atlantic.

National Security Council Review

The National Security Council began preparing another National Security Study Memorandum in mid May that re-evaluated American strategic interests in the Indian Ocean in light of recent events in the Middle East and attempts to justify the Diego Garcia base expansion.

Executive Agreements versus Treaties

Several Senators were attempting to use the Diego Garcia expansion to express opposition to executive agreements in general, as opposed to treaties, which require Senate approval. The Senate Foreign Relations Committee recently approved an amendment to the State Department-United States Information Agency authorization bill, requiring that any agreement on Diego Garcia with Britain be approved by Congress.

House and Senate Conferees

The House and Senate conferees met on 20 May 1974, to resolve differences in the Supplemental Bills. They adjourned without reaching agreement. They reconvened two days later, and this time they came into agreement. On 24 May 1974, the Conference Report on H.R. 12565 was printed. The report noted that the House approved the $29,000,000 project by a vote of 255 to 94, and that the Senate denied the request, stating that the expansion required a complete review of United States policy in the Indian Ocean. The Senate also emphasized their objection to projects inclusion in a supplemental authorization request. The House conferees, with the understanding and assurance that this project would be given careful consideration by the Senate in the Military Construction Bill for fiscal year 1975, reluctantly receded and accepted the Senate recommendation to deny the authorization request at this time. The action taken by the conferees was without prejudice to the merits of the project.

Cost Increases

A meeting was held in the Pentagon on 24 May 1974. Attending were Mr. Edward Sheridan, Mr. Evan Harrington, and Mr. Van Bandjunis of the Office of the Assistant Secretary of Defense for Installations and Logistics; and Admiral A.R. Marshall, Commander of the Naval Facilities Engineering Command, and Admiral F.M. Lalor, Jr., the Chief of Naval Operation's Director of Shore Facilities Programming Division. The meeting was called to discuss cost increases for Diego Garcia construction. An approval letter was held up to allow completion of actions on the fiscal year 1974 Supplemental. Notification to the appropriate House and Senate Committee staffs was discussed, but this was not considered necessary. The Navy representatives said that if the decision was not made by 15 June 1974, certain work would have to be stopped, and some work would remain uncompleted. The fiscal year 1970 authorization was escalated 20 percent, and the fiscal year 1972 authorization was escalated to 35 percent. Both escalations used the energy related escalation flexibility in the fiscal year 1975 Military Construction Authorization Act.

House Armed Services Subcommittee Hearing

Rear Admiral C.D. Grojean, Director of the Politico-Military Policy Division in the Office of the Chief of Naval Operations and Admiral A.R. Marschall testified before the House Armed Services Subcommittee on Military Construction on 4 June 1974. Mr. Pike chaired the hearing.

Rear Admiral Grojean concluded his statement by pointing out that the United States deployment of Naval Forces in the Indian Ocean stemmed from longstanding national policy. Regardless of the decision concerning facilities at Diego Garcia, it is in United States interest to maintain a naval presence in the Indian Ocean. Denial of logistic facilities on Diego Garcia would inhibit implementation of the policy and increase the cost of our periodic deployment to the region. The Admiral emphasized that Diego Garcia was not a base. Chairman Pike asked for a definition of a base. Grojean responded, "A base is a location which ships and/or aircraft will routinely operate out of, and I say routinely, to the extent that we usually put the families there."

Referring to the inclusion of families in the definition of a base, Chairman Pike said, "I think that is the most fascinating definition of a base I have ever heard of in my life, Admiral."

Admiral Grojean explained that United States Navy ships do not go into Indian ports because the Indians require all ships coming in to declare whether they have nuclear weapons on board or not. The Navy also did not go into South Africa ports because of the policies that country has toward racial discrimination.

Senate Subcommittee Hearing

The Senate Armed Services Subcommittee on Military Construction met on 11 July 1974 to take up the Navy's proposal to expand facilities at Diego Garcia as part of the fiscal year 1975 request. The Subcommittee met in Room 212, Russell Senate Office Building; Senator Stuart Symington Chaired the subcommittee. Senators Dominick and Taft were in attendance. Navy witnesses included Rear Admiral Charles D. Grojean, Director of the Politico-Military Policy Division within the Office of the Chief of Naval Operations, Rear Admiral A.R. Marshall, Commander Naval Facilities Engineering Command; and Captain W.C. Giovanetti and Lieutenant Colonel David J. Cade of the Air Force.

Central Intelligence Agency

On 11 July 1974, William Colby, Director of the Central Intelligence Agency testified before the Senate Armed Services Subcommittee on Military Construction. The subcommittee met in executive session (Closed) in Room 212, Russell Senate Office Building. Senator Symington chaired the hearing, and Senators Dominick and Taft were present. Also present were Gordon Nease, Professional Staff Member;

Joyce T. Campbell, clerical Assistant; and Kathy Smith, Assistant to Senator Symington.[22] In Mr. Colbey's opening statement, he outlined Soviet strength and strategy in the Indian Ocean.

The Soviet presence in the Indian Ocean began in March 1968, when four ships from Vladivostok made a "good will" visit to most of the littoral countries. By mid-1973, the typical Soviet Indian Ocean force included five surface ships—one gun armed cruiser or missile-equipped ship, two destroyers or destroyer escorts, a minesweeper and an amphibious ship. There was also usually a diesel submarine, and six auxiliary support ships, one of which was a merchant tanker. Recently a Soviet intelligence collection ship has deployed for the first time since the India-Pakistan War. Additionally a group of Soviet minesweepers arrived from the Pacific to conduct mine-clearing operations in the Gulf of Suez. United States and United Kingdom ships were also helping clear mines. The length on station for the Soviet ships seems to be increasing, up to a year on station. Colbey described the Soviet naval facilities in the Indian Ocean:

1. Socotra. A bare island. There is nothing there except for a small garrison from South Yemen. The only airstrip is an old World War II airstrip which is not feasible for modern operations. The Soviets have used Socotra as an anchoring place for their ships, and spend a considerable time at anchor.
2. Chagos Archipelago. The Soviets have set up some mooring buoys there in international waters so they can just come on and hook onto them.
3. Berbera, in Somalia. A communication station, with barracks, repair ships, and other facilities. A small installation which will handle two or three ships. The Soviets have been building an airstrip there for about a year, but have not gotten very far.
4. Mogadiscio, Somalia's capital. The area within the breakwater is somewhat shallow water; you have to anchor offshore and

bring in lighters. There is an airstrip 30 to 40 miles away northwest which the Soviets were gradually improving.

5. Umm Qasr, in Iraq. The so-called port is about four, five or six buildings, a place where you can anchor. It is complicated to get through the delta down to the Persian Gulf.

6. Aden. The former British base at Aden is a good base. It is a good harbor. The Soviets have not used it much. The airfield has a short runway, not big enough to handle the TU-16s and larger aircraft.

7. Vizakhapatnam, India. The Soviets helped build India's naval base at Vizakhapatnam, and have equipped the Indian Navy with minor warships and diesel submarines. New Delhi has not granted the Soviets free access to Indian ports.

8. Singapore. A very well equipped port. The Soviets have bunkered there. Singapore sells to whoever happens to go by.

9. Mauritius. Port Louis is a very good port. Soviet ships have bunkered there.

10. Overtures. The Soviets have made overtures to Sri Lanka and Chittagong, Bangladesh.

Colbey said that he expected a gradual increase in Soviet presence in the Indian Ocean area, and that if there was some particular American increase, that the Soviets will increase that gradually to match any substantial American involvement. Colby also observed that the Russian units left port only after United States or United Kingdom carrier task groups had departed for, or arrived in, the Indian Ocean. All indications were that Moscow was chiefly responding to deployments rather than initiating a unilateral buildup. He said that Moscow assigns a lower military priority to the Indian Ocean than to the United States, China, Europe or the Middle East.

Senate Armed Services Committee Decision

The Senate Armed Services Committee recommended, on 23 August 1974, authorization in the amount of $14,802,000 for the expansion project at Diego Garcia for the Navy, and $3,300,000 for the Air Force project. Their draft bill, however, included a provision that would require the President of the United States to revalidate the requirement for these facilities, and that afterwards a joint resolution of the House and Senate be passed approving the construction.

Armed Services Committee Impasse

The House and Senate Armed Services Subcommittees on Military Construction completed their markup of the fiscal year 1975 Military Construction Authorization Request on 9 October 1974, with only one exception—that pertaining to the restrictive language proposed for the Diego Garcia authorization. The Senate version would require a Presidential certification of essentiality to the national interest and a resolution of joint concurrence by both houses before construction could proceed. The House had proposed alternative language that would permit the construction to go forward 60 days after the certification unless both houses had acted to indicate their disapproval. The impasse on resolution of this point has prevailed for over a week, although the respective Chairmen have met several times. The House and Senate recessed for the elections without resolving their differences.

During the recess, Chairman F. Edward Hebert instructed the subcommittee's counsel, Mr. James Shumate, to prepare a short form military construction bill that would provide for continuing the support and maintenance of military family housing, NATO Infrastructure, and any other essential item, but would omit any authorization for all other new military construction. Mr. James

Shumate requested that the Office of the Assistant Secretary of Defense for Installations and Logistics provide such a bill as a drafting service. Chairman F. Edward Hebert warned that if the Senate does not accept the House version of the Diego Garcia language, there simply will be no new construction authority for fiscal year 1975.

Although Chairman John C. Stennis favors the House version, he was constrained by two major considerations. One of these was that the Senate voted specifically to support the Senate version by an overwhelming 83 to 0. The other was that Senator Mike Mansfield has privately advised Senator John Stennis that if the Senate defers to the House in conference, he will attach a provision to the appropriation bill restoring the Senate language. Another problem was that if there were no agreement by the time the present Congress recesses for the holidays, the bill automatically expires and would have to be reintroduced as a new bill for the 94th Congress. This would effectively kill it. The impact of the loss of all the $1.9 billion military construction in fiscal year would be substantial. Assistant Secretary of Defense for Installations and Logistics, Arthur I. Mendolia reluctantly provided a short draft bill to the House Armed Services Committee on 7 November 1974.

Appropriation Committee Approval

The House Committee on Appropriations approved $14,802,000 for the Navy that was authorized and $3,300,000 for the Air Force missions at Diego Garcia on 19 November 1974.[23] The Committee report stated that they had been assured that the facilities to be provided are not designed for the basing of nuclear weapons' delivery systems or for the storage of nuclear weapons at Diego Garcia.

Chief of Naval Operations Assurances

Admiral J. L. Holloway III, Chief of Naval Operations discussed Diego Garcia with Senator John C. Stennis, Chairman of the Senate Armed Services Committee on 26 November 1974. Admiral Holloway offered Chairman Stennis the following points:

- The Indian Ocean is an all weather transit route for the Soviet Navy between Europe and Asiatic Fleets; therefore, we can expect the Soviet Navy to be in the Indian Ocean regardless of United States presence.
- The oil routes from the Persian Gulf to the United States and our allies in Western Europe and Japan run through the Indian Ocean. A periodic United States Navy presence in the Indian Ocean will be required, both to protect those supply routes in the event of hostilities, and to demonstrate to our friends in the Middle East, evidence of United States interest and support.
- The naval base facility on Diego Garcia will be only a replenishment stop intended to support task groups in the Indian Ocean *when* the President determines naval forces should be deployed there.
- There will be no combat forces permanently based on Diego Garcia.
- Without Diego Garcia, United States Navy Task Groups in the Indian Ocean will have to be supported from Subic Bay that is over 5,000 miles away.
- Diego Garcia will not require additional United States Navy forces but, in fact, will compensate for programmed reductions in force levels.

Admiral Holloway stated in a follow up letter that other than the $14,802,000 in fiscal year 1975, the $13,800,000 in fiscal year 1976 proposed for the fleet logistic support function, and the $6,900,000 programmed for fiscal year 1977 for improvements in the original communications facility, the Navy had no plans for future military construction programs for Diego Garcia.

OECD

The United States responsibility to help its Allies protect their source of oil stemmed from a 1974 International Energy Agency agreement, whereby the organization of Economic Cooperation and Development established the international energy program committing all to share the oil should there be a net shortfall of 7 percent or greater.

Somalian Invitation

President Siad of Somalia offered in November 1974 to permit United States ship visits to Somalia leading toward improved political relationships. Present United States restrictions and technical aid to Somalia were imposed in 1971 because ships from other nations bearing the Somali "flag of convenience" were transporting cargoes to Cuba and Vietnam. In July, Somalia and the Soviet Union concluded a friendship treaty.

British Defense Review

On 3 December 1974, the British Labor Government, in its report to Parliament on the British Defense Review, approved United States plans to upgrade facilities at Diego Garcia. The formal signing of the ad referendum Agreement negotiated in London in February 1974 was still to be accomplished.

Authorization Conference Agreement

On 14 December 1974, the Senate approved the conference report on the fiscal year 1975 military construction authorization bill. Senator Symington informed the Senate that language was worked out that satisfies the House and accomplishes the purpose intended by the Senate. This provision provides that none of the funds authorized to be appropriated under this act for the construction at Diego Garcia could be obligated until certain specified conditions are met. These require that the President certify to the Congress in writing an evaluation by him of the need for, and the essentiality of, these facilities. Further, 60 days of continuous session of Congress must have expired following the certification—with the further condition that within that 60 days period either the House or the Senate may pass a resolution of disapproval for the project, thereby precluding obligation of any funds authorized pursuant to this act for the project.

Language was also included which in substance precluded parliamentary tactics aimed at delaying a vote on the Senate floor regarding a resolution of disapproval. Therefore $14,802,000 was authorized for Navy and $3,300,000 authorized for the Air Force at Diego Garcia. The Secretary of Defense was authorized to use existing funds for obligation without reprogramming action after the 60-day period expired without Congressional disapproval.

Improvements After Expansion of Diego Garcia

- An anchorage that will be capable of mooring a six-ship carrier task group. The lagoon dredging will also provide an explosive anchorage for ship to ship transfer ordnance.
- A fuel and general purpose pier capable of loading and unloading 180,000 barrel tanker in a 24 hour period.
- An increase in POL storage capacity from 60,000 barrels to 640,000 barrels.
- Lengthened the 8,000-foot runway to 12,000 feet to permit its use by tactical aircraft assigned to a carrier.
- Airfield improvements to permit aerial resupply for the task group, basing of patrol aircraft and recovery of tactical jet aircraft in emergencies.
- Parking apron extension to accommodate an additional C-141, four P-3 Orion antisubmarine patrol planes, one carrier on board delivery (COD) and twenty divert aircraft.
- Additional personnel quarters, to accommodate a total of 609 people.

Senate-House Appropriation Conferees

On 18 December 1974, Senate-House conferees agreed to deny the Navy $18.1 million to build up its base on Diego Garcia. The House had approved $18.8 million in the appropriations bill, but the Senate knocked out the Diego Garcia funds, questioning the extent of the Soviet threat in the Indian Ocean. Under the Senate-House agreement to drop the funding, the Navy still could seek a restoration of the funds 60 days after Congress convenes 14 January 1975. But President Ford would first have to certify that the base was essential to the national interest, and if neither house passes a resolution of disapproval.

Fly-speck

Outgoing U.S. Ambassador to India, Daniel Patrick Moynihan has accused Washington of touching off a wave of anti-Americanism by its handling of the decision to build a refueling base in the Indian Ocean. He said that Washington decided to proceed with plans for the refueling post despite a United Nations resolution every year since 1971 declaring the Indian Ocean a "zone of peace." He said congressional opposition has forced President Ford, in order to gain a $18.1 million appropriation for the move, "to tell the whole world that fly-speck called Diego Garcia is necessary to the security of America." After two years as ambassador to India, Ambassador Moynihan, was succeeded in February 1975 by former Attorney General William B. Saxbe.[24]

Draft Presidential Determination

A draft Presidential Determination on Diego Garcia was prepared on 17 January 1975 by Glenn E. Blitgen, Deputy Director for International Security Affairs for Near Eastern and South Asian Affairs for review and comments within the Pentagon. On 18 February 1975, the draft was forwarded to the National Security Council.

Mercy Mission

The *Enterprise* caused considerable speculation when she left the Seventh Fleet near the Philippines and Vietnam and passed into the Indian Ocean through the Strait of Malacca in January 1975. There was widespread speculation that the *Enterprise* was making a show of the flag for political reasons near the oil-rich Persian Gulf, but the Navy has never disclosed the purpose of the voyage or the destination of the task force. It was learned that the *Enterprise* was near Mombasa when heavy fighting in Eritrea between rebel forces and the Ethiopian army erupted. Some sources said the carrier was in the area to lend a hand if needed when more than 100 American and other foreign nationals were evacuated.

The Nuclear aircraft carrier was now involved in a major mercy operation at the storm-stricken Indian Ocean island of Mauritius. Mauritius was struck by a powerful cyclone that caused extensive damage to the island and its half-million inhabitants.[25] The *Enterprise* sent 800 volunteers ashore to help clear the roads of fallen trees and restore damaged water and electrical facilities. Its underwater demolition experts were put to work blowing up huge banyan trees blocking roads. The relief assistance cost the United States more than $300,000 which included money, supplies, and manpower. In addition, the United States pledged $25,000 to assist victims of the cyclone. The other powers acted likewise, presumably to convey the same message, and French and Soviet aircraft carriers also came running to the rescue. Probably the isle has never seen such a stream of warships into its waters, each one trying to outdo the other in showing the benefits of its presence. The "open port" policy had advantages.

Fiscal Year 1976 Second Increment

On 7 February 1975, the Navy submitted justification documents for the Fiscal Year 1976 construction program that included $13,800,000 for the second increment of facilities expansion at Diego Garcia. The Navy assumed that Congress would authorize and fund the Fiscal Year 1975 projects that had been deferred from the Fiscal Year 1974 Supplemental Request.

Senator McClellan presided over the Senate Appropriations Committee on 27 February, and Secretary of the Navy Middendorf and Chief of Naval Operations Holloway reviewed Indian Ocean operations.

Admiral Holloway said the establishment of modest support facilities on Diego Garcia was essential to insure the proper flexibility and responsiveness of United States forces to national requirements in a variety of possible contingencies, and that there were three alternatives to the development of Diego Garcia.

- First, without Diego Garcia, the United States must depend on support from littoral countries; the availability of this support, however, depends on the existing political situation and may not be forthcoming during a time of political crisis.
- Second, without Diego Garcia, the nearest fuel supply and support facility is Subic Bay, 5,000 miles from the Persian Gulf.
- Third, without Diego Garcia, it requires four oilers to maintain a carrier task group in the Indian Ocean for 60 days; with Diego Garcia, this is reduced to two. Task forces have been sent into the Indian Ocean about once every three months to remain there for 30 days to 60 days, since the October 1973 War to provide a United States presence in the area.

Trials of the Presidential Certification

Colonel Ellis, in the Office of the Assistant Secretary of Defense for International Security Affairs tracked the progress of the draft Presidential Certification. On 4 April 1975, the draft Presidential Certification was forwarded to the President by the National Security Council. The justification forwarded with the Certification said that Diego Garcia was essential to insure the proper flexibility and responsiveness of United States forces to national requirements in a variety of possible contingencies. The alternative would be an inefficient and costly increase in naval tankers and other mobile logistics forces. The

President had the papers with him in California, and the Defense Department was waiting for his decision. Colonel Ellis said that Senator Kennedy had proposed a resolution that the President not certify until talks were completed with the U.S.S.R. on force reductions in the Indian Ocean.

On 16 April, the National Security Council withdrew the Presidential Determination from President Ford, based on the State Department's Congressional Relations view that Senator Mansfield had all the votes necessary to pass a resolution of disapproval of the Presidential Determination. An internal memorandum from the Political-Military Affairs Director to the Secretary of State was prepared and contained four possible options:

- Submit the Presidential Determination,
- Submit to Congress in order to support the Administration's position in possible talks with the U.S.S.R.,
- Postpone sending the Presidential Determination and take no further action vis-a-vis with the U.S.S.R.,
- Postpone submission to Congress while renewing efforts to discuss the Indian Ocean with the Soviets.

The Assistant Secretary of Defense for Legislative Affairs made an assessment that the chances of the survival of the Presidential Determination were good, and passed this assessment to the National Security Council. The Presidential Determination was returned to the President for his consideration.

The Presidential Determination was forwarded by mistake to the Congress and published in the Congressional Record and Federal Register on 12 May 1975. It was intended that the actual forwarding of the Determination be delayed, at Senator Stennis's request, until congressional work on the Defense Budget was completed, about mid June. The message to the Congress read:

"To the Congress of the United States:

In accordance with Section 613(a)(1)(A) of the Military Construction Authorization Act, 1975, (Public Law 93-552), I have evaluated all the military and foreign policy implications regarding the need for United States facilities at Diego Garcia, On the basis of this evaluation and in accordance with Section 613(a)(1)(B), I hereby certify that the construction of such facilities is essential to the national interest of the United States." Gerald R. Ford.

The principal issue expected to be raised in opposition was the request that the Administration undertake arms limitations talks with the U.S.S.R. prior to congressional approval of the Diego Garcia expansion. Unaware that the Presidential Determination had been forwarded to Congress, the Senate Armed Services Subcommittee deleted the $13,800,000 project for Diego Garcia from the fiscal year 1976 request.

The House Appropriations Subcommittee on Military Construction met on 12 May 1975 to hear testimony on the $13,800,000 second increment of facilities expansion at Diego Garcia. Admiral Marschall testified to the need of a super filling station in the Indian Ocean, and referred to Dr. Schlesinger's testimony concerning the rapid buildup of Soviet facilities in Berbera.

The next day, Admiral Marschall appeared before the House Armed Services Subcommittee on Military Construction. Representative Richard H. Ichord chaired the hearing. Again the hearing was brief, with most of the discussion on the congressional response to the Presidential Certification, and the language added by the Senate which required congressional action to kill the prior Diego Garcia authorization.

Diego Garcia Restored

The full Senate Armed Services Committee restored the $13,800,000 project for Diego Garcia on 15 May 1975, but added language that tied approval to the Presidential Determination and the 60 days in which either the House or Senate could vote a resolution. (The United States action in recovering the merchant ship *Mayaguez* and its 39 crewmen seized by the new Cambodian Government may aid getting Senate support for the Diego Garcia base expansion.)

Senator Mansfield was expected to introduce his resolution of disapproval. It was expected to be referred to the Senate Armed Services Committee. A Senate Armed Services hearing was scheduled for the week of 2 June when Central Intelligence Agency Director Colby was to testify. Senator Mansfield submitted Resolution 160 on 19 May 1975, disapproving the expansion of Diego Garcia. The resolution read, "Resolved, that the Senate does not approve the proposed construction project on the island of Diego Garcia, the need for which was certified to by the President and the certification with respect to which was received by the Senate on May 12, 1975."

Construction Begun?

Senator Mansfield inserted an item from the 1 June 1975 *Washington Post* newspaper that indicated that construction of air and naval facilities had begun on the island of Diego Garcia. Senator Mansfield said, "I do not know what the commitments are. I do know that Congress has not yet approved the proposal of the President of the United States. I hope that here, again, the words would be muted until the facts are laid out and a decision is reached."

Special Subcommittee on Investigations

The Special Subcommittee on Investigations of the House Committee on International Relations, chaired by Lee H. Hamilton, met on 5 June 1975 at 1:32 P.M. in Room 2172, Rayburn House

Office Building, to examine the reasons behind the decision of the United States to try to develop base support facilities on the island of Diego Garcia.

Witnesses for the Ford Administration were George S. Vest, Director of the Bureau of Politico-Military Affairs at the Department of State, and James H. Noyes, Deputy Assistant Secretary of Defense for International Security Affairs. George Vest said that the United States is not a latecomer to the Indian Ocean, that the United States had a long association with the area, and that United States deployments were not a threat. He pointed out that in 1974, about 26 percent of America's petroleum and petroleum products imports, direct and indirect, came from the Persian Gulf. The comparable figure for Western Europe was about 65 percent; for Japan, over 70 percent. "Clearly, it is in our interest that the vital sea lines of communication over which this oil flows remain open to all nations."

James Noyes spoke of the various United States naval deployments to the Indian Ocean, and noted with irony that the United States often ranked third in numbers of naval combatants in the Indian Ocean after France and the Soviet Union. Since the July 1974 friendship treaty between Somalia and the Soviet Union, the United States was aware of construction of a major air strip, greatly enhanced POL storage facilities, and most importantly, a missile storage and handling facility at Berbera.

Soviet Naval Deployments

James Noyes provided the following information concerning Soviet vessel activities:

"On the basis of ship days spent in the Indian Ocean by Soviet naval units during 1974, the normal Soviet presence averaged between 20 and

21 ships at any given time. This figure does not include harbor clearing operations in Bangladesh or the Strait of Gubal.

Approximately one half of these units were combatants and the remainder were support ships. Using the same measure for the period through May, 31, 1975, the average Soviet presence was approximately 20 ships at any given time. The slightly lower figure is a result of the unusually high Soviet naval presence in the Indian Ocean in early 1974 in the months following the October 1973 Arab-Israel War. During the first week of June 1975, the Soviet presence in the Indian Ocean consisted of two guided missile destroyers, two destroyer escorts, an attack submarine, two minesweepers, an amphibious landing ship, five naval support vessels, a space recovery ship, two oceanographic ships, and two naval-associated tankers."

In 1974, Soviet naval deployments to the Indian Ocean constituted 20 percent of all Soviet naval out of area deployments in all oceans of the world. In that year, Soviet ship-days in the Indian Ocean were approximately 30 percent greater than out of area deployments in the Pacific, approximately 25 percent less than comparable deployments to the Atlantic, approximately half the level of Soviet deployments to the Mediterranean, and more than eight times the level of Soviet deployments to the Caribbean. The Subcommittee inquired when the last time that a member of the Arms Control and Disarmament Agency visited the Persian Gulf area. Mr. George Vest didn't know, but provided for the record that in February-March 1974, Dr. John Lehman, Deputy Director of the Arms Control Disarmament Agency, visited the Persian Gulf and Indian Ocean areas, including the island of Diego Garcia.

Soviet Missile Base

The Senate Armed Services Committee met on 10 June 1975 on the Special Resolution of disapproval of the funds for Diego Garcia. Present for the hearing were Senator Stennis (presiding), Symington, McIntyre, Bryd, Jr., Culver, Hart, Leahy, Thurmond, Goldwater, and Bartlett. Attending witnesses were General George S. Brown, Chairman, Joint Chiefs of Staff; and George S. Vest, Director, Bureau of Politico-Military Affairs, Department of State.

Much of Defense Secretary Schlesinger's testimony focused not so much on the Pentagon's plans to construct an air and naval support base on Diego Garcia as on Soviet activities in developing what he described as a "significant new facility" in Somalia to support Soviet naval and air operations in the northwest Indian Ocean near the Persian Gulf.

Schlesinger showed the committee aerial reconnaissance photographs that he said were taken in April of Soviet naval facilities at Berbera. He said the photographs showed that the facility was designed to handle surface-to-surface missiles which could be fired by Soviet warships against enemy shipping and probably air-to-surface missiles which could be carried by Soviet planes flying out of the airstrip at Berbera.

Secretary Schlesinger defended the proposed Diego Garcia base as necessary to offset what he described as "steady growth of Soviet military activity in the region" in the last seven years and to insure "the stability of nations" in the region. The principal purpose of Diego Garcia, he said, would be to provide a logistics base to support periodic naval operations in the Indian Ocean, thus "permitting us to maintain a credible presence" in the region.[26]

Chairman Stennis supported the Navy's expansion plan because "the evidence is clear and convincing that we need this service station in the

Indian Ocean." Senator Symington disagreed. Senators Thurmond and Goldwater openly favored the expansion plan.

Secretary of Defense Schlesinger said the principal objective of the facility was to provide secure access to logistical support for our forces operating in the Indian Ocean. The additional fuel storage would allow a normal carrier task group to operate for about 30 days independent of other sources of supply. He said that the first Soviet deployments to the Indian Ocean in 1968 were small and tentative in nature. But by the time of the Arab-Israel War of October 1973, the Soviets were able to introduce and sustain an armada of more than 90 ships, including the most modern in their inventory.

Somalia

As early as 1962, the Soviets agreed to assist the Government of Somalia in constructing port facilities at Berbera, a small port overlooking the entrance to the Red Sea. The harbor was completed in 1969, and in 1971, 16 Soviet ships paid visits to the port. In 1972, Marshall Grechko visited Somalia for the signing of a Soviet-Somali agreement. In late 1973, the U.S.S.R. began construction of a missile storage and handling facility. In July 1974, the U.S.S.R. signed a treaty of friendship and cooperation with Somalia, similar to those signed with Egypt, Iraq, and India. Following after the signing of the treaty was the beginning of expansion of POL storage, additional housing ashore, and a long airstrip.

Secretary of Defense Schlesinger noted that the entire buildup in the Indian Ocean has occurred during the period since the Suez Canal closed in 1967. With the canal again opened in June 1975, increases in Soviet merchant ships were expected.

Secretary Schlesinger brought photographs taken in April 1975 of the ongoing activities at Berbera. The photographs showed the Berbera port facilities, housing for 1,500 people, long-range communications facilities, the POL storage facilities, with a total capacity of 170,000 barrels, the new airfield, with cleared areas of 16,000 to 17,000 feet, and the missile handling and storage facility.

Chairman of the Joint Chiefs Brown, spoke of the strategic importance of the Indian Ocean. Not only are the lines of communication across the sea that carry oil, but also minerals from the coast of Africa to the United States. Secretary of Defense Schlesinger said that there was a revision to the Diego Garcia executive agreement in February 1974.

Committee Vote

The Senate Armed Services Committee voted 10 to six on 17 June 1975 approving expanding the base at Diego Garcia. The vote was against the resolution by Majority Leader Mike Mansfield disapproving the project. Chairman John C. Stennis said the Committee was influenced by the testimony of Defense Secretary James R. Schlesinger and the photograph which indicated that a missile storage facility was being considered in Berbera, Somalia.

Senate Delegations To Somalia

Senator Dewey Bartlett lead a Senate delegation that visited Somalia during the July 4 recess. The members of the group agreed that the Soviets do have some facilities in Somalia—missile storage and communications. The latter are definitely under Soviet control; the former may be. The group also agreed that the Soviets have access to other facilities—an airfield and port facilities. But, the group members differed in their interpretations of the military capabilities and significance of the facilities they saw. Some felt that the Soviet military potential in Somalia was significant and helps justify construction on Diego Garcia—others considered the Soviet potential less substantial.

The harbor at Berbera, one mile long and two miles wide, had depths of 50 to 60 feet. Berbera at the present time has ample depth and space for a large task force. There was also adequate berthing space, material handling equipment, storage space, and access roads to enable the port facility to serve a naval task force. The communications facility was a long-range, high-powered facility of very long transmissions and receptions, completely under the control of the Soviets.

The open bay missile handling building was about 45 by 120 feet, with 30 feet of vertical clearance, there was a 25-ton crane, capable of handling any missiles that the Soviet Navy would use. The storage bunkers were approximately 30 by 250 feet, and included sophisticated temperature and humidity controls. The airport, still under construction, will be 13,000 to 14,000 feet long. There was much construction going on, including housing, new water supply, and other buildings that the Soviets identified as a "hospital." The Soviets there numbered about 1,500. The fuel storage was being expanded from 40,000 to 170,000 barrels. The Berbera facilities, combined with the Aden facilities, could control the confluence of the sea lanes from the Suez Canal and the Red Sea into the Persian Gulf and the Indian Ocean.

Senate Delegation To Soviet Union

Senator Humphrey led another delegation of Senators to the U.S.-U.S.S.R. Parliamentary Conference. Senator's Culver, Hart, and Leahy discussed the Indian Ocean situation with several Soviet officials. The Russians said they received indications that their Government might be willing to negotiate a limitation of naval arms in the Indian Ocean. The Senators relayed their impressions to the Secretary of State urging that he further explore the possibility of such negotiations.

FIGURE 9 Map of Diego Garcia showing FY 1974 Supplemental

3

Senate Debate on Diego Garcia

On 28 July 1975, the United States Senate debated Senator Mansfield's Resolution 160, a resolution disapproving construction projects on the island of Diego Garcia. Five hours was allotted for the debate.

Arguments For Construction

1. To enable the United States to counter the increasing Soviet presence in the Indian Ocean.

The Soviet threat in the Indian Ocean has gradually increased by one or two ships per year in the past few years. They now maintain a force of 15-20 ships of which half can be classified as combatants. The United Sates maintains a small task-force on station in the Indian Ocean about one-third of the year and in addition has three ships stationed permanently at Bahrain.

Very recently the Soviet Union has greatly increased its capability to operate in the Indian Ocean. First, the Suez Canal has been reopened, and second, the Soviet Union was nearing completion of a naval support facility at Berbera, Somalia, that includes a major runway, housing for 1,500 personnel and a missile storage and repair facility. The expansion at Diego Garcia would provide the United States a comparable capability to sustain naval operations in the Indian Ocean area, and the Senate Armed Services Committee was convinced that it is necessary to counter the increased Soviet capability and to maintain the balance of power in the Indian Ocean.

2. To enable the United States to protect its vital interests in the Indian Ocean—access to crude oil and freedom of the seas.

The United States and the other industrialized nations of the world depend heavily on the Indian Ocean sea lanes that lead from the vast natural resources of Africa, India and the Middle East. This reliance can be most readily illustrated by a few facts concerning oil. More than two-thirds of the known reserves of crude oil in the world are found in the Middle East and Africa. Today approximately 20 percent of the crude oil that the United States imports comes from the Middle East; Europe is 75 percent dependent on Middle East oil and Japan 85 percent dependent. The oil embargo in the Fall of 1973 provided a warning of the consequences that would result from a loss of imported crude oil. At any time, 50 percent of the sea borne oil was in transit on the Indian Ocean sea lanes. The United Sates and the remainder of the industrialized free world cannot afford to let any nation restrict those Indian Ocean sea lanes.

The Administration has opposed the establishment of a peace zone in the Indian Ocean on grounds that it would restrict "freedom of the seas."

3. To provide secure support, at a reasonable cost, to the United States forces in the event of contingencies.

The expanded fuel storage requested for Diego Garcia will increase U.S. operating flexibility in the Indian Ocean by providing contingency support for U.S. naval force operating in the area. In absence of Diego Garcia the nearest independent U.S. fuel supply was now 4,000 miles away at Subic Bay in the Philippines.

Arguments Against Construction

1. Prior to embarking on construction, we should try negotiation.

Prior to embarking on construction, we should try negotiation. Despite congressional interest in negotiation—expressed in the Armed Services Committee report at the time that the Congress voted to require Presidential certification of the essential need—no attempt to engage the Soviets in discussions or negotiations for mutual restraint in the Indian Ocean were made. Most, if not all, the nations of the area would support mutual restraint.[27]

2. The publicly stated opinions of the littoral nations should be respected.

To disregard the public statements of leaders in the area could create ill will toward the United States. None of the 29 nations bordering on the Indian Ocean has given public support for the expansion of the Diego Garcia base. India, the nearest major power, opposes the base, our closest allies in the area, Australia and New Zealand, have publicly expressed their opposition. However, a State Department survey taken in May 1975 indicated that of the 29 countries polled, nine supported the United States planned expansion, seven opposed, and the remaining nations took no position at all.

3. The Soviet presence in the area, including the reported facility at Berbera, was limited.

It provides no major challenge to the American, French, and British forces in the area that collectively are much stronger than Soviet forces in the area and have access to a greater number of ports. The French alone have a great number of port facilities and a greater number of ships permanently deployed in the Indian Ocean than any other power.

4. The Soviet facilities at Berbera are not as ominous as the Department of Defense claims.

The Soviet presence in Somalia represent a potential threat in the future, but not a current risk to U.S. interests. The tactical and strategic balance in the Indian Ocean still favors the United States and its allies.

5. The United States has no treaty obligations in the area.

Since we have no obligation to consider deployment of forces into countries of the region, there was no need to expand facilities on Diego Garcia in order to adequately support a larger contingent of forces in the area. Our interests in maintaining freedom of the seas and safer transit for oil supplies can be served by working in concert with other nations.

6. While stability in the Indian Ocean was important to us, it was less essential to our security than to the security of our allies.

We should act in concert with them, rather than attempt to unilaterally police the area. It was reasonable to assume that France and Britain, which are far more dependent than the United States on Persian Gulf oil and which retain facilities in the area, would act to protect their access to oil supplies and freedom of navigation.

7. The primary threat to United States, French, and British interests was a cutoff of oil supplies.

This was a threat posed by Persian Gulf nations, not the Soviet Union.

8. There was no firm agreement on usage of the facilities on Diego Garcia.

The ad referendum agreement reached provides for use of the facility for routine operations. The British have publicly stated that use of the facilities other than for routine purposes would "be a matter of joint decision of the two governments." The British will not sign the ad referendum agreement until Congress approves the construction.

9. Expansion of facilities on Diego Garcia would not provide us with sufficient capabilities to conduct major military operations in the Indian Ocean area.

The expansion of facilities on the island was not necessary if our only goal was to show the flag. If our goal was greater, this and the associated costs of a three-ocean Navy—$5 to $8 billion operating costs—should be acknowledged.[28]

Senator Mike Mansfield quoted Senator Richard Russell who long ago had warned, "If we make it easy for the Navy to go places and do things, you can be assured that they will always be going places and doing things." The Navy has wanted a base at Diego Garcia since the late 1950's.

In the face of increasing Soviet presence in the Indian Ocean, the Senate voted 53 to 43 on 28 July 1975, approving expanding the base at

Diego Garcia. The vote was against the resolution by Majority Leader Mike Mansfield disapproving the project.

Leggett Amendment Fails

On 28 July 1975, Congressman Robert Leggett offered an amendment, which would terminate new construction authorization for Diego Garcia in the Indian Ocean, during the House debate on the fiscal year 1976 military construction bill. Congressman Leggett said, "In summary: If you liked Vietnam, you will love Diego Garcia. The amendment was rejected. There were three views expressed in the debate. The extreme view of the right was to build Diego Garcia into a major base. The extreme view on the left was that we should do nothing in Diego Garcia. The House took the middle view that we maintain our communication facility on Diego Garcia, and build it up by only the $13,800,000 appropriation—sufficiently top support a periodic presence of American naval forces in the Indian Ocean. The House passed H.R. 5210, the Fiscal Year 1976 Military Construction Authorization Bill by a vote of 369 to 47.

Status of Diego Garcia

Admiral J. L. Holloway III, the Chief of Naval Operations, provided the Secretary of Defense James R. Schlesinger the status of execution plans for Diego Garcia, as of 9 August 1975, in view of the defeat of the Mansfield Resolution and the expiration of the 60 days from the time of the Presidential certification.

- Naval Mobile Construction Battalion THREE was on site with seven hundred plus men working on previously authorized projects at the Communication Station. Construction operations for the new facilities can start upon the signing of the Ad Referendum Agreement of February 1974 that authorizes the expanded mission. The signing of the agreement was expected in about 30 days. The Navy requested the State Department to obtain informal concurrence from the British to start site preparation work immediately.

- A request for apportionment of the fiscal year 1975 Military Construction was forwarded to the Assistant Secretary of Defense (Comptroller). Procurement of the materials and equipment to be used by the Seabees to construct the new facilities will be started immediately upon the apportionment of funds.

- Approval to design the facilities in the fiscal year 1975 program has been received from the Senate Armed Services Committee. (In February 1974, Senator John Stennis requested that the Navy delay award of architect-engineer Contracts.) Complete design was expected in less than a year, however, material procurement and construction work will be carried out concurrently with the design effort.

- The fiscal year Military Construction Bill includes an additional $13,800,000 for the Logistic Support Facility. The design of these facilities will commence along with the fiscal year 1975 effort. The fiscal year 1978 program will contain the remaining $5,900,000 for communication station facilities.

- The estimated completion of major portions of the fiscal year 1975 work are: airfield expansion by April 1977, 550 foot pier by February 1978, support facilities by October 1978, and POL expansion by 1979. To meet this schedule and phase into the work that will be associated with the fiscal year 1976 and fiscal year 1978 increments of the program, Seabee strength on the island will grow as necessary to achieve optimum progress.

Commanders Digest

The 25 September 1975 Commanders Digest was devoted to Diego Garcia, featuring an article by Deputy Assistant Secretary of Defense for International Affairs James H. Noyes. The article addressed the basic questions about Diego Garcia. Secretary Noyes wrote that the additional facilities would provide an assured access to logistical support that could sustain the operation of a normal carrier task group in a contingency situation for a period of about 30 days. In a world of great economic and political uncertainty, that margin of time could mean the difference between an orderly, efficient resupply of United States forces and a hasty, ad hoc, expensive operation requiring a significant diversion of support assets from other areas.

Evicted Islanders Petition for Relief

More than a thousand of the inhabitants of Diego Garcia were forcibly removed and relocated to Mauritius late 1971. The islanders are now living in abject poverty, and have been petitioning the British and American embassies as well as the Mauritian government for help. Britain gave the Mauritian government about $1.4 million in 1972 to provide housing, social services and other resettlement assistance, but the people say that little of this money reached them. The U.S. State Department disavowed any responsibility to an American relief organization.

Interviews with some of the former inhabitants revealed that there were more than 300 families, between 1,200 and 1,400 people, living on Diego Garcia and the two neighboring islets, many of them third and even fourth generation inhabitants. The transplanted people feel they are neglected and were not compensated for losses. In 1974, the Diego Garcian organized, and drew up a formal petition and presented it to the British embassy, with copies delivered to the American embassy, and Mauritian Prime Minister Seewoosagur Ramgoolam.

The petition began, "We the inhabitants of the Chagos Islands—Diego Garcia, Peros Banhos and Salomon—have been uprooted from those islands because the Mauritian government sold the islands to the British government to build a base. Our ancestors were slaves on those islands, but we know that we are the heirs of those islands. Although we were poor there, we were not dying of hunger. We were living free. Here in Mauritius when animals are debarked, an enclosure with water and grass is prepared for them. But we, being mini-slaves, we don't get anybody to help us. We are at a loss, not knowing what to do. We (want to) let the British government know how many people have died through sorrow, poverty, and lack of food and care. We have at least 40 persons who have died." The British told the islanders to address their petition to the Mauritian government.

One of the principal leaders, Christian Ramdas, was born on Diego Garcia as were his parents, grandmother and most of his children. He was not allowed to return after a vacation in Mauritius after formation of the British Indian Ocean Territory. Working conditions on the Chagos Islands appear to have been close to those of slavery. The plantation workers were given food, housing and the equivalent of about $4 a month to buy clothes, tea and coffee from the company store. But "The life was easy," according to Ramdas. A recent survey of the Diego Garcian found that only 17 percent of family heads had full-time jobs, 33 percent were unemployed, and 50 percent worked part time. Some of the men, such as Ramdas, would like to return to Diego Garcia to work on the American base and look after the church and cemetery where their relatives are buried.[29]

The revelation of the plight of the former inhabitants was like a bomb shell exploding in Congress. Opponents of the base were furious, and believed that they had been purposely mislead by administration witnesses. Senators John Culver and Edward Kennedy attached an amendment to the Department of State Authorization, 1976, demanding that President Gerald R. Ford report by 1 November on why inhabitants of Diego Garcia were removed to another Indian Ocean island to make way for a U.S. Navy outpost. The senators said that throughout the Diego Garcia debate, administration witnesses assured the Congress that this island was uninhabited and had no indigenous population. For example, General George S. Brown, Chairman of the Joint Chiefs of Staff, testified before the Senate Armed Services Committee on 10 June 1975, that Diego Garcia was "an unpopulated speck of land." "But if the claim was based on the actions reported in the *Washington Post*, then the administration was clearly misrepresenting the case," said Senator Edward Kennedy. Nevertheless, on 7 November, the Senate approved the fiscal year 1976 Military Construction Authorization Bill after delaying funds for Diego Garcia. The 51 to 44 vote on the amendment by Senator John Culver delayed spending any more on the base until after July 1. The House passed its own military construction bill approving the Diego Garcia base. The Senate and House versions will have to be reconciled in a conference. Senator Hart asked the Comptroller General of the United States, Elmer B. Staats, to investigate and report how the dislocation of the inhabitants of Diego Garcia and of its associated islands was financed and whether United States law was violated.

Senates Passes Bill

The Senate passed the Military Construction Bill recommended by the Senate Armed Services Committee. However, by a 51 to 44 vote on an amendment by Senator John Culver, who in an emotional speech said that in order to build the base, the island's natives were being told to move or starve to death, would delay spending any more on the base until after July 1.[30]

Resettlement 1975 Report

Senators John Culver and Edward Kennedy submitted Amendment 884 to Senate Bill 1517 that required the President to submit a report by 1 November 1975, detailing the history of the United States Government's agreements, commitments, financial arrangements, understandings, and other relevant communications concerning the people who used to inhabit Diego Garcia. In addition, the amendment requests a judgement on the current status of any United States Government obligations to those people, or proposed efforts to assist them. Pending disposition of the amendment in conference, the State and Defense Departments provided on 10 October 1975, a nine page "Report on the Resettlement of Inhabitants of the Chagos Archipelago."

Architect-Engineer Slate

On 6 October 1975, Deputy Assistant Perry J. Fliakas approved the Navy's slate of architect-engineers for the Diego Garcia project. The slate included Lyon Associates; Louis Berger International Inc/Van Houten Associates; and Daniel, Mann, Johnson and Mendenhall. The architect-engineer fee was estimated at $800,000.

Appropriations Conference

The House Appropriations Conferees discussed the Senate's Diego Garcia amendment at length. House conferees expressed agreement with their Senate counterparts that negotiations regarding mutual arms restraints in the Indian Ocean are highly desirable and should proceed at the earliest practical time; however, the Senate amendment would have the undesirable effect of prolonging completion of the Diego

Garcia project and increasing costs significantly as a result of split procurement and escalated prices.

After much discussion, the conferees agreed to modify the Senate amendment with the full expectation that the Administration would report to the Committee on Appropriations and Armed Services of the Senate and the House of Representatives, the Committee on Foreign Affairs of the Senate and the Committee on International Relations of the House of Representatives regarding negotiation initiatives before 15 April 1976.

However, the Navy would be permitted and was expected to arrange its procurement contracts to minimize cost and delay in procurement of materials for the fiscal year 1976 increment of facilities by the use of fiscal year 1975 appropriations for construction at Diego Garcia that have been already made available. Such projects may proceed provided that neither cumulative obligations nor cumulative expenditures by 15 April 1976, on projects authorized for fiscal year 1975 and fiscal year 1976 will exceed $18.1 million, or that amount authorized and appropriated for fiscal year 1975, except that funds in the amount of $250,000 from the fiscal year 1976 appropriations may be used to procure, construct and install aircraft arresting gear prior to 15 April 1976, as authorized by law.

The conferees' intent was to prohibit construction of projects on Diego Garcia using fiscal year 1976 funds before 15 April 1976, but not to delay planning or the procurement of long lead time items.[31] President Ford signed the bill into law on 28 November 1975.

Special Subcommittee on Investigations

The Subcommittee of the House International Relations Committee on Investigations reconvened in Room H-236 in the Capital, on 4 November 1975, chaired by Congressman Lee H. Hamilton. Ford

Administration witnesses were George T. Churchill, Director of the Office of International Security Operations from the State Department and Commander Gary S. Sick, Director for the Persian Gulf and Indian Ocean within the Office of the Assistant Secretary of Defense for International Security Affairs.

The Subcommittee wanted an update from the Executive Branch on what was taking place on Diego Garcia now that the final efforts in Congress to stop development were defeated, and to explore the circumstances under which the former inhabitants of Diego Garcia were removed.

George Churchill and Commander Sick had developed a nine-page report concerning the former inhabitants of Diego Garcia, which had been sent to the Congress on 10 October 1975. Senator John Culver was the first witness. Senator Culver discussed the diplomatic backlash as a result of the Senate's vote on 28 July 1975, allowing a go-ahead on Diego Garcia construction. He said that Somalia, which had been receptive to the suggestion of a United States naval visit, perhaps as a way of reducing its current dependence on the Soviet Union, deferred any scheduling of such a visit because of the atmosphere after the debate earlier this summer was not conducive to a friendly visit.

Delegates to the British Commonwealth Parliamentary Conference, meeting in New Delhi in September 1975, criticized the United States base expansion. The opening day of the conference devoted all its working sessions to discussion of the tension that is being generated because of the American decision to go ahead in spite of opposition from all littoral and hinterland countries.

George Churchill testified that most of the information concerning the 10 October 1975 report came from British sources. He said that with few exceptions, the inhabitants of Diego Garcia and the other Chagos islands were contract laborers and their families whose livelihood depended on the coconut plantations and whose ties to the island were tenuous. The settlements on Diego Garcia appeared to have been something more than work camps, but considerably less than free indigenous communities. Everyone worked for the company, lived in a company house, were issued rations and bought his few rations at the company store.

The British Government had assured the United States that they were prepared to make appropriate arrangements for resettlement, including an assumption of compensation costs. The United Kingdom and Mauritius Governments reached agreement in 1973 for $1,400,000 in relocation funds to cover 1,151 persons that provided about $1,220 per person in a country with an average per capita income that was about $265 in 1972. George Churchill contended that the United States' position was that "these people originally were a British responsibility and are now a Mauritian responsibility."

GAO Report

The General Accounting Office completed its report, requested by Senator Gary Hart on 11 September 1975, concerning the financing of the dislocation of Diego Garcia inhabitants and whether United States law had been violated in late January 1976.[32] Comptroller General Elmer B. Staats reported that the United States waived $14 million under the Polaris Sales Agreement to cover its share of the British Indian Ocean Territory detachment costs. See Tables 4 and 5. Because of limitations placed on access to records by the Departments of State and Defense, the General Accounting Office was unable to satisfy themselves about the financing methods considered by the Department of Defense or to learn the total extent of United States financial participation. The General Accounting Office noted that United States economic assistance has been provided to the islands since the United States became involved in this area.

From the information made available to the General Accounting Office, they were unable to say that United States law was violated. However, they considered the method used as circumvention of congressional oversight authority. It was not until 1969 that the financial arrangements were first disclosed to a member of Congress.

TABLE 4

ACCRUED RESEARCH AND DEVELOPMENT SURCHARGES
Against the Polaris Sales Agreement
As of 18 September 1975
$ in Millions

FY	Cost
1964	0.224
1965	1.819
1966	1.724
1967	1.984
1968	3.621
1969	1.031
1970	0.251
1971	0.140
1972	0.188
1973	0.177
1974	0.155
1975	0.209
July 1975	0.019
Total	11.542

Economic Assistance

Since the early 1960s, Mauritius has been receiving a small amount of United States assistance, mostly under Public Law 480 (Food for Peace). This averaged about $100,000 a year until 1968, when it increased to $800,000. In 1969, assistance decreased to $100,000, and during 1970-1974 it ranged from $1.1 million to $3.3 million. Proposed assistance programs for 1975 and 1976 were $1.2 million and $1.8 million, respectively. Thus, total assistance to Mauritius since the United States became involved in the area, approaches $16 million. The increased assistance to Mauritius roughly corresponds with two events: (1) The relocation of inhabitants from Diego Garcia to Mauritius, and (2) The independence of Mauritius on 12 March 1968.

Both State and Defense officials said there was absolutely no connection between economic assistance to Mauritius and United States military programs. One State Department official observed that the Unites States normally did not give much assistance to dependencies and that the increase could probably be related to Mauritian independence. The Seychelles, still a British Crown Colony, has been provided assistance primarily under Public Law 480 totaling about $300,000 during 1962-74. Proposed assistance programs for 1975 and 1976 were $26,000 and $143,000, respectively.

FIGURE 10 A view of the Diego Garcia communication complex in November 1976. U.S. Navy Photo

FIGURE 11 Heavy equipment of NMCB 133 at work on the runway lengthening project in November 1976. U.S. Navy Photo

TABLE 5
BRITISH DETACHMENT COSTS
As of 19 September 1975, the British stated they had
incurred the following detachment costs.
$ in Millions

Detachment Items	Cost
Compensation to Mauritius for loss of sovereignty	8.40
Chagos Agalega Copra Plantation for transfer of freehold	3.78
Compensation to Seychelles for transfer of sovereignty, Construction of Mahe Commericial Airfield	17.36
Compensation to Mauritius for relocation of inhabitants	1.82
Total	31.36

1977 Program Slipped

Secretary of Defense Donald H. Rumsfield responded to a question during the Secretary's Posture Hearing on 15 January 1976, "that there were no funds in the fiscal year 1977 Defense Budget to support construction at Diego Garcia other than the amounts for military salaries and normal operation and maintenance functions. As testified to by the Navy last year, the construction planned for fiscal year has been slipped to fiscal year 1978." The project funding was slipped because of the

Congressional restrictions placed on commencement of construction of the fiscal year 1976 project.

Ad Referendum Signed

The British Indian Ocean Territory Agreement of 1976 was effected in London by the exchange of notes between the British Minister of State for Foreign and Commonwealth Affairs, signed by Roy Hattersley, and signed by the American Charge d'affaires ad interim, Ronald I. Spiers, on 25 February 1976. The new agreement allowed the development of the communications facility on Diego Garcia into a support facility. The agreement limited access to Diego Garcia to members of the military forces, representatives of the two Governments, and contractor personnel. The Diego Garcia Agreement of 1972 was replaced with the 1976 version. British Vice Admiral R.D. Lygo and American Admiral D.H. Bagley signed a supplementary arrangement, which detailed procedures for manning the facility, logistical support, telecommunications, and access to research groups. A related note listed the additional construction proposed to make Diego a Navy Support Facility.

Four months later, the United States and the United Kingdom signed an agreement on 22 and 25 June 1976, which modified the 30 December 1966 Agreement, by deleting reference to the islands of Aldabra, Farquhar and Desroches, leaving the 1966 agreement covering only the island of Diego Garcia and the remainder of the Chagos Archipelago. The 1976 amendment was signed by the American Ambassador Anne Armstrong and signed by E. N. Larmour for the British Secretary of State for Foreign and Commonwealth Affairs Anthony Crosland. This agreement was made preceding the Agreement between the United Kingdom and Seychelles of 29 June 1976 (Independence Day) which made provision for the United States rights of access, entry, use or establishment with respect to Seychelles.[33] Concurrently, the United States and the Republic of Seychelles signed an agreement on 29 June 1976 allowing the United States to establish, in the island of Mahe, a tracking and telemetry facility for orbital control and data acquisition.[34]

Report on Indian Ocean Arms Limitation

Assistant Secretary for Congressional Relations Robert J. McCloskey forwarded the statement of the administration's position on Indian Ocean arms limitation initiatives to the Appropriations, Armed Services Committees, Foreign Relations, and International Relations Committees of the House and Senate, on 15 April 1976, as was requested in the Conference Report, and later enacted into law, on the Military Construction Appropriation Act for Fiscal Year 1976.[35] The statement read:

"The Executive Branch has given careful consideration to the issues involved in arms limitation in the Indian Ocean area. We have examined the technical problems involved in any such limitation and we have considered the issue of arms limitation in the broader political context of recent events in the region, as well as our overall relationship to the Soviet Union. We have concluded that although we might want to give further   consideration to some arms limitation initiative at a later date and perhaps take up the matter with the Soviet government then, any such initiative would be inappropriate now.

The situation in the Indian Ocean cannot be considered in isolation from the past and possible future events on the African mainland. Soviet activities in Angola and the Soviet buildup of facilities in Somalia have raised major questions about the intentions of the Soviet Union in areas bordering on the Indian Ocean. While reemphasizing our support for majority rule in Africa and for political solutions of regional problems by regional states, we have made clear that we cannot acquiesce in the use of Soviet or surrogate forces as a means of determining the outcome of local conflicts.

We are now seeking to encourage the Soviet Union to conduct itself with restraint and to avoid exploiting local crises for unilateral gain. An arms limitation initiative at this time in a region immediately contiguous to the African continent might convey the mistaken impression to the Soviets and our friends and allies that we were willing to acquiesce in this type of Soviet behavior.

For these reasons, we could not consider seriously an arms limitation initiative focused on the Indian Ocean without clear evidence of Soviet willingness to exercise restraint in the region as a whole. This view has been reinforced by our examination of the technical issues which would be involved in any arms limitation negotiations. Although the technical complexities do not in themselves preclude negotiations, it is evident that a successful arrangement could occur only within a general political framework of mutual restraint in the region.

Clearly, it is not in our interest for this region to become a theater of contention and rivalry, nor would the states of the area welcome such a development. In fact, over the past two years the naval deployments of the United States and the Soviet Union have remained relatively stable. For our part, we will continue a policy of restraint in our military activities in the Indian Ocean area. We intend to proceed with our planned improvements to the support facilities on Diego Garcia, but there is no present intention to go beyond the plans as presented to the Congress last year or to increase our naval deployments to the area.

We, of course, hope that the Soviets will exercise restraint in the area. We will watch carefully to determine the impact on the Soviet military presence of their expansion of naval and air support facilities in Somalia. Restraint in Soviet Indian Ocean deployments, coupled with a more general forbearance from adventurism in the region as a whole, would provide a better context for considering the possibilities for arms limitation in the Indian Ocean. Thus, while we will keep open the matter of a possible future arms limitation initiative as a potential contribution to regional stability and to our relationship with the Soviet Union, we do not perceive it to be in the United States interest just at this time."

Assistant Secretary McCloskey noted in his forwarding letter the new call for initiatives on Indian Ocean arms limitations, and for a report to the Congress thereon by 1 December 1976, in legislation now before the Congress.

Construction Proceeds

Chief of Naval Operations Admiral James L. Holloway, III sent a message on 5 March 1976 to the Commander, Naval Facilities Engineering Command. The message authorized commencement of construction of the fiscal year 1975 increment and the aircraft arresting gear of the fiscal year 1976 increment. The message cautioned that no other portion of the fiscal year 1976 could proceed prior to 15 April 1976.

On 16 April 1976, Navy Secretary J. William Middendorf, II sent a memorandum to Defense Secretary Donald H. Rumsfield. The memorandum advised, "The report of the Committee of Conference on the Fiscal Year 1976 Military Construction Appropriations Bill (Report No. 94–655) expressed the expectation that a report will be made by the Administration to six Congressional Committees prior to 15 April 1976, regarding negotiating initiatives leading towards mutual arms restraint in the Indian Ocean.

Since it is anticipated that this report will be forwarded to the Congress in the very near future, the Navy proposes to proceed with the authorized construction project for Diego Garcia, on 16 April 1976, as previously scheduled."

The Chief of Naval Operations message on 1 May 1976 to the Commander, Naval Facilities Engineering Command authorized commencement of construction on the remainder of the fiscal year 1976 projects at Diego Garcia.

Full Scale Investigation

Senators John Culver; Mike Mansfield who accused the Ford Administration of arrogance, duplicity and deception; Stuart Symington; Edward M. Kennedy; and Claiborne Pell backed a draft study resolution to learn about the costs, conditions and diplomatic actions involving the Diego Garcia base. The dispute was revived by three developments:

- Receipt of the 15 April 1976 report from the State Department indicating that the administration has ignored the congressional mandate to try to negotiate a mutual arms restraint agreement with the Soviets.
- Testimony on 4 May 1976 by the former United States Ambassador to Saudi Arabia James Akins that the State Department had ignored an offer by Saudi Arabia to finance aid to Somalia in order to eliminate the Soviet presence. The Democratic Senators suggested that the offer was ignored because elimination of Russian influence would rob the Pentagon of its excuse for building the Diego Garcia base.
- A charge by Senator Mike Mansfield that a congressional delegation to Somalia had been steered away from Saudi Arabia for fear the mission would learn of the offer.[36]

Joint Resolution 193

Senator John C. Culver, for himself, Senators Edward M. Kennedy, Claiborne Pell, and Stuart Symington, on 6 May 1976, introduced Senate Joint Resolution 193, a joint resolution which would prohibit the use of funds for "any construction in the Indian Ocean area" for a period of 180 days after enactment. This prohibition could be terminated at an earlier date by the adoption of a concurrent resolution expressing the sense of Congress that all reasonable diplomatic efforts have been made to achieve (1) a reduction of the Soviet military presence in the Indian Ocean and in Somalia, and (2) an agreement with the Soviet Union regarding mutual limitations on the military presence of both the United States and the U.S.S.R. in the Indian Ocean and adjacent land areas."

The Department of State draft letter of 20 June 1976, to Senate Foreign Relations Committee Chairman John Sparkman, contained the coordinated views of the Executive Branch on Senate Joint Resolution 193. "The Executive Branch is strongly opposed to this resolution. The questions relating to construction at the Navy facility on Diego Garcia have been thoroughly scrutinized by Congress and funds for this purpose have been authorized and appropriated on the basis of detailed justification. Further delay in the ongoing construction while another review was undertaken would therefore, be unwarranted. Such a delay would greatly increase the costs of the project and would detract from the attainment of operational objectives intended to be served by this approved facility."

Soviet Fleet

Twenty Soviet naval ships were operating in the Indian Ocean in June according to Australian Defense Minister James Killen. The fleet comprised four destroyer-frigates, one submarine, two mine sweepers, one landing ship, four oilers, one oceanographic ship, two support ships, one stores ship and one intelligence collecting ship.[37]

July 1976 Program Status

The designs for the fiscal years 1975 and 1976 facilities were essentially finished with the in-house designs completed and the architect-engineer designs scheduled for completion in July 1976. Procurement of material commenced in November 1975, and most long-lead procurements have been initiated. As of 30 June 1976 approximately 50 percent of the total fiscal years 1975 and 1976 programs had been obligated for material procurement or committed for shipping procured materials.

Construction of the fiscal year 1975 facilities commenced upon signing of the Ad Referendum Agreement with the British. Construction of the fiscal year 1976 facilities commenced in May 1976 after the requirements imposed by the Conference Committee on Military Construction Appropriations were satisfied. The first of the fiscal year facilities were be completed in November, and all fiscal years 1975 and 1976 construction were to be completed in calendar year 1979. Except for dredging and POL tanks, all construction was being done by approximately 750 Seabees.

House and Senate Conferees completed action on the fiscal year 1976 and the transition year budget to the new budget year Military Construction Appropriations on 12 November 1976. The conferees discussed the Senate's amendment at length and modified the amendment requiring the Administration to report negotiating initiatives before 15 April 1975. The modified amendment did not delay construction long lead time items.[38]

Expansion Plan Final Increment

The Navy's fiscal year 1978 military construction program for the Naval Support Facility, Diego Garcia proposed:

- An aircraft direct fueling station, and an aircraft taxi-through rinse rack. The existing refueling procedure required aircraft to utilize small and slow tank trucks that conveyed fuel from storage to the aircraft's parking apron. There was no facility for rinsing the salt deposits from the aircraft.
- Communications improvements, including additions to the receiver and generator buildings. The new terminal portion of the project was for a Defense Satellite Communications System line to Clark Air Force Base in the Philippines and to Landstuhl, Germany to provide better communications with a Defense System satellite directly over the Indian Ocean.
- An aircraft crash/rescue fire station in the air operations area, and a structural fire station convenient to the cantonment and receiver area. The existing aircraft fire and crash rescue trucks were in a temporary shed that was to be demolished. The other fire truck was housed in a wooden temporary facility in the cantonment area. The new buildings were to be constructed with concrete masonry units.
- Conversion of an existing warehouse into a public works and vehicle maintenance shop, and modification of the existing public works shop.
- Two general warehouses, a Navy Exchange warehouse, medical storage spaces, and an armory. These were needed to store supplies for a four month period.
- Four buildings to provide adequate living quarters for 172 enlisted personnel.

• A pavilion, playing field, officer/Chief Petty Officer Club, a combined hobby shop and special services issue office, and an education center. The only permanent fleet recreation facilities were a softball field, a volleyball court, and a cleared beach area with a picnic table and a couple cabanas. The only permanent morale facilities were a chapel, library, bowling alley, and a gymnasium. No women were stationed at Diego Garcia.

Manpower Increase

There were two basic changes that developed subsequent to the fiscal year 1976 hearings: a 172-man Bachelor Enlisted Quarters was added to support the planned manning level, and satellite communications was added to meet operational requirements. Based on previous testimony before the Congress, permanent island manning was established at 583 officers and men. The Commander in Chief Pacific Fleet and the Commander Navy Telecommunications Command indicated the need to increase the manning level to a total of 797 officers and men, including permanently assigned and transient personnel to adequately accomplish previously authorized missions. The fiscal year 1978 military budget submission to the Office of Secretary of Defense included an additional 171 man Bachelor Enlisted Quarters for $2,500,000 to accommodate this increased requirement. Reductions in the scopes of other projects contained in the Diego Garcia program were made to accommodate the Bachelor Enlisted Quarters in order to remain within the $7,300,000 program total.

Congressional approval of this new Bachelor Enlisted Quarters project would in effect approve the increased manning level just as the Congressional approvals of the previous Bachelor Officer and Bachelor Enlisted Quarter projects established the 583 man level. The $7,300,000 proposed for fiscal year 1978 was the final increment of the construction expansion plan certified by the President in May 1975 to be essential to the United States national interest.

TABLE 6 MANPOWER REQUIREMENT

Activity	Officers	Enlisted	Total
Support Facility	19	386	405
Communications Station	7	161	168
Security Group	2	72	74
Weather Service	1	15	16
VP/VQ	26	71	97
Transient	2	8	10
FASU	3	24	27
British	2	22	24
Totals	62	759	821

Anticipating congressional questions about the substantial increased manning, the Navy offered the following explanation. "During our testimony on the Navy's FY 1975 and FY 1976 programs, we indicated that the total permanent island manning would be approximately 600 people. Since that time, two factors have led to an increase in manning requirements. First, there have been some important political changes in the Indian Ocean area. The loss of support from Utapao in Thailand, and the British giving up their base in Gan, from which we received weather service support, compel our activities on Diego Garcia to operate more independently, which increases manning requirements. Secondly, we now have significant experience in operating and maintaining equipment and facilities in this remote area. I am of course most familiar with facilities; I know from my visits to the island that facilities maintenance and vehicle maintenance is very difficult. The atmosphere is laden with salt and highly corrosive. I know that this causes similar headaches in communications and aircraft maintenance as well. Based on our experience to date, we know additional personnel are required to operate and properly maintain our facilities and equipment.

The new BEQ in this request would enable us to support a total United States Navy manning level of about 800 personnel, including transients. As you know, we also provide space for 24 Royal Navy personnel on the island, and this requirement is included on the DD 1390."

No Negotiations

On 1 December 1976, another report was made to Congress which, while fully recognizing the sense of Congress that the United States should enter into negotiations with the Soviet Union intended to achieve agreement limiting United States/Soviet military deployment in that region, still did not judge that circumstances were appropriate for an initiative of the type.

National Security Council Inquiry

On 24 February 1977, a meeting was called by Randy Jayne of the National Security Council at the Old State Department Building to discuss the problem between Defense and State regarding the increase in manning for Diego Garcia. Representing Defense were Jack Gaardsmoe from the Comptroller's Office, Van Bandjunis from Installations and Logistics, Commander Ron Zwart from International Security Affairs, Steve Nash from Navy's Comptroller's Office, Commander J.B. Green,

Jr. from the Chief of Naval Operation's Shore Facilities Programming Division, Franz Kretzman and Bruce McDonald from the Office of Management and Budget, and Commander Jack Burgess from the State Department. The meeting was attended by action officers in hopes of reaching an agreement on the Diego Garcia manning problem.

State Objection to Barracks Project

The memorandum from the Office of Management and Budget Assistant Director for Legislative Reference James M. Frey of 11 March 1977 to Defense Secretary Harold Brown cleared the draft fiscal year 1978 Military Construction Authorization Bill. The Office of Management and Budget noted that the Department of State objected to the inclusion of a $2,500,000 barracks project at Diego Garcia due to international concerns. For this reason, the barracks were not approved unless the differences between the State Department and Defense were resolved. Defense Secretary Harold Brown met with State Secretary Cyrus R. Vance at a luncheon on 13 March 1977. Afterwards, State agreed to withdraw its objection.

The increased manning was not based on new mission capabilities. The 83 additional support facility men were required for administrative requirements, increased air operations, increased fire fighting capability, to establish a preventive maintenance program, increased vehicle maintenance, essential facilities maintenance, essential utilities support, aircraft maintenance, and 24 hour aircraft fuel service. The communication station needed 39 more people for high frequency support to P-3 Orion airplanes, submarine communications, and for satellite capability. The Security group needed 10 more people so they could make full use of the CLASSIC WIZARD system. The patrol and reconnaissance squadrons needed 49 people to increase patrol squadrons and reconnaissance squadron crews. Weather Service needed six people for aircraft and ship weather service, and the FASU needed 27 people for intermediate avionics maintenance support for VP/VQ operations.

Loss of the additional men would have a severe effect on operations at Diego Garcia. In the Support Facility there would be a critical shortage in supply and mess cooks, a critical shortage in public works resulting in RPMA from PWC Subic, loss of AMD Officer, across the board reduction of base support functions. The communications station could not provide fleet satellite communications or Defense Satellite communications, SI and Genser support reduced, ship communications limited to high frequency. The Security Group would have to reduce CLASSIC WIZARD capability from 24 hour coverage to 16 hours. The patrol and reconnaissance squadrons would have to eliminate reconnaissance operations, eliminate one patrol plane crew that could provide for two P-3 aircraft rather than three. There would be incomplete Indian Ocean weather data available. The FASU would be eliminated.

The Department of State opposed the large manning increase because Congressional opponents of the joint United State-United Kingdom facility could seize upon the permanent increase implied by this project to challenge again the United States military presence in the Indian Ocean, and any increase at Diego Garcia until the Administration determined its overall policy toward the Indian Ocean. Further, State feared that a new public controversy could be generated that might impact adversely upon State Secretary Vance's intent to sound out the Soviets on Indian Ocean arms limitations during his forthcoming visit to Moscow.

Sense of Congress

The Sense of Congress concerning force limitation negotiations was contained in the International Security Assistance and Arms Export

Control Act of 1976, Public Law 94-329. Section 407(a) of the that Act stipulated that:

"It is the sense of Congress, that the President should undertake to enter into negotiations with the Soviet Union intended to achieve an agreement limiting the deployment of naval, air, and land forces of the Soviet Union and the United States in the Indian Ocean and littoral countries. Such negotiations should be convened as soon as possible and should consider, among other things, limitations with respect to— (1) the establishment or use of facilities for naval, air, or land forces in the Indian Ocean and littoral countries; (2) the number of naval vessels which may be deployed in the Indian Ocean, or the number of "ship-days" allowed therein; and (3) the type and number of military forces and facilities allowed therein."

The United States Government in March 1977, approached the Soviet Union about entering into negotiations on force limitations in the Indian Ocean.

Steps Toward Demilitarization

President Jimmy Carter mentioned the Indian Ocean to Soviet Ambassador Anatoly F. Dobrynin as part of a long list of arms control topics that should be considered in the future. Department of State and Defense officials were surprised in early March 1977 by the President's revelation that he had broached the subject before a policy had been worked out. In President Carter's address to the General Assembly of the United Nations in March 1977, the President declared, "We will seek to establish Soviet willingness to reach agreement with us on mutual restraint in the Indian Ocean."

The United States Navy thought that it had enough ocean in which to hide its nuclear missile-launching submarines without using the Indian Ocean, although if there were a major breakthrough in antisubmarine warfare, it might be an advantage to have another ocean available. Submarines in the Indian Ocean would open up a new Soviet Union southern flank to possible attack.

President Carter's ideas on "mutual restraint" in the Indian Ocean were put forward in Moscow by Secretary of State Cyrus R. Vance. Secretary Vance said that the Indian Ocean was a good place to make some hard progress on detente, and proposed a limit on the number of ships the Soviet Union and the United States could have in the Indian Ocean. The Soviets agreed to establish a working group to study the issues involved, leading toward a meeting in May 1977 of the two foreign ministers.

The Soviet Union had almost finished construction of a long runway, ammunition and petroleum storage areas were near completion, and a floating drydock for Soviet warships in the Indian Ocean was being commissioned at Berbera in Somalia. The nuclear carrier *Enterprise* (CVAN-65) and escort vessels were in the Indian Ocean. The Soviets had a light cruiser shadowing the nuclear-powered *Enterprise*.[39]

One of the first Pentagon's concerns about the possible demilitarization of the Indian Ocean was the loss of the communications facility at Diego Garcia. A second worry was the difficulty in running P-3 Orion antisubmarine patrol missions in the area if the island's airstrip were closed down. "No matter how we demilitarize, we'll need intelligence to determine whether the other side is holding their part of the bargain." The United States Navy neither operated nor maintained any airfields in the littoral countries of the Indian Ocean. They did rely on a number of non-United States airfields in the littoral countries to provide refueling and crew rest in conjunction with P-3 operations. These airfields were located at Bandar Abbas, Iran; Karachi, Pakistan; Masirah, Oman; Djibouti, formerly the French Territory of Afars and Issas; Mahe, Seychelles; Nairobi and Mombasa, Kenya; and the Cocos Island, Australia.

Navy P-3 Orion reconnaissance planes based at Diego Garcia had been landing at the British base on Masirah Island, Oman, on an irregular basis with Oman's permission. The United States Navy expected to continue making occasional use of the airport after Britain's Royal Air Force closed its operations there in March 1977.[40]

Diego Garcia Opened to Journalists

For the first time in its four years of operation, the Navy base at Diego Garcia was opened on 6 April 1977 to journalists. The reporters, 16 from America and four from British media, were taken on a five-hour closely guided tour. When it was over, most of the newsmen wondered what all the secrecy had been about. The 1,400 Americans were commanded by Captain Philip F. Yosway. The 25 Royal Navy Party were led by Lieutenant Commander Arthur G. Portwine, Jr.[41] The only part of the Island that was ruled off-limits to the reporters was the security area known as CHARLEY Site, which relays submarine radio traffic and does other unspecified secret tasks.

The newsmen saw three airplanes on the ground, one of them a P-3 Orion surveillance plane, and two C-141 Starlifter transports, one of which brought them on a six-hour flight from Singapore. They saw bulldozers, graders and other heavy equipment, operated by a contingent of 850 Seabees of the 30th Naval Construction Regiment under the command of Captain Philip Oliver, Jr., being used to extend the island's runway from 8,000 to 12,000 feet. Men and machines were paving an enlarged parking area for airplanes and others were putting in foundations for eight 80,000 barrel fuel tanks. The tankage was of sufficient complexity, as far as welding, to be done by a private contractor. And, except for dredging, all the rest of the construction was accomplished by rotating one of the eight regular Naval Construction

Battalions on a cycle of eight months on island and six months back at home port.

The newsmen also saw the numerous recreational facilities many of which were self-help projects that the Seabees had constructed since they arrived. A gymnasium, a four-lane bowling alley, hobby shops, softball and baseball fields; volley ball, tennis, and handball courts; a large swimming pool still under construction; separate clubs for enlisted, petty officers, and officers; and fishing, boating, and skin-diving offered recreation for the Seabees that put in a six-day work week. Entertainment came in the form of two movies a night, closed circuit television, and USO shows from the Philippines. The tremendous number of recreation facilities reported by the visiting newsmen did not go unnoticed by congressional staffers in Washington.

Australia Backs Diego Garcia Base

Australia's Foreign Minister, Andrew S. Peacock, said the United States base on Diego Garcia island in the Indian Ocean should be maintained until the Soviet Union agrees to "a mutual reduction" of its base at Berbera, Somalia. "You can talk about disarmament or a zone of peace, but before you can have a zone of peace, you have got to have a zone of balance," he said in an interview with the newspaper The Australian.[42]

Fiscal Year 1978 Project Hold

Senator John C. Stennis, Chairman of the Senate Armed Services Committee, wrote a letter on 6 May 1977 to President Jimmy Carter and requested that "..before any project authorized for Diego Garcia for Fiscal Year 1978 is allowed to proceed to construction, that the decision to proceed be carefully considered in light of the current negotiating situation, and that the Armed Services Committees of Congress be notified of your intent to proceed together with the considerations involved in such a decision." In a reply to Senator Stennis the Deputy Assistant to the President for National Security Affairs stated that "…no fiscal year 1978 funds will be expended for the aircraft maintenance and barracks construction on Diego Garcia until the Administration has completed an Indian Ocean policy review and has had an opportunity to evaluate the results of discussions with the Soviet Union in Indian Ocean Arms control."

Task Group

A four-ship United States Navy task group headed by the guided missile cruiser *Sterett* (CG-31), including the destroyer *Morton* (DD-948), the frigate *Bradley* (FF-1041), and the oiler *Mispillian* (TAO-105) entered the Indian Ocean on 14 May 1977. The task group entered the Indian Ocean through the remote Lombok Strait. Asked why it deployed warships into the Indian Ocean after President Jimmy Carter raised the demilitarization issue, the Navy indicated it would continue to do so until the Russians agree to keep their warships out. "Any substantial changes in our periodic deployment policy would have to occur within a context of mutual United States-Soviet Union military restraint in the region," the Navy said.[43]

National Press Club Luncheon

During the question and answer session at the National Press Club luncheon on 25 May 1977, Defense Secretary Harold Brown responded, "With respect to Diego Garcia, it's not a massive Navy base. What it is is some communication equipment, and a gas station. We would like to see the Indian Ocean, like other parts of the world, more peaceful than it is now, but that's not the way it is now. As you pointed out, the Soviets have been building bases around the periphery—or gaining base rights around the Indian Ocean—and we believe that while we work with them, if they're willing to, to reverse that trend. It's important that we in the interim, preserve our ability to operate in that part of the world."

Demilitarization Downgraded

President Jimmy Carter and Australian Prime Minister Malcolm Fraser agreed on 22 June 1977 on the current goal of seeking a freeze, or "balance," of American and Soviet military forces in the Indian Ocean. The initial target was "complete demilitarization."

Brzezinski Limitation

In September 1977, Dr. Zbigniew Brzezinski, President Carter's National Security Advisor, signed a memorandum requesting that Secretary of Defense monitor closely the pace of construction at Diego Garcia in light of the Indian Ocean Arms Control negotiations that were underway at the time. The memorandum was issued by Dr. Brzezinski in response primarily to the congressional restraints placed on the Department of Defense in developing Diego Garcia.

Sadat and Begin

On 19 November 1977, Anwar el-Sadat flew from Abu Suwayr airfield to Ben Gurion Airport. Within 16 months, Sadat and Israeli Prime Minister Menachem Begin, urged by President Jimmy Carter, concluded a treaty that ended a 31-year state of war and gave the Jewish state the security that peace and diplomatic recognition from its largest neighbor and former enemy could bestow.

Talks Snag

The Carter Administration talks with the Soviet Union on mutual restraint in the Indian Ocean seem to have hit an embarrassing snag by December 1977. The White House found that the American Navy's carrier task groups and missile submarines contrasted with the Russian's small surface ships, forcing the Administration to reduce the negotiating goals from "complete demilitarization" to "mutual military restraint." The Russians recently lost their major littoral foothold, in Somalia. Since being thrown out, it was reported, they had decided that it was not enough to stabilize the situation; what was needed was to reduce the big-power military presence and, specifically, to exclude nuclear-powered vessels. Such restrictions would bear considerably more heavily on the United States. The Diego Garcia base was undertaken on the grounds that the Russians already had a base at Berbera. Now Berbera was wiped out, but the work proceeded apace at Diego Garcia.[44]

Naval Support Facility Established

Captain Bobie Andrews commissioned the Naval Support Facility on 1 October 1977, and became its first commanding officer. Commander C.R. Scobee, Jr. was reassigned as commanding officer of the communications station. The senior official attending the combined change of command and change of claimancy ceremony was Rear Admiral L.F. Eggert, COMFAIRWESTPAC. Incident to the change of claimancy, the Commander, Naval Telecommunications Command, assigned the United States Naval Communications Station,

Philippines, fiscal and accounting responsibility for the communications station at Diego Garcia.

The Support Facility's mission was to provide air terminal operations, search and rescue, aerology services, aviation shops, and fuel and supply support for planes and ships. The Naval Support Facility was the central point for all personnel and material movements throughout the Indian Ocean and was a critical link in the logistical chain stretching from both coasts of the United States to the Indian Ocean Battle Groups operating in the North Arabian Sea.

The new command supported the communications station, the Resident Officer in Charge of Construction, the NWSED, NAVBC-STSVC, 374th Tactical Air Wing from Clark Air Base in the Philippines, the Defense Mapping Agency that operated a small navigation satellite tracking station for geodetic survey purposes, and the United Kingdom Royal Navy Party.

The destroyer *Stein* (DE-1065) took on 30,000 gallons of JP-5, and loaded 3,000 coconuts on 5 March 1978 to enable former Diego Garcia residents relocated in the Seychelles to establish a coconut plantation.

In July, the enlisted men's club was dedicated in honor of CECN Howard F. Turner (1954–1976) who had been killed in an accident during the construction of power transmission facilities on Diego Garcia.

Gene Klebe, a 76 year old artist from Bristol, Maine, came to Diego Garcia in 1978 to paint the projects that were under construction. The water color paintings were to be displayed in Washington.

Fiscal Year 1978 Projects to Start

The Navy was authorized by the Assistant Secretary of Defense for International Security Affairs David E. McGiffert in January 1978 to proceed with construction of the fiscal year 1978 program for Diego Garcia, except for the airfield facilities and barracks. Procurement of materials for shipment to the island followed shortly after. As the Chairman of the Senate Armed Services Committee was assured in May 1977, the Carter Administration consulted fully with Congress before expending funds on the airfield and barracks.

Negotiation Update

David E. McGiffert, the Assistant Secretary of Defense for International Security Affairs wrote a letter on 8 March 1978 to John C. Stennis, Chairman Senate Armed Services Committee concerning the review of the Indian Ocean policy. McGiffert said that the policy review was completed in the June-September 1977 period, and resulted in a decision to maintain a minimal military presence in the area while remaining capable of making surge deployments in a crisis. At the same time, the Carter Administration attempted to negotiate an arms control agreement with the Soviet Union to prevent Indian Ocean naval arms competition, to lessen potential for United States-Soviet Union conflict in the region, and to ensure that the United States would continue to need only a minimal military presence in the area in the future. The first meeting was held in Moscow and ended on 2 June 1977.

The United States was negotiating with the Soviet Union on an agreement to stabilize United States and Soviet Union naval and military air deployments to the Indian Ocean. Under stabilization, each side would be limited to deployment levels and patterns of the recent past. However, Soviet activity in the Horn of Africa and the related increase in Soviet naval forces had a negative effect on the negotiations. The second meeting was held in the United States on 26 September to 3 October 1977, and the third in Berne, Switzerland.

The fourth round of talks, which took place in February 1978, was completed in Berne, Switzerland, with little or no progress toward resolving outstanding differences, and the advisability of convening the next round was questionable until the situation in the Horn has stabilized. Should an accord be reached with the Soviets, it would take the form of an Executive agreement and would be submitted to the Congress for approval. Ambassador Paul C. Warnke, then Director of the Arms Control and Disarmament Agency headed the United States delegation to the Indian Ocean Forces Limitation negotiating sessions. Vice Admiral Marmaduke Bayne, USN (Retired) was the senior United States military and represented the Joint Chiefs of Staff at all rounds in the negotiations. The Joint Chiefs of Staff opposed formal arms control in the Indian Ocean, and recommended on 30 January 1978 that talks be suspended.

Under a stabilization agreement, the United States would keep its Diego Garcia facility. However, the United States indicated to the Soviets that the United States did not intend to go beyond currently programmed construction. In short, with the completion of the planned construction, Diego Garcia would remain a modest facility that should in no way hinder serious United States and Soviet efforts to negotiate an arms control agreement for the area.

In light of these considerations, McGiffert said that Defense could now proceed with the construction of the barracks and aircraft maintenance facilities. Both were considered important to the conduct of operations, and a decision not to go forward could be misinterpreted by the Soviets as an indication that the United States firm commitment to the planned construction was negotiable. The aircraft refueling station would result in a more efficient alternative to the tank truck method, and the aircraft wash rack would help prevent salt-induced deterioration of aircraft metals. The barracks was needed to house personnel required to operate authorized missions. Chairman Stennis concurred with Assistant Secretary McGiffert's assessment.

Culver Relents

Senator John C. Culver wrote to President Jimmy Carter on 18 March 1978 concerning mutual arms limitations in the Indian Ocean. Senator Culver noted that while a diplomatic initiative had long been urged by the Congress, it was not taken until President Carter took office.

In December 1977, Senator Culver met with the United States Delegation just before the third session of the Indian Ocean arms limitation talks in Berne. He was impressed with the seriousness of purpose which both sides brought to the talks. Although those talks were temporarily eclipsed by other matters, he urged the President to press ahead. Recent troubles in the Horn of Africa demonstrated the importance of reaching agreements that could prevent or at least limit outside military involvement in the Indian Ocean area. Senator Culver wrote that he believed that the modest construction plans previously authorized by the Congress could be completed without jeopardizing broader goals of military stabilization and restraint.

Remainder of Fiscal Year 1978 Projects Released

Walter Slocombe, the Acting Assistant Secretary of Defense for International Security Affairs wrote to the Deputy Chief of Naval Operations for Plans, Policy, and Operations on 12 April 1978 and authorized the Navy to expend funds appropriated for all projects in the fiscal year 1978 Diego Garcia military construction program. The Acting Secretary referred to the letter sent to the Chairman of the Senate Arms Services Committee on 8 March 1978 and the Chairman's concurrence, and to Senator Culver's letter of 18 March 1978 to President Carter.

MIDEASTFORCE Augmentation

In the spring of 1978, growing tension in the Horn of Africa, occasioned by the Somalia-Ethiopia conflict, resulted in the decision to augment the Middle East Force with ships from both the Atlantic Fleet and the Seventh Fleet. In April 1978, the guided missile cruiser *Fox* (CG-33) became the first ship of her type to serve in the Middle East Force.

Panel on Forces and Arms Limitation

G.V. (Sonny) Montgomery was the Chairman of the House Armed Services Committee Panel on Indian Ocean Forces Limitation and Conventional Arms Transfer Limitation. The Panel held hearings on three and 10 October 1978 with representatives from the Department of State, Arms Control and Disarmament Agency, Secretary of Defense, and Joint Chiefs of Staff. The purpose was to review:

- The current policies of the United States governing Indian Ocean force limitations and conventional arms transfer;
- The present state of United States proposals for limiting forces in the Indian Ocean, and for limiting conventional arms transfers;
- The projected timetable for negotiations;
- The major security implications of these negotiations; and;
- The procedures for developing negotiating positions and obtaining decisions within the Executive Branch.

The Panel's report on 16 January 1979 concluded that "The negotiations that were the subject of the Panel's inquiry have not been given the priority of other proposed agreements, such as Salt II. In addition, they involve extremely complex and difficult policy questions. As a result, little actual negotiating progress has been made to date."

An example of the difficulties involved in the negotiations was that the geographical area subject to negotiation had not been defined. The Panel believed it would be some time before any substantive agreement was concluded, if at all, on the Indian Ocean.

Logistics/Airfield Expansion Summary

The follow-on development authorized and funded in fiscal years 1975 through 1978 for Diego Garcia was designed to provide minimal support to task groups that would operate in the Indian Ocean. Logistically, Diego Garcia would serve as an outpost base where ships could perform limited in port upkeep, receive periodic devices from a tender and receive critical supplies via the Military Airlift Command aircraft. Diego Garcia would also serve as a base for patrol aircraft providing air surveillance support to the ships in the Indian Ocean.

The major facility improvements approved were:

An anchorage that would be capable of mooring a six-ship carrier task group, the lagoon dredging also provided an explosive anchorage for ship to ship transfer of ordnance.

A fuel and general purpose pier that would be capable of loading and unloading a 180,000-barrel tanker in a 24 hour period. This rapid loading capability would increase the fuel endurance of the task group during critical operations when tanker assets were limited.

The POL (JP-5) storage capability on the island was increased from 60,000 barrels to 640,000 barrels. This POL storage represented that amount necessary to support short notice deployment of forces to the Indian Ocean until a POL tanker pipeline independent of Middle East sources could be established; or support deployment of reinforcements in the event of hostilities until pipelines could be increased; and could provide accessible POL support to combat forces to accommodate temporary area POL fluctuation in the area due to varying consumption rates or attrition of pipeline assets. The Diego Garcia supply would sustain a typical Indian Ocean task group for approximately 28 days. Additionally, the supply was designed to serve Air Force contingency needs. JP-5 was the only fuel on the island.

Airfield improvements would allow aerial resupply for the task group, basing of patrol aircraft and recovery of tactical jet aircraft in emergencies. A 4,000-foot runway extension (1,000 feet on north end, 3,000 feet on south end) would provide for the safe recovery of tactical jet aircraft under a range of adverse conditions with the conduct of air training exercises by a carrier task group within the vicinity of Diego Garcia. The runway would also accommodate KC-135 aircraft.

Aircraft maintenance, a hangar, an aircraft rinse and rack and an aircraft ready-issue-refueler would provide necessary operational/maintenance support for the patrol (VP/VQ) aircraft operating from the island. Ready issue storage for antisubmarine warfare and other aircraft ordnance would be constructed in the airfield area. Two standard magazines for storage of antisubmarine warfare ordnance used by P-3 aircraft would be constructed in an area more remote to populated areas of the island. An open munitions storage area, comprising 20 earthen bermed modules, for contingency ordnance storage, primarily for Air Force requirements, would also be constructed in this area.

A parking apron extension to accommodate an additional C-141 Starlifter cargo plane, four P-3 Orion antisubmarine patrol planes, one carrier on board delivery, and twenty divert aircraft from a carrier. Additional 25,000 square yards are provided for Air Force Contingency Airlift use. The original parking apron was 600' x 300', the expanded apron measured 1,950' x 525'.

Other airfield improvements, which included an operations building extension for the patrol operations, an air cargo transit shed and a crash fire station.

Additions to the personnel support complex were required to support the personnel to be assigned to both the communications mission and the fleet support mission. Bachelor enlisted quarters extensions for 449 men (277 men in fiscal year 1976 and 172 men in fiscal year 1978), over the previously constructed 250 man barracks, and a bachelor officers quarters facilities for 32 officers would be built. The combined officer and enlisted subsistence facility would be expanded to serve the added men.

Structural Fire Station, to house fire fighting equipment and personnel to provide protection against structural fires.

Other Storage comprising three general warehouses, a Navy Exchange warehouse, and additional cold storage would be constructed in a new warehouse complex north of the airfield complex. An armory and medical storage facility would be constructed in the cantonment area.

Power Plant, three 1,200 KW diesel units would be added to the existing five units to support the increased power demands of the additional island population and the POL storage and pumping system.

Utilities Distribution. Power and water distribution systems would be improved and increased in capacity to provide reliable electrical power and fire protection to all new construction.

4

Rapid Deployment Force

Continuous Naval Deployments

On 15 November 1978, the guided missile cruiser *Sterett* (CG-31), along with the guided missile destroyer Waddell (DDG-24), the frigate *Bradley* (FF-1041), and the oiler *Passumpsic* (TAO-107) entered the Indian Ocean to usher in an era of almost continuous United States naval ship deployments to the area.[45] On 7 January 1979, these ships were joined by the guided missile destroyers *Decatur* (DDG-31) and *Hoel* (DDG-13), the destroyer *Kinkaid* (DD-965), and the replenishment oiler *Kansas City* (AOR-3).

The Naval Support Facility at Diego Garcia assumed a major role in contingency operations in the Arabian Sea. Patrol plane detachments increased from three to eight P-3 Orion antisubmarine patrol planes, the Air Force had established a four aircraft KC-135 tanker detachment, and Military Airlift Command flights increased from two C-141 Starlifter cargo planes to six, plus one C-5A Galaxy transport. Through put of cargo, mail, and personnel increased by factors of seven, six, and five, respectively. The total island population increased from 1,450 to nearly 1,900 people, straining housing accommodations. The station gymnasium and lounges in bachelor living quarters were pressed into service.

Shah of Iran

The Shah of Iran left in January 1979, following mass demonstrations against his rule. The next month, the revolutionaries took control of Iran's government. Armed Iranian rebels attacked the United States Embassy in Tehran on 14 February 1979. On 21 February, the Middle East Force flagship *LaSalle* (AGF-3) and five destroyers participated in the evacuation of more than 400 persons, including 200 United States citizens, from the Iranian ports of Bandar Abbas and Chah Bahar.

Ayatollah Ruhollah Khomeini declared Iran an Islamic Republic. For the first year after the revolution, a Revolutionary Council appointed by Khomeini carried out the policies of the new government. In 1980, the Iranian people elected the first president and the first Majlis of the republic. After the Shah was deposed, Iran no longer provided the security buffer for the Persian Gulf States sought by the United States. Consequently, the United States had to change its strategy for the region.

New Security Framework

National Security Advisor Zbigniew Brzezinski's memorandum of 28 February 1979 to President Carter proposed that a new security framework be established in the Southwest Asia region to reassert American influence and power.[46] The new approach completely reversed President Carter's 1977 plan that called for demilitarization of the Indian Ocean area. Events in the area that Brzezinski called the "arc of instability" continued. The border conflict between North and South

Yemen erupted. On 8 March, the Department of Defense announced that the aircraft carrier *Constellation* (CVA-64) had been deployed to the Indian Ocean and that the guided missile cruiser *Sterett* (CG-31), the guided missile destroyer *Waddell* (DDG-24), and replenishment oiler *Kansas City* (AOR-3) had been extended in the area in a show of support for the Yemen Arab Republic (North Yemen) in a conflict with South Yemen. At the request of Saudi Arabia, two United States Air Force air warfare control planes were dispatched. By 6 April, combined Indian Ocean-Middle East Force strength amounted to 15 ships.

In March, justification and guidelines for the expanded United States role were developed by the National Security staff. The United States would shore up friendly nations, and augment military power. A rapid deployment force, based in the United States, but ready to move to trouble spots was conceived.

President Carter temporarily put aside the security framework for Southwest Asia while negotiating the peace treaty between Egypt and Israel. The Camp David Treaty between Israel and Egypt was signed on 26 March 1979, and provided for the gradual withdrawal of Israel troops from the Sinai.

In May 1979, the Soviet carrier *Minsk* (117), the amphibious warfare ship *Ivan Rogov* and a "Kara" class cruiser conducted a demonstration cruise for South Yemen officials while visiting Aden. That same month, two Soviet Il-38 aircraft on maritime patrol in the Arabian Sea flew within 500 feet of the U.S. carrier *Midway* (CV-41), causing the Midway's aircraft in the landing pattern to take emergency evasion action.

Working from a four-option Pentagon paper, the National Security Council recommended that the number of regular United States naval task force annual deployments in the Indian Ocean be increased from three to four. On 9 July, a five-ship task force of combat vessels entered the Indian Ocean for what the Navy called routine operations.

Readiness Improvement

Russell Murray, the Assistant Secretary of Defense for Program Analysis and Evaluation, proposed on 23 October 1979 to expand the capability at Diego Garcia to support United States Marine Corps Maritime Prepositioning Ships, and to handle additional airlift throughput. Military construction funding was estimated to be $10,000,000 in fiscal year 1981, $40,000,000 in fiscal year 1982, $40,000,000 in fiscal year 1983, and $10,000,000 in fiscal year 1984. Two days later, Secretary of Defense Harold Brown approved Russell Murray's proposal in band 4 of the budget decisions.

The Carter Administration instituted a zero based budgeting system that placed every budget item in the five-year plan in a priority listing. Theoretically, once a budget dollar level was set, the programs that were within this budget level were approved. Zero based budgeting caused an immense amount of paper work that seemed to slow down the budget review process. Band 4 was not a very high priority item. In discussing the make up of the $80,000,000 proposed construction for Diego Garcia, Ken Hotel, from the Program Analysis and Evaluation Office explained that $2,000,000 was for water upgrade, $6,000,000 for a pier and causeway, $8,000,000 for an airfield apron, $12,000,000 for a taxiway, $6,000,000 for a high capacity fuel handling system, and $46,000,000 for 200,000 barrels of additional fuel storage. At that time there were no plans or specifications for the construction, and no State Department clearance or British approval. The $10,000,000 proposed for fiscal year 1981 was not defined, other than it was mostly for the Air Force.

American Hostages

The seizure by armed Iranian students of the United States Embassy in Tehran on 4 November 1979 marked the beginning of a painful ordeal for the American people and for 52 countrymen held hostage in Iran. By the end of the month, total United States navy ship strength in the region had grown to 21. At least two carrier battle groups would be maintained in the Indian Ocean for two years after the seizure of the embassy. The Iranians said they would release the hostages if the United States returned the Shah to Iran for trial.

In a meeting with Defense Secretary Brown at Camp David on 24 November 1979, President Carter ordered a full report on what could be done quickly to provide emergency United States operating access to the region, including overflights of friendly nations, and transit and operating facilities. The second aircraft carrier task force entered the Indian Ocean, to join the carrier *Midway* (CV-41) and its task force on the same day President Carter was discussing the report with Secretary Brown. Sustaining these ships strained Navy resources. The cost of the additional presence in the Indian Ocean of two carrier battle groups through the end of January 1980 was $110 million. The Navy had to delete four of the planned 63 ship overhauls to pay for the operations.

Gulf Area Bases

At a National Security Council meeting on 4 December 1979, it was decided to initiate exploration of improved United States "access" to facilities rather than attempt to build United States bases because of Arab nations reluctance to have foreign bases on their territories. The State Department initially had objections, but on a Friday, 14 December 1979, after a meeting between National Security Advisor Zbigniew Brzezinski, Secretary of Defense Harold Brown and Secretary of State Cyrus R. Vance, President Jimmy Carter ordered that a team be sent to Saudi Arabia, Oman, Somalia, and Kenya at once. The team departed on Monday. Access to facilities in several countries would increase politico-military flexibility. This facility network would be centered around the Navy's base at Diego Garcia.

Oman, Kenya and Somalia agreed to the Carter Administration plans for giving American air and naval forces increased access to bases, government officials said.[47] Leaders of the three countries accepted a proposal, brought with an American team visiting the area, which would allow American forces to pay regular visits to bases and would enable the United States military forces to store limited amounts of equipment and fuel on their territories. The American team was led by Reginald Bartholomew, the State Department's director of political-military affairs. The team returned from the visit with favorable responses from Oman, Kenya, and Somalia, just as Soviet troops entered Afghanistan. In January 1980, another team of technical experts visited, inspected, and developed plans to construct military facilities in the three countries. The Carter Administration had also engaged in secret talks with France over gaining increased naval access to the port at Djibouti, the former French colony on the Horn of Africa.

In Somalia, the Carter Administration was most interested in making use of the base at Berbera, a port that had been used by the Soviet navy until 1978. While the port required massive repair, a 15,000-foot runway nearby could be used by American surveillance aircraft and fighter planes. State Department experts were concerned that American military support for Somalia could lead the country's leader, President Mohammed Siad Barre, into stepping up his conflict with neighboring Ethiopia; a development that could weaken American influence in Africa.

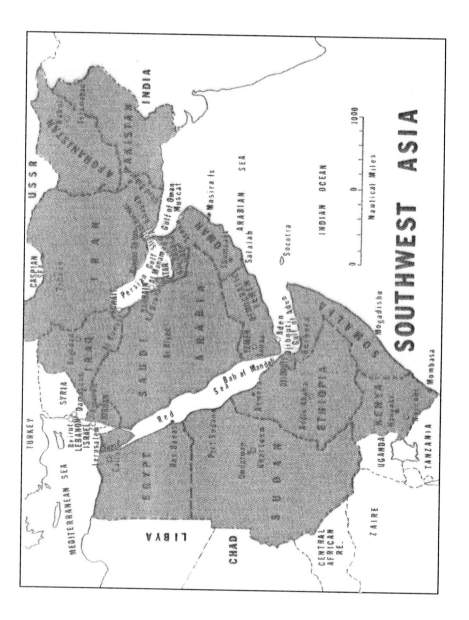

FIGURE 12 Map of Southwest Asia

In Oman, the Pentagon was seeking increased access for aircraft at the airstrip on Masirah Island and for warships at the port of Muscat. Kenya's port of Mombasa, which American warships had occasionally visited in the past, could also be used to support naval presence in the area.

Pentagon officials said that the administration wanted to deploy more tanker aircraft on Diego Garcia, and that it was examining a proposal for widening the airstrip to accommodate B-52 bombers.

The Pentagon was also formulating a plan that would call on Saudi Arabia to construct several new air bases around the country, which would be designed to meet American needs and be stocked with large amounts of American weapons and fuel.

Marines Form Rapid Reaction Force

Against the backdrop of the Soviet brigade in Cuba and turmoil in Iran, Marine leaders disclosed on 5 December 1979 that they had been ordered to organize a 50,000-man spearhead for President Carter's Rapid Deployment Force.[48]

The first of three brigades of 16,500 Marines was to be ready for airlifting to distant trouble spots by 1983, Major General Paul X. Kelley, Marine planning chief, said in describing the Corp's role in the quick reaction force.

Although planning for this outfit, which the Army called the Unilateral Corps, preceded the current crisis in Iran, Pentagon officials said that rising concern about the oil-rich Persian Gulf was providing a sense of urgency to implement these plans. The basic idea was to give the President more military options in the Third World.

Each brigade was to be supported by five supply ships deployed ahead of time, near likely trouble spots around the world. Kelley said a Marine brigade could operate on its own, though presumably not fight any kind of major battle, for 30 days before having to depend on the ships for resupply.

White House budget chiefs approved about $80,000,000 to start development of a successor to the C-5 Galaxy transport plane for airlifting troops and supplies, and $220,000,000 for the first two of a fleet of cargo ships. Defense officials said that over the next several years about $9 billion would go for the new C-X transport airlift, with about 50 planes costing $180,000,000 each. Another $3 billion in the quick reaction force account was earmarked for 16 ships to be loaded with Marine gear and prepositioned near likely areas of conflict.

The Army's 82nd Airborne Division and armored units from Fort Hood, Texas, and Fort Carson, Colorado were expected to be designated as part of the force. Their heavy tanks and other weaponry were expected to take up most of the space on the fleet of C-X planes.

Some Navy leaders were cool to the idea of building special cargo ships for the Marines and deploying them near likely trouble spots. They believed that such ships would take money out of their already strained shipbuilding budget, and predicted that warships ultimately would have to be assigned to protect them.

Defense Secretary Harold Brown overrode those objections. Not only did he direct the Marines Corps to bring its 50,000 member special airlift force into being by the middle 1980s, but he approved extra money so the Corps did not have to go through with its planned cut of 10,000 men.

To ease the Corps' budget crunch, Marine Commandant Robert Barrow had decided to reduce his force from 189,000 to 179,000 by the end of fiscal 1981. The extra money approved by Defense Secretary Brown, Kelley said, would enable the Marines to field a force of 185,200, a cut of only 3,800.

Kelley said the Marines wanted to brief reporters on the Rapid Deployment Force because some "of our friends" had gotten the idea that the Corps' mission was being changed. He said that, on the contrary, the Corps was enthusiastic about its new role.

"In looking at the 1980s," Kelley said, "It becomes obvious that we need a sharper focus for the Third World." The United States would "do well to sharpen that focus before we let it slip through our fingers," he said.

Kelley said the Marines have traditionally designed their forces to go into battle in a hurry, but that a "glaring deficiency" was the shortage of long-range planes to carry them to crises. He said the present airlift force of 70 C-5 Galaxy transports and 234 C-141 Starlifter cargo planes were not enough to carry troops and weaponry to distant points. The new C-X cargo plane, he added, would help close that gap. To fly just one brigade of 16,500 Marines in a quick reaction unit would require 130 round trips of 14 C-5s and 102 C-141s, and 14 wide-bodied civilian transport planes pressed into service as part of what is called the Civil Reserve Air Fleet. The transport planes, as well as the fighter-bombers that would support the Marine ground troops, would have to be refueled enroute by Air Force flying tankers.

Kelley said the Marine brigade would not be targeted on any specific area of the world, but could go anywhere. Asked about getting to the Persian Gulf, he said that one option would be to fly Marines from Okinawa to Diego Garcia in the Indian Ocean.

Although he did not volunteer it, when pressed by reporters Kelley said Diego Garcia could indeed become the "linchpin" as the United States increased its military presence for conflicts in the Middle East and Africa.

In the past, some members of Congress had been reluctant to increase the United States presence on the island for fear of making the Indian Ocean a new area of confrontation for the United States and Soviet Union. Senator Sam Nunn led a delegation of the Senate Armed Services Committee to the Persian Gulf in early 1980 to assess the need for additional United States military facilities in the area, including

Diego Garcia. One staffer on the Senate Foreign Relations Committee, who had observed the Senate's efforts in past years to restrict military activities on Diego Garcia, said: "That was a different era. Iran has changed all that."

Invasion of Afghanistan

In April 1978, Mohammed Daoud was overthrown in a coup staged by the leftist Khalq (or People's Democratic) Party, whose leader, Noor Muhammad Taraki, became president. But Muslim tribesmen, resenting the government's attempts to change their traditions and fearing its closeness to the Soviet Union, rebelled and soon controlled much of the countryside. Taraki was ousted in September 1979 by his own prime minister, Hafizullah Amin, a hard-liner. But in December Amin was ousted by yet, another leftist, Babrak Karmal, with the help of 30,000 Soviet troops that entered the country on 27 December. In four days, Soviet troops totaled 85,000.

Because of the Soviet invasion, the Soviets gained an important strategic position that posed a threat to the West's dependence on Persian Gulf oil. The Soviets outflanked Iran, threatened the frontier of Pakistan and enhanced the prospect of a Soviet presence on the Indian Ocean or Persian Gulf littoral.

Carter's Pledge

During his State of Union message on 23 January 1980, President Jimmy Carter said, "Any attempt by any outside force to gain control of the Persian Gulf region will be regarded as an assault on the vital interests of the United States of America, and such an assault will be repelled by any means necessary, including military force." He had ordered the Pentagon to organize a 110,000-man Rapid Deployment

Force, designed expressly to fight in such distant places as the Persian Gulf. A Rapid Deployment Joint Task Force Headquarters at MacDill Air Force Base, Florida, became operational on 1 March 1980 under the command of Lieutenant General P.X. Kelley. His new defense budget called for developing a fleet of C-X cargo planes to deliver the heavy tanks and other armor such a force would need. The purchase of 14 new Maritime prepositioning ships was also planned. But both the Rapid Deployment Force and the C-X were still on paper, with 1983 the earliest that the spearhead of the special, long-distance reaction force would be ready for battle. Carter's decision to seek registration of draft-age youths came after the Joint Chiefs of Staff said that step was vital to gearing up for war. The Defense Authorization Act of 1981 mandated that the Department of Defense submit to the Congress a Mobility Study.

President Carter also ordered B-52 surveillance missions over the Indian Ocean/Persian Gulf region from the mid-Pacific island of Guam as a part of his effort to show the Soviets United States resolve. The round trip from Guam to the Arabian Sea took about 30 hours, prompting the Air Force to find a closer platform, such as the Navy's airfield at Diego Garcia.

Indian Ocean Interests

Robert W. Komer, the Under Secretary of Defense for Policy, developed the strategy concerning United States interests in the Persian Gulf, Middle East, and Indian Ocean areas. Ambassador Komer focused on United States interests in those areas before several congressional committee hearings in early 1980: first, to assure flow of oil from the region; second, the long standing interest in the security of Israel that President Jimmy Carter advanced with the peace treaty between Egypt and Israel; and third, the independence of other sovereign states and their freedom from Soviet domination. Ambassador Komer tried to assure the congressional committees that the United States military profile would remain low, and that most of the heavy equipment and ammunition would be stored on cargo ships.

Diego Garcia FY 1981 Program

The fiscal year 1981 Military Construction Program submitted to Congress on 28 January 1980 included the following Navy projects at the Naval Support Facility, Diego Garcia:

($ in Millions)

Project	Cost	Remarks
Ocean Surveillance Building Addition	2.977	Existing building to be expanded to house four additional computers for expanded ocean surveillance.
Dredging (1st Increment)	13.000	To raise the elevation of portions of the island.
Utilities and Facilities Upgrade	2.000	To correct existing deficiencies in fresh water supply, elevate the control tower, and improve Fuel facilities.
Total	17.977	

To support the increased naval presence in the Indian Ocean, the Naval Support Facility also had the following projects planned for the out years:

| | $ in Millions | | |
Facility	FY 82	FY 83	FY 84
Dredging (2nd Increment)	12.0		
Taxiway	16.0		
Parking Apron	33.0		
High Speed Arcrft Refueling (AF)	6.0		
Hazardous Cargo Pad	2.0		
POL Storage (AF)		16.5	
Pier		24.2	
Potable Water System Improvement		10.9	
Totals	69.0	40.7	10.9

The island of Diego Garcia was in for a major expansion so it could handle the biggest planes and aircraft carriers, billet troops and store tons of gear. The price tag could end up being many times the $170 million already earmarked for the island's improvement over the next five years.

Assistance to Kenya, Oman, Somalia

The Carter Administration asked Congress for $90 million to $100 million in military and economic assistance to Kenya, Oman, and Somalia in return for expanded access to ports and air units.[49] The aid package was to be spread over two years, fiscal year 1980 and 1981, and would include money to finance credit purchases of military equipment, economic support funds and some development and food aid. The agreement to use Kenyan facilities was reached on 20 February 1980, during a meeting between President Carter and visiting Kenyan President Daniel arap Moi.

Australian Carrier Group

An Australian carrier task group led by the aircraft carrier HMAS *Melbourne* was deployed in the Indian Ocean to help strengthen the western position in that region following the Soviet invasion of Afghanistan. That decision was announced at the conclusion of a meeting on 27 February 1980 of foreign ministers of ANZUS, the defense alliance linking Australia, New Zealand and the United States.

Contingency Construction Questioned

Congress approved the establishment of an emergency construction authority under the appropriation "Military Construction, Defense Agencies." This authority provided the Secretary of Defense with a capability to react to unforeseen situations involving the need for construction of military facilities where that requirement was determined vital to the security of the United States, and the where the need was of such urgency and impact that construction could not await approval through the regular authorization-appropriation process. The Committees on Armed Services and Appropriations were to be notified immediately by the Secretary of Defense upon his determination to invoke this authority, including complete disclosure of the facts pertaining to its use. Legislation required a 21-day waiting period following notification of the Committees before funds could be obligated.

FIGURE 13. A July 1980 view of the buildings constructed for the 1,500- man military camp. U.S. Navy Photo

FIGURE 14 Senior Chief Builder Pepin, center, describes pier construction operations to Chief of Naval Operations ADM Thomas B. Hayward, left, in July 1980. Accompanying Hayward on the tour is Captain L.K. Donovan, right, the Commander of the 30th Naval Construction Regiment. U.S. Navy Photo

FIGURE 15 A July aerial view of the temporary camp and fuels storage in foreground, and the main camp, cantonment area in the distance. U.S. Navy Photo

Admiral Maurice F. Weisner, Commander in Chief, Pacific, decided that a temporary 1,500 man camp was badly needed at Diego Garcia because of the buildup due to moving the aircraft carrier *Nimitz* (CVN-68) around, and adding to the battle groups that were in the Indian Ocean that added to the required logistic support during the last six months. Military people were sleeping in gymnasiums and hanger spaces, or wherever they could find a spot. The temporary camp, estimated to cost $8,600,000, was to be composed of a combination of South East Asia huts and several small preengineered buildings for air operational and support facilities. (See Figure 13)

Aware that the cargo ship *Private Leonard C. Brostrum* (AK-255) was about to commence loading supplies destined for Diego Garcia on 16 February 1980, and that it was scheduled to arrive at Diego

Garcia about mid-March, and that the next supply ship would not arrive on island until July 1980, the Navy decided to use construction material and equipment from existing consumable supplies, and load them aboard the then available supply ship. In addition, certain high priority common construction material that were not available from stock was purchased on the open market. The Navy planned to pay the cost of this material and its transportation to Diego Garcia from the Secretary of Defense's contingency funds. The Navy wanted to start construction of the camp with Naval Construction Forces by April 1980, and planned to completed the austere camp by December 1980.

FIGURE 16. Prepositioned ships at anchor in Diego Garcia lagoon. U.S. Navy Photo

The Joint Chiefs of Staff requested that Secretary Harold Brown approve the project under his authority, utilizing funds available to the Secretary of Defense. Secretary Brown approved the use of the contingency authority on 18 March 1980 for construction of the camp at Diego Garcia. The Armed Services and Appropriation Committees were then notified, as was required by law. The supply ship, loaded with construction materials, had departed a month before the use of the authority was approved, and seven days before the Congressional committees were informed.

The previous Fiscal Year 1980 Appropriations Conference Report stated that prior approval of the committees should be obtained before using the emergency construction fund. House Appropriations Subcommittee Chairman Gunn McKay believed the Department of Defense misused the contingency authority, and asked Deputy Assistant Secretary of Defense Perry J. Fliakas, during a hearing on 24 April 1980, if he were aware of the prior approval requirement. Perry Fliakas replied, "Yes, Mr. Chairman; I am aware of it. There was sufficient prior year funds available and accordingly we do not believe that prior approval as requested or directed by the committee was applicable in this case to use 1979 prior year funds that had been made available through the contingency fund."

Chairman McKay replied, "You are playing a little semantics here, aren't you, Perry?" Rear Admiral William Zobel, Vice Commander of the Naval Facilities Engineering Command, later added, "The decision was made to preposition that material that had been purchased, not with construction funds, it was coming primarily out of our prepositioned war reserve stocks. We decided to preposition that material on the island so when the approval was obtained, we could move out." Perry Fliakas acknowledged that if Secretary of Defense Brown had objected or did not see fit to approve the temporary camp, or if the committee objected, it was not irreversible. The materials that were being shipped out, couldn't have been used for that project.

Logistics Ships Readied

The Pentagon planned to send the first equipment-loaded ships to the Indian Ocean in the summer of 1980 to be ready for any emergency deployment of a 10,000-man Marine brigade and several jet fighter squadrons, a Pentagon spokesperson said on 5 March 1980. Deputy Defense Secretary W. Graham Claytor, Jr. announced the interim move, which would use seven cargo and tanker ships, referred to as near term prepositioning ships, in testimony before the House Armed Services Seapower Subcommittee.

The aim was to establish the interim depot ship force afloat at an Indian Ocean anchorage, probably the British-owned island of Diego Garcia. At least four of the ships were owned by the Navy, and the others probably would be chartered. The first of the near term prepositioning ship was to start from the West Coast to the East Coast, picking up equipment being readied in Barstow and Albany and would arrive in Diego Garcia in July 1980. One of the seven ships would hold water, another fuel, and another Air Force ammunition. Five of the ships were chartered from private industry. In the long term, Defense planned to either lease or purchase 15 maritime prepositioning ships. (Figure 16 shows a September 1980 port bow view of the Military Sealift Command breakbulk ship *American Champion* anchored in the Diego Garcia lagoon in the company of several other MSC ships. In background MSC Ship *American Courier*. These ships were part of a prepositioned seven-ship stand-by force in the Persian/Arabian Sea area. The force was capable of responding to a crisis within days rather than weeks.)

The total United States Navy ship count reached 31 on 16 March 1980, with the arrival of a Seventh Fleet amphibious task group with 1,800 Marines embarked. Included were the helicopter assault ship *Okinawa* (LPH-3), dock landing ship *Alamo* (LSD-33), attack cargo

ship *Mobile* (LKA-115), and tank landing ship *San Bernardino*
(LST-1189). This was the first of four such task groups to deploy to the
Indian Ocean, resulting in a Navy-Marine amphibious team on station
almost continuously until March 1981. By the end of April 1980, the
Navy had 37 ships deployed in the area.

In April 1980, six months after the seizure of the American Embassy
in Tehran, the Soviets had 30 ships in the Indian Ocean. Following the
release of the United States hostages by Iran, and coincident with the
gradual reduction of United States naval forces, the Soviet naval posture
in the Indian Ocean underwent a similar reduction.

Revised Budget

On 31 March 1980, President Jimmy Carter, forwarded to the
Congress revisions to the Federal Budget for fiscal year 1981 and a supplemental for fiscal year 1980 because of the immediate need to
improve logistical support of operations in the Indian Ocean area. Most
of the funds in the supplemental and amendment were for design and
construction of Navy and Air Force facilities in Diego Garcia, Oman,
Somalia, and Kenya. Some facilities in the Azores were also included.

Lajes

Lajes Field, located on the Atlantic Ocean island of Terceira, in the
Azores and 865 miles off mainland Portugal, provided a base for
American naval antisubmarine warfare operations and service to mili-
tary aircraft on intercontinental missions to and from the European
continent. A study in 1980, done by a private contractor, proposed that
the United States build additional aircraft fuel storage at Lajes Field.
The additional fuel storage needs were based on projected Southwest
Asia contingency requirements, and the assumption that United States

access to Spanish bases would be denied, as it was during the 1973 Middle East War.

The Army's fiscal year 1980 supplemental included $4,300,000 for planning and design of a first increment of an intermediate divisional staging base camp, however, no government in the area had been approached about the location. The total military construction requirement, including planning and design, was $126 million for fiscal year 1980 through fiscal year 1984. The $21,361,000 for construction in the fiscal year 1981 amended Army program was for starting the first increment of the intermediate staging base to accommodate approximately one third of a division force in the Indian Ocean.

The Army amended budget also contained $5.9 million to continue planning and design of future facilities. The Army's staging base was to consist of tent frames on concrete floor slabs for housing and dining facilities; prefabricated steel frame motor repair shops, dispensaries, unit headquarters and supply buildings, battalion headquarters and supply facilities and bathhouses on concrete slabs; pit latrines; hardstands; and roads.

The Navy's fiscal year 1980 supplemental included $23.5 million for the facility expansion at Diego Garcia, and $19 million for planning and design of facilities in Kenya and Diego Garcia. The Navy projects included an air cargo terminal to provide adequate support for the expanded air operations; dredging to provide fill material for stabilizing buildable areas of the island; a ground support equipment shop to provide adequate maintenance and repair of aircraft support and towing equipment; a vehicle maintenance shop to provide services necessary to keep vehicles in operational use; a general warehouse to serve both forces ashore and afloat; a hazardous storage facility to provide adequate storage and control of hazardous materials; adequate housing for 256 additional personnel; and increased power plant capacity and expanded electrical distribution system.

The Air Force fiscal year 1980 supplemental included $24.7 million for planning and design of which $20.5 million was for design of projects in Oman, $2.0 million for planning and design of projects at Diego Garcia, and $2.2 million for design of projects at Lajes Air Base in the Azores.

Navy's amended 1981 budget totaled $104 million. Included were a wharf and waterfront transit shed to provide facilities for increased ship visits and for barge operations, helo-lift operations, and small craft operating between anchored ships and the island; dredging for the wharf construction, access to the wharf and for fill material for stabilizing buildable areas of the island; and facilities for upgrading the telephone system and for ship-to-shore helicopter operations; magazines to provide additional ordnance storage for supporting increased tempo of operations; expansion of cold storage warehouse capacity to support additional personnel ashore and afloat and to provide capacity for a normal resupply period; open storage to support increased operations and provide adequate storage of materials not requiring cover; additional administrative space to support increased operations and personnel loading; adequate housing and dining facilities for additional enlisted and officer personnel to support an island population of 2,150; expanded and upgraded sewage system; increased potable water system; expanded power plant capacity; additional and improved roads and parking.

The Navy and Air Force programs, as amended, for Diego Garcia in fiscal year 1981 included $104 million for the Navy and $23.7 million for the Air Force to complete facility requirements for the expanded mission of supporting a deployed battle group or an amphibious ready group and air lift operations. The funds programmed in the out years, $115 million for the Navy and $125 million for the Air Force, was for completion of facilities to support the rapid deployment force concept.

Air Force projects included in the fiscal year 1981 amendment included $85.7 million for facilities in Oman, and included runway extensions and improvements, apron construction, runway barriers, navigation aids, run-up pads with tie downs, arm and disarm pads, power check pads, fuel storage, ammunition storage, general purpose warehouse, maintenance hangar, water desalinization plants, water storage, water distribution system, power generation and distribution system, billeting facilities, messing facilities, security fencing, and a cargo processing terminal.

The $23.7 million at Diego Garcia was for fuel storage tanks; and the $27.8 million at Lajes Field, Azores, was for fuel storage, airfield pavements, power plant, communication—navigation facility, rehabilitate various buildings, fire station, security fencing, and a water system.

President News Conference

President Carter suggested in his 17 April 1980 news conference dealing with military costs resulting from the Iranian crisis that he would ask Congress for discretion authority to pay reparations to the hostages and their families out of the more than $8 billion in frozen Iranian assets. Those assets would be available to satisfy contracts and other commercial claims to American firms against the Iranian Government entities and to reimburse claims of the United States for the heavy military and other costs incurred because of Iran's illegal actions.

When Department of Defense witnesses were asked if this would be a source of funding for the fiscal year military construction 1980 supplemental and 1981 amended budgets, the Defense witnesses responded that it was determined that Defense costs were incurred directly or indirectly as a result of the Iranian hostage situation, they saw a potential for a claim against frozen Iranian assets. They saw that more as a reimbursement for costs incurred rather than a way of financing military construction.

Subcommittee Hearing

The House Appropriations Subcommittee on Military Construction met on 24 April 1980 to hear testimony in executive session (closed) on the Fiscal Year 1980 Supplemental and Fiscal Year 1981 Amendment. The Subcommittee was Chaired by Congressman Gunn McKay. The Department of Defense sent Perry J. Fliakas, Deputy Assistant Secretary of Defense for Installations and Housing to the hearing.

The changes to the fiscal year 1980 and 1981 budgets were required to reflect updated fuel costs, to adjust for new inflation assumptions, and for the financing of facilities to support increased military operations in the Indian Ocean area. The budget revision included new military construction requirements totaling $117.4 million for fiscal year 1980 and $407 million for fiscal year 1981.

The projected 5-year construction cost estimate to support the Indian Ocean/Persian Gulf operations totaled about $1.5 billion. The estimate was based on a Joint Chiefs of Staff plan for constructing facilities in Oman, Somalia, and Kenya with additional support facilities for Diego Garcia and Lajes Field, Portugal. Lajes Field, in the Azores, was included because of its key role in establishment of an air line of communication link to sustain potential force deployments to the Middle East. Planning and design costs for all Persian Gulf/Indian Ocean facilities in the fiscal year 1981-84 period was estimated to be $71.45 million, of which $19.2 million was for Army facilities, $27.55 million for Navy facilities, and $24.7 million for Air Force facilities.

Access to facilities in several countries stemmed from the need to increase politico-military flexibility while building on existing arrangements. Logistical flexibility and redundancy, especially during a crisis, was critical to ensure the United States forces ability to support a wide range of military operations. Negotiations of the facility access agreements with Oman, Somalia, and Kenya were still in progress. The items being discussed included aid, status of forces agreements, extensive discussion of facilities for naval and air facilities, and contracting arrangements, but did not raise the question of ground base facilities. The Army could not design their intermediate divisional staging base camp until they had an approved location. Agreements with the three countries could take six more months.

The State Department had initiated consultations with Great Britain about the improvements to Diego Garcia. British approval was not yet in hand, but was expected soon. The Navy and Air Force facility requirements for Diego Garcia were to support the expanded mission of supporting a deployed battle group on an amphibious ready group and air lift operations. The Navy planned to construct the new facilities at Diego Garcia by a combination of Seabees and contractors. The Seabees would do horizontal work, and contractors would do the vertical work and dredging.

The Carter Administration worked with the NATO allies to increase overall Allied security efforts in response to the situation in Southwest Asia. They asked the Allies to renew efforts to achieve 3 percent real annual increase in defense spending and to accelerate implementation of selected defense measures contained in the NATO Long Term Defense Program. They indicated areas of NATO defense in which the Allies might pick up any slack occasioned by allocation of United States assets to Southwest Asia. They were also encouraging those Allies who could provide military training and assistance to countries in Southwest Asia, and without diminishing significantly their capabilities for defense in Europe, to deploy even on a temporary basis some military forces to the area and to develop the capability to help reinforce in the area. Finally they asked Allies to help ensure that their facilities would be available when United States forces had to be moved into and supported in Southwest Asia.

Rotational Services

With the increased population at Diego Garcia, in May 1980 the Navy brought in 55 Philippine nationals to replace 55 Seabees working in the dining facility on a ninety-day turnaround basis. A contracted messing service for the 1,500 man temporary camp was also instituted because of the high demand for military in other functions. The Navy also rotated 244 maintenance personnel to Diego Garcia from the Public Works Center at Subic Bay.

Oman Facilities

For a while, Oman threatened to cancel its agreement with the United States in wake of the aborted United States hostage rescue mission in Iran on 24 April 1980 after United States C-130 transport planes used airfields in Oman without asking permission from the Government of Sultan Qaboos bin Said.

On 4 June 1980, Ambassador Marshall W. Wiley for the United States and Minister of State for Foreign Affairs Qais A. Al-Zawawi, for the Sultanate of Oman signed a single page country-to-country economic and military agreement that referred to discussions regarding a "framework for bilateral cooperation relating to economic development and trade, and to defense equipment, training and development, in order to enhance the capability of Oman to safeguard its security and territorial integrity, and to promote peace and stability."[50]

The agreement allowed American use of sea and air bases in Oman in return for United States technical, economic, and military aid, including $25 million in foreign military sales credits in both fiscal years 1980 and 1981, and an additional $5 million in economic support to help establish a joint economic commission between the United States and Oman. The United States was responsible for paying a reasonable proportion of the cost of maintaining the facilities used. The agreement allowed the United States use of air facilities at Seeb International Airport, Masirah Island, Khasab and Thumrait and port facilities at Raysut (Salalah) and Port Qaboos (Mutrah) were to be available for contingency situations only.

Kenya Facilities

The access agreement with Kenya, signed on 26 June 1980, provided for United States use of airfields and ports at Nanyaki and Mombasa. Kenya expected to receive military and economic aid in fiscal years 1981 and 1982. The military aid for fiscal year 1981 included $6 million Foreign Military Sales credit for purchase of United States weaponry; $.5 million International Education and Training Program funds; $5.5 million Economic Support Funds.

The military aid for fiscal year included $51 million Foreign Military Sales credit (all concessional); $1.3 million International Education and Training Program funds; $10 million Economic Support Funds. Economic aid for fiscal year 1981 was $21.1 million; $23.7 million (PL-480). For fiscal year 1982, $34.5 million; $19.2 million (PL-480). Kenya was unhappy when the United States agreed to provide Somalia with antiaircraft missiles, which would enable the Somalis to shoot down the aircraft that the United States had previously supplied to Kenya.

Enacted Fiscal Year 1980 Supplemental

The Supplemental Appropriations and Recision Act, 1980 (Public Law 96-304) was enacted on 8 July 1980. Congress reduced the total requested for planning and design from $48 million to $22 million because of lack of overall planning and absence of signed county-to-country agreements. The Congress funded only $7.5 million of the $23.5 million requested for Diego Garcia construction. Congress also rejected the Department of Defense's plan to pay for the additional design and construction by transfer from the Navy's ship building account. Instead, they provided some new appropriations and transferred some funds from the NATO Infrastructure account as a message that NATO needed to participate in the Persian Gulf venture.

Further, the Congress legislated an American preference in Indian Ocean construction, stressing prequalification for United States contractors, use of United States labor and materials, and use of joint ventures to satisfy existing agreements. The Act also closed the loophole concerning the prior approval of the Secretary of Defense's emergency construction fund, as was done with the approval of the 1,500 man temporary camp at Diego Garcia, and included legislation that required that none of the funds available for the emergency construction fund could be obligated until 21 days after the Secretary of Defense notified the Appropriations Committees.

Appeal to Subcommittee

On 23 July 1980, Secretary of Defense Harold Brown wrote to Walter Huddleston, Chairman of the Appropriations Committee Subcommittee on Military Construction concerning the House version of the fiscal year 1981 Military Construction Appropriation Bill. Secretary Brown said he appreciated approval by the House of certain Indian Ocean access projects previously disallowed from the fiscal year 1980 Supplemental Appropriations Request.

Concerning the Indian Ocean/Persian Gulf Area construction, Secretary of Defense Brown noted that "the House approved only $153,500,000 of the $208,800,000 requested for fiscal year 1981, plus $20,200,000 deferred from previous requests. It is imperative that we rapidly strengthen our capabilities in this vital region, particularly by funding forward facilities for crisis use in the Persian Gulf/Indian Ocean area itself. Without these, it will not be possible to assure preservation of Western oil access. Without that access, the Alliance will fragment and the economies of the industrialized democracies will fail. The great distances and logistic difficulties for us, the proximity of the Soviets to an area so vital to us that we cannot opt out of the competition, are serious enough handicaps. We must not add to them by failing to establish facilities where we can." In July 1980, the Chief of Naval Operations visited Diego Garcia. (See Figure 14)

Mauritius Claim

Sir Seewoosagur Ramgoolam, the Prime Minister of Mauritius, met with British Prime Minister Margaret Thatcher at 10 Downing Street on 7 July 1980 concerning the Mauritius claim to the right of ownership of Diego Garcia. While recognizing British sovereignty, Mauritius wanted Diego Garcia returned without compensation when it was no longer needed as a base. No promises were made.

Somalia Facilities

The access agreement with Somalia, signed on 22 August 1980, gave the United States access to the airfields and ports at Berbera and Mogadishu. Military construction projects, however, were not a part of the access agreement. Negotiations had become stalled over Somali demands for economic and military assistance of $2 billion over a ten year period. There were also concerns that the United States could be dragged into the continuing battle between Somalia and Ethiopia over the Ogaden desert region dispute. Somalia formerly was a Soviet ally complete with a Soviet base, and Ethiopia was an American ally with

United States bases. The countries changed partners after the 1974 Ethiopian revolution.

The agreement provided for the United States to supply $20 million in military sales credits in fiscal year 1980, and another $20 million credit plus $3 million in budgetary support the following year. The United States planned to spend another $11 million to improve the Somali ports of Berbera and Mogadishu. Although the State Department testified in support of reprogramming fiscal year funds that Somalia had given up plans for a military takeover of the Ogaden, and had no significant troops there, the Central Intelligence Agency informed the Foreign Affairs Subcommittee that elements of three Somali battalions, plus up to 1,000 Somali regulars were serving with insurgents in the Ogaden. Somali agreed in writing that it would not use American supplied equipment to fight in Ethiopia.

All of the agreements required prior consultation with the host government concerning the use of the access facilities. Typically, the United States would be able to exercise there, have maneuvers and joint exercises, and store fuel and ammunition.

Appeal to Conferees

Secretary of Defense Harold Brown appealed to the Chairmen of the House and Senate Armed Services Committees on 22 September 1980 before their conference on the fiscal year 1981 Military Construction Authorization Bill. The Department of Defense had requested $315,538,000 to support Indian Ocean area basing initiatives. The House approved $298,177,000 and the Senate approved $200,000,000 for a mid-east base construction contingency fund. The Department of Defense supported the House position. The Navy projects at Diego Garcia were well defined and construction could commence upon enactment of authorization and funding. The Air

Force projects at Lajes, Portugal, and Diego Garcia should not be included in a "contingency fund." The remaining projects concerned construction at other locations in the Indian Ocean that were vital to the success of the regional defense strategy. Agreements with Oman, Kenya and Somalia to use such facilities were now complete and had been formally supplied and transmitted to Congress to comply with House requirements for beginning work. The Senate's proposal for a Middle East base construction fund would be more acceptable as an alternative if the authorization level were raised to the $298,200,000 as approved by the House.

Iran-Iraq Hostilities

Shortly after the outbreak of hostilities between Iran and Iraq on 22 September 1980, Britain began maintaining an average of eight Royal Navy ships in the Gulf of Oman. In late October 1981, the French increased their forces in the Indian Ocean to approximately 25 ships. India protested the build up of United States, British, and French warships as a threat to the peace and stability in the region and as a contribution to the aggravation of the Iraq-Iran conflict.

Appeal to Conferees

Secretary of Defense Harold Brown appealed to the House and Senate Appropriations Committees on 23 September 1980 on the fiscal year 1981 Military Construction Appropriation Bill. Concerning the Indian Ocean Access/Persian Gulf/Rapid Deployment Force construction, he noted that the House denied funding of $107.8 million; the Senate denied $70.5 million. Defense supported the Senate funding level of $245,000,000 since that level more nearly approached Defense's needs. Secretary Brown warned that "Failure to support these projects will severely limit Defense's capability to project military power in this crucial area, since existing facilities were insufficient to support major deployment efforts. We cannot emphasize enough the importance of this construction effort as an integral part of support of Rapid Deployment contingency requirements. We also request the Conferees to fund the projects through the individual construction accounts rather than through a central fund. This is requested in an effort to speed construction."

Special Contingency Fund

The Armed Services Committees conferees agreed to use a contingency approach in order to provide the Secretary of Defense with flexibility to program construction in Southwest Asia while meeting the political and military uncertainties facing the United States at that time. They authorized a $150 million special contingency facilities construction fund, rather than the $200 million amount initially recommended by the Senate. Diego Garcia was excluded from the special contingency fund since it was an established installation and requirements could be approved in the normal fashion. The Armed Services Committees supported the Army's plan to construct a division sized facility in the Middle East/Indian Ocean for the Rapid Deployment Force when a site decision was made.

The Appropriations Committees conferees provided $105 million for the special contingency facilities construction fund. The special contingency fund legislation required that preference be given to United States materials, vessels, and contractors, with the host nation providing the bulk of the labor requirements. (See Figure 16)

By October 1980, more than 60 American, British, French, and Australian warships were in the Arabian Sea and the Indian Ocean. In 1980, a massive increase in Soviet submarine was observed. Before

1980, Soviet submarine patrols had been limited to one diesel boat plus a four and one-half annual excursion by an older nuclear submarine from their Pacific Fleet. 1980 brought a nearly continuous Pacific Fleet nuclear submarine presence, an increase in diesel patrols and two "Victor"-class submarines from their northern Fleet. Soviet Il-38 "May" aircraft in South Yemen and Ethiopia conducted surveillance of American battle groups. The Soviets had about 29 ships in the region by October 1980. Iran threatened to mine the Persian Gulf and the Strait of Hormuz if the United States or other Western countries helped Iraq in the war.

Foreign Affairs Study Report

The House Committee on Foreign Affairs sent a staff study mission to nine countries in the Persian Gulf, Middle East, and Horn of Africa during October and November 1980.[51] The study mission examined the security, economic, and foreign policy implications of the Carter Doctrine to United States interests in the Persian Gulf. The study mission concluded that the steps the United States had taken to implement the Carter Doctrine were not adequate to assure United States interests in the Persian Gulf. The study mission noted that the Gulf States which did not want a United States military presence or facility access agreement may be willing over time to consider participation in quiet forms of United States military cooperation, such as strategic dialogue, prepositioning of United States equipment, familiarization of the United States with local military assets and capabilities, and communications, navigational and air defense systems helpful to the United States in a time of conflict. The staff report stressed speed and more coordination in implementing the Carter Doctrine.

Soviet Doctrine

Soviet President Leonid Brezhnev, in a major foreign policy address to members of India's Parliament on 10 December 1980, proposed a "Brezhnev Doctrine" that would ban establishment of foreign military bases in the region.[52] Brezhnev's doctrine had five major points. These points called for the United States, other Western powers, China, and Japan to agree:

- Not to set up foreign military bases in the Persian Gulf area and on adjacent islands; not to deploy nuclear or any other weapons of mass destruction there;
- Not to use or threaten to use force against the countries of the Persian Gulf and not to interfere in their internal affairs;
- To respect the status of nonalignment chosen by states of the Persian Gulf area; not to draw them into military groupings with the participation of nuclear powers;
- To respect the sovereign right of the states of that area to their natural resources;   and
- Not to raise any obstacles or pose threats to normal trade exchanges and to the use of sea lanes linking the states of that area with other countries of the world.

Architect-Engineer Notification

On 9 December 1980, a Section 612 Notification was made to the Armed Services Committee, notifying them that the Navy planned to start planning and design of a $27,000,000 project proposed for fiscal year 1983. The fee was estimated at $1,500,000.

Hostages Released

The American hostages were released on 20 January 1981. The United States maintained two carrier groups until 21 October 1981, when strength dropped to one battle group for the first time since November 1979, the month in which the embassy was seized. The single battle group consisted of six combatant ships plus seven to 12 P-3 maritime patrol aircraft operating from Diego Garcia.

By mid 1982, Soviet ship count averaged about 25 and by year's end had fallen to approximately 20, with not more than two major surface combatants in the Indian Ocean area for any sustained period.

Within the first two months of 1983, the Soviets were maintaining only about 15 ships in the Indian Ocean, including a "Kashin"-class guided missile destroyer and an "Echo II" submarine.

Multi-year Regional Plan

On 21 January 1981, Perry J. Fliakas, the Deputy Assistant Secretary of Defense for Installations and Housing, submitted to the Chairmen of the Armed Services and Appropriations Subcommittees on Military Construction a Joint Chiefs of Staff developed multi-year regional plan for Oman, Kenya, and Somalia in accordance with the provisions of Section 405 of Public Law 96-418. The plan had been reviewed by President Ronald Reagan and endorsed by his Secretary of Defense Caspar W. Weinberger. The regional plan included project listings and justifications for the $105 million Persian Gulf Contingency Fund. Legislation required the Department of Defense to wait for 30 days after submission of the plan before proceeding with construction to allow review of the plan by congressional committees. Included were $3 million for runway facilities at Khasab, in the northern noncontiguous Omani Musandam Peninsula at the Straits of Hormuz, and $82.5

million for Masirah Island in Oman; $19.7 million for dredging Kilindini Harbor and a parallel taxiway and aircraft parking for Navy aircraft at Mombasa, Kenya; and a $400,000 project at Berbera, Somalia. Most of the contingency funds were allocated to the Island of Masirah.

Masirah

Masirah Island, located 15 miles off the mainland, was in a remote area, had no civilian population, and was considered a good place to support current fleet operations. The island is 44 miles long and ranges in width from about 18 miles to only a few miles at its narrowest points. The island had no fresh water. It is the main breeding ground for the loggerhead sea turtle. Masirah had some drawbacks too. Monsoons made Masirah unreachable by ship four months a year, and the strong crosswinds during monsoons made takeoffs and landings difficult. In a conflict, Masirah would be vulnerable to an air attack.

The Congressional Committees were also provided copies of the Reagan Administration's "Southwest Asia Facility Access and Development Strategy."

Kilindini Harbor

Initially Defense had envisaged a larger program for Somalia, but Congress wanted Somalia out of the Ogaden first, and it was not until January 1981 that this requirement was validated. The Somali Government also undertook some of the improvements at Mogadishu Airfield, and requested that the United States concentrate upgrading at Berbera. The remaining funds planned initially for Somalia were switched by Defense for dredging Kilindini Harbor to a depth of 45 feet, which was a Commander-in-Chief, Pacific high priority. With deeper water, a carrier task group could enter the harbor and berth at this international port and recreation site for Navy personnel assigned to ships on nearly continuous duty in the Indian Ocean.

TABLE 7—SPECIAL CONTINGENCY FACILITIES CONSTRUC-
TION FUNDS
$ in Millions

Location	Project	$
OMAN (AF)		
KHASAB	Realign and Upgrade Runway	3.000
MASIRAH	Mobilization Camp/Security	5.000
	*Water Desal., Storage & Distribution (Phase	3.500
	*Power Generation & Distribution (Phase 1)	3.900
	Ext. Main Runway & Overlay (Incl. Runway	9.500
	POL Storage & Distribution (Phase 1)	6.100
	Hydrant Refueling (5 Point)	4.000
	Extend Parallel Taxiway & Overlay	7.600
	Apron	7.500
	Overlay Existing Apron	2.500
	*Ready Magazine	0.100
	Ammunition Storage Igloos (Phase 1)	5.300
	Munitions Maintenance Facility	3.000
	Arm/Disarm, Power Check Pad	0.800
	*Consolidated Transient A/C Maintenance	3.000
	*Cargo Terminal	2.900
	*Unaccompanied Personnel Housing	5.000
	*Dining Hall w/Cold Storage	2.200
	*General Purpose Warehouse	4.800
	Extend Secondary Runway	5.800
	Subtotal OMAN	85.500
KE YA ( )		
MOI AIRPORT	Parallel Taxiway	1.650
	Aircraft Parking Apron	0.870
MOMBASA NB	HE Magazines	0.390
MOMBASA	Dredging	16.190
	Subtotal KENYA	19.100
SOMALIA		
BERBERA	Airfield Improvements and Facility	0.400
TOTAL	* Includes both Air Force and Navy	105.0

5

Naval Air Facility

A separate United States Naval Air Facility was established on Diego Garcia on 26 February 1981 under the command of Commander D.L. Nesbitt. The Naval Air Facility operated the airfield and served the aircraft detachments and units assigned to Diego Garcia.

Sadat Offers Base Access

President Anwar el-Sadat, in his letter of 27 July 1981 to President Reagan, invited the United States the use of Egyptian military facilities in the case of emergency contingencies, but President Sadat would not sign any agreement or allow an American flag to fly over any Egyptian facility. Egyptian Defense Minister Kamal Hassan Ali first offered the United States use of Egyptian military facilities in January 1980, during the ninth summit conference between Egypt and Israel.[53] Egyptian and United States air forces conducted joint exercises as a test for United States planes operating from Egyptian bases. The Egyptians wanted the United States to preposition F15 fighters and other sophisticated equipment in Egypt. Egyptian pilots would operate them, but would turn the equipment over to United States crews during a crisis.

The Egyptians made a serious distinction between facilities and bases. They had historic experiences with the Turks, British, and the Soviets involving bases that they found politically repugnant and caused domestic political problems for the Egyptian leadership. Sadat had expelled Soviet military advisors from Egypt in 1972. President Sadat's letter, stated, "Egypt will give full facilities to the United States to defend any Arab country that is exposed to foreign invasion from Iran or the Soviet Union."

The United States military planners were sent to Egypt and they believed they could use some of the Egyptian facilities, and began revising their plans for access in the Indian Ocean and Persian Gulf area to include use of the Egyptian base at Ras Banas where a C-141 Starlifter cargo jet could go and where there was access by sea. The Egyptian air base at Ras Banas, which was built by the Egyptians with Soviet aid and advisors, was directly on the air and sea lines of communication between the United States and potential conflict areas in the Indian Ocean/Persian Gulf.

Ras Banas was located in an isolated desert location on the Red Sea in southern Egypt, near the border with Sudan, and was across from an Arabian refinery at the port of Yanbu, which was to be on the line about 1982. Ras Banas had an 8,500 foot runway, some underground bunkers, and aircraft shelters. There was an existing fuel loading pier, and a cargo pier. The base was subject to occasional flooding, which caused some Soviet mines to be shifted about and had to be located. The annual mean maximum temperature for Ras Banas was 83 degrees Fahrenheit, with an all-time record high of 104 degrees.

Ras Banas was ideal as a rear-staging area with adequate area for prepositioning equipment and fuel for United States ground and tactical air units that could arrive early in a crisis. Its accessibility by either air or sea, distance to critical objective areas, defensibility against enemy attack or harassment, and remoteness from major population centers made Ras Banas the best available rear-staging location essential to the United States Southwest Asia defense strategy.

The total construction cost for developing Ras Banas facilities based on a preliminary master plan was almost $400 million, of which $231 million for Air Force facilities, and $167 for Army facilities. As a result of later architectural-engineering cost estimates, the Air Force portion rose to $299 million. The revised amount included $19 million for the runway, $29 million for the taxiways, $76 million for aprons, $30 million for fuel storage and distribution, $17 million for munitions storage, $19 million for water supply and storage, $18 million for electrical power supply and distribution, $23 million for cantonment facilities, $14 million for airfield operations and maintenance facilities, $19 million for supply facilities and $35 million for site preparation, grading, drainage and roads.

Fiscal Year 1982 Program

The Reagan Administration added about $117 million to the fiscal year 1982 construction program for Southwest Asia after reviewing the Joint Chiefs of Staff developed regional plan. However, Deputy Secretary of Defense Frank C. Carlucci was asked to review by the end of April 1981 the decision concerning B-52 bomber capability. Defense had the funds in the supplemental for design and potentially the funds in the 1982 or 1983 to build the bomber capability. Perry Fliakas testified that the basing mode was being reviewed, but also that a deliberate decision had been made to proceed with double track design so as not to impact on the Initial Operational Date. The B-52 capability at Ras Banas, Egypt, would be reflected in the fiscal year budget.

B-52

At Diego Garcia, construction for the B-52 capability meant adding a nine-inch concrete overlay as well as a 25-foot shoulder on each side of the existing runway, as well as changes to the aprons and taxiways to enable them to be used as a temporary runway while the main runway was being rebuilt. The British Government had been consulted and approved the improvement plan for Diego Garcia.

The additional cost of providing B-52 bomber capabilities at Ras Banas was about $102 million, including $6.6 million for upgrading the runway, $9.6 million for the taxiway, $38.3 million for the apron, $5.6 million for the hydrant refueling system, $6.6 million for fuel storage, $7.8 million for munitions storage igloos, $5.9 million for the cantonment area, $6.4 million for the pro rata share of the other base utility support, $1.3 million for a squadron operations facility, $2 million for a general purpose warehouse, $11.8 million for the pro rata share of site preparation, and $.6 million for the demineralized water plant.

The fiscal year 1982 construction program was intended to provide enroute airlift support and rear staging and support bases for expeditionary forces required in contingency situations. Construction at Diego Garcia was to support an airlift of a Marine amphibious brigade, and a classified mission. The Navy wanted to build a parallel taxiway and aircraft parking apron to support expanded air operations for fleet support and the Rapid Deployment Force. Also included at Diego Garcia were waterfront facilities for loading, off-loading, and storage of prepositioned materials and equipment for the Rapid Deployment Force. At Lajes Field, Azores, it would increase C-141 equivalent airlift sorties to support projected airlift requirements. In Egypt, for the first time, it would support airlift operations as well as provide the first of two rear-staging areas for the Army. In Oman, it would support tactical aircraft operations at Seeb International Airport at Muscat, on Masirah Island, and at Thumrait.

The fiscal year 1982 construction program also had Navy projects at Kenya, to continue the dredging the harbor channel at Mombasa, to allow a full carrier group to enter and to berth there so the crews could go ashore for liberty, to provide an access road at Mombasa, to provide communications and navigational aids at Moi International Airport, and to provide some storage facilities at both locations. The Navy planned to spend a total of $62.9 million for dredging at Mombasa. At Somalia the Navy wanted to extend the quay at Berbera to provide limited fleet support. Some of the previously Soviet built facilities were available now to the United States Navy.

Defense Secretary Caspar W. Weinberger, in a television interview on "Face the Nation," said that the United States needs enough of a military presence in the Middle East to convince the Soviets that any interference in the area would carry an unacceptable risk.

Somali Funds Approved

The House Appropriations Foreign Operations Subcommittee conditionally approved in October 1980, the State Department's request for a $20 million arms sale to Somalia, in return for the United States's use of Somali facilities that might be needed during a conflict. The sole condition imposed by the House subcommittee was that the Department of Defense must first certify that all Somali troops were completely out of the Ogaden.

Subcommittee Hearing

On 31 March 1981, the House Appropriations Subcommittee on Military Construction met to review the amended fiscal year 1982 request for $522 million for construction in the Persian Gulf, and $425 million for the Pacific. Presiding the subcommittee was Congressman Bo Ginn. The Defense witnesses were headed by Perry J. Fliakas, the Deputy Assistant Secretary of Defense for Installations and Housing.

The construction program in the Persian Gulf region had grown in the last year from the development of the base at Diego Garcia to the planned expenditure of about $1.5 billion for a network of facilities in the next four years in five countries. The construction was designed to improve four types of facilities in the Indian Ocean/Persian Gulf:

- Facilities to support peacetime presence; included were port improvements such as dredging, warehouses, communication facilities and administrative functions; fleet logistics support activity such as runway improvements, cargo terminals, billets and navigation and communication aids; and support for surveillance missions;
- Facilities to support sea control operations; such as in Oman, Kenya, and Somalia that were situated near three choke points: the Strait of Hormuz, the Bab al-Mandab, and the Mozambique Channel. Access to these facilities was considered vital to keep oil flowing and to protect movement of sealift in a crisis;
- Rear-staging facilities for use in crisis; such as Ras Banas were considered critical for closing units to the region as a deterrent to hostilities and for delivering and sustaining large combat units; and
- Forward operating facilities for use in a conflict. These facilities would be needed to bed down tactical fighter aircraft and as in theater terminus for sealift and airlift.

TABLE 8
TENTATIVE RAPID DEPLOYMENT TASK FORCE COMPOSITION

Army Forces	Air Forces	Naval Forces
XVII Airborne Corps, HQ	Air Force,	(1) Surface action
24th Infantry Division (Mech.)	(4) Tactical fighter wings	(3) Carrier battle groups
9th Infantry Division	(2) Tactical RECCE squadrons	(1) Marine Amphibious Force
82th Airborne Division	(2) Tactical airlift wings	(5) Patrol Squadrons
101st Airborne Div. (Air Assault) Assault)t)	Other classified	
6th Cavalry Brigade Air Combat		
194th Armored Brigade		
1st/75th Infantry Battalion (Ranger)		
2d/75th Infantry Battalion (Ranger)		

Host Nation Support

Since some American NATO allocated forces might have to be deployed to Southwest Asia in time of conflict, the United States asked it's Allies to pick up the slack by such steps as providing Host Nation Support for United States stationed/reinforcing forces. Secretary of

State Alexander M. Haig, Jr., visited Saudi Arabia the following month to discuss proposals for facility access.

Gulf Cooperation Council

On eight to 10 March 1981, the six state Gulf Cooperation Council met for the second time to define their roles in the region. The states were Saudi Arabia, Kuwait, Qatar, Bahrain, United Arab Emirates, and Oman. The purpose was to develop a pact aimed at protecting the oil exporting region and keeping out foreign powers. Saudi King Fahd Khalid had said, "Security comes from placing confidence in God and ourselves," at the first meeting in Riyadh in February. On 25 May 1981, the six states signed a charter for economic and technological cooperation, and deferred discussions on defense issues. Summit leaders issued a statement declaring the "Security of the region and its stability are the responsibility of its peoples and states." The statement demanded that the Gulf be kept "outside the sphere of international conflict, particularly the presence of foreign fleets and bases."

Enacted FY 1981 Supplemental

The fiscal year 1981 supplemental request included $59 million for planning and design funds related to the rapid deployment force initiatives in the Indian Ocean and Persian Gulf, and $9 million for dredging the harbor at Mombasa, Kenya. Only $33 million was approved for planning and design. The $6 million for planning and design of Ras Banas facilities was denied because the Appropriations Committees believed Army had sufficient funds to develop preliminary plans and cost estimates while policy issues were resolved. The $3 million Navy requested for planning and design of Indian Ocean and Persian Gulf facilities was approved, but the Air Force request of $50 million was reduced to $30 million because of uncertainties and the problem of obligating the funds in the final quarter of the fiscal year.

The Committees were concerned that designs were being made prior to firm decisions or need or purpose of the installations. The only construction funds requested, the dredging the Mombasa harbor, were denied. The Committees noted that funds were available in the Persian Gulf Contingency Fund, subject to congressional approval.

Construction Policy

The Department of Defense developed in November 1980 a construction policy for the Indian Ocean/Persian Gulf that provided preference to United States firms to insure a dependable, technically proficient, and responsive regional construction capability. The policy required that for projects costing over $5 million, the construction agent was permitted to determine if there was sufficient American interest. If the construction agent determined that there has been sufficient competition, then an award would be made to an American contractor. If there was insufficient interest or competition, then the agent was free to extend the bidding to international competition. The United States dredging contractors were provided with a 20 per cent bid factor advantage, in accordance with the provisions of Public Law 97–106.

The Associated General Contractors believed the policy was beneficial because it provided for a viable, dependable construction capacity in the region, provided for an increased return to the economy, and finally enhanced the United States construction's industry's competitive position overseas. Then, there were 950,000 United States construction tradesmen out of work, about 20 per cent of that sector.

Diego Garcia Dredging

In spite of the 20 percent bid factor advantage for American firms, a Japanese firm, Penta-Ocean Construction Co., Ltd., was awarded the fiscal year 1981 dredging contract for $17.9 million at Diego Garcia. The lowest American bid from the Great Lakes Dredge and Dock was $42 million. The agreements with the host nations required construction participation by host nation firms. At Diego Garcia a joint venture partnership had to be formed.

Diego Garcia Contractor

Seventeen firms responded to the Navy's announcement in the November 1980 Commerce Business Daily concerning the $70 to $90 million construction project at Diego Garcia. Eight were selected and in March 1981 they were taken to Diego Garcia. The Navy selected one through a competitive negotiation process. The Navy planned to award the contract in June 1981.

Lajes Field Agreement

In the Rapid Deployment Force exercises in 1980, the Government of Portugal denied access to Lajes Airfield. But Lajes was at the right distance in the Atlantic and close enough to the Mediterranean, making it an ideal location. There was an exchange of notes between the United States and Portugal on 18 June 1979 that extended the original 1951 defense agreement to continue through February 1983.

Regional Plan

Including the fiscal year 1981 supplemental, there remained $916 million for construction in the Indian Ocean/Persian Gulf. Additionally the United States planned to construct another $134 million of facilities at Lajes, Portugal. The plan in brief was:

$ in Millions

	IO/PG	Lajes
Fiscal year 1981 supplemental	9.0	—
Fiscal year 1982	473.0	49.6
Fiscal year 1983	297.0	84.0
Fiscal year 1984 and beyond	137.0	—
	—	—
Totals	916.0	133.6

It was a huge construction undertaking, the design alone was estimated to cost $96.4 million for facilities in the Indian Ocean/ Persian Gulf area and another $11.2 million for facilities at Lajes. Contracts for the design work were awarded by the Atlantic Division, Naval Facilities Engineering Command, and the United States Army Engineer Division Rear at Winchester, Virginia to United States firms. The Navy was designated as the design agent for the work in Kenya, Somalia, and Diego Garcia. The Corps of Engineers was assigned as the design and construction agent in Oman and Egypt.

Diego Garcia Population

In March 1981, there were about 3,000 people on Diego Garcia. The Naval Support facility had about 800. Primary tenants were the communications station, a security group, an antisubmarine warfare patrol squadron, and a reconnaissance squadron, totaling about 900 people. Other tenants, including Air Force detachments, a carrier beach detachment, and others totaled 450. There were also 850 Seabees working on construction on the island.

Resettlement Talks

The British Government had offered 1,250,000 pounds sterling and a further 300,000 pounds sterling in aid to Mauritius to achieve a final settlement on compensation for the islanders displaced ten years ago from Diego Garcia and the other parts of the Chagos Archipelago. Talks between a delegation from Mauritius lead by Ragkeswur Purryag and the British Foreign Office broke down on 2 July 1981. Mauritius had asked for eight million pounds sterling besides the 650,000 pounds sterling agreed to in 1973. Mauritius was also calling for the return of the islands.[54]

Lajes

The House Armed Services Committee initially denied the requested facilities at Lajes Field, Portugal, because of concerns about Portuguese commitments to the use of Lajes for the Rapid Deployment Force. Defense argued that these facilities could be used for either Southwest Asia or NATO requirements, and that the new fuel storage capacity would increase the airlift capacity for the Rapid Deployment Force. The Armed Services Committees conferees restored the construction at Lajes with fencing language for Rapid Deployment Force use.

B-52 Decision

Secretary of Defense Weinberger had decided by November 1981, not only to receive strategic and tactical airlift of Army land forces and to achieve rear staging of tactical aircraft and ground forces capability at Ras Banas, Egypt, but to proceed there to accommodate the Strategic Projection Force (B-52 Bombers). The United States had received a commitment in the 27 July 1981 letter from former President Anwar el-Sadat inviting the United States the use of Egyptian military facilities. President Hosni Mubarak, who became President after President Sadat's assassination, indicated in October 1981 that he would honor the commitment. Both the Senate Foreign Relations Committee and the House Foreign Affairs Committee agreed that further pursuit of any other written agreement would have a negative effect on relations with the Government of Egypt.[55]

The House Appropriations Committee, still unconvinced, denied all construction funds for Ras Banas until their questions concerning the program, country-to-country agreement, and design were resolved. The Rapid Deployment Force projects at Lajes Field were approved, but funds could not be obligated until the Government of Portugal approved the construction plan, and the House Appropriations Committee had assurances that facilities could be used for intended purposes.

Raymond, Brown & Root, and Mowlem

On 14 July 1981, the Navy awarded a cost-reimbursable contract (cost-plus-award fee) to Raymond International Builders, Inc.; Brown & Root, Incorporated, of Houston; and John Mowlem International, Limited, of Middlesex, England, a joint venture, to construct facilities programmed for fiscal years 1981 and 1982, with an estimated cost of $285 million. This contract joint venture followed ten years of construction work by the Naval Construction Forces, which had provided the infrastructure for support of limited United States military operations in the Indian Ocean. The administration of the contract was the responsibility of the Pacific Division, Naval Facilities Engineering Command, which appointed an Officer in Charge of Construction. The OICC's headquarters was collocated with that of the contractor's in Houston, Texas. On Diego Garcia, the Deputy OICC's staff consisted of three resident OICC's and about 30 civilians.

Under the cost-reimbursable contract, practically all costs incurred by the joint venture were reimbursed by the government. The Navy chose the cost-plus-award fee contract because that contract form provided the flexibility to cope with various uncertainties in the program. The General Accounting Office in its investigation reported in May 1984[56] that because of ineffective management and information and materials control systems, unnecessary costs were incurred and construction delays were exacerbated. The joint venture contractor employed about 1,400 people on Diego Garcia. The first contractor personnel arrived on Diego Garcia for preliminary investigation of the site in July 1981, and construction started in early 1982.

By November 1981, the joint venture contractor had started construction of the contractor's camp on Diego Garcia. Early in February, construction of the first facility, an 8,000-KW power plant started.

Comptroller General Report

The Comptroller General completed the "United States Facility Access Initiatives in Support of Southwest Asia Contingencies—Achievements and Future Challenges Report" to the Committee on Foreign Relations, United States Senate, in September 1981.

Operation *BRIGHT STAR 82*

Operation BRIGHT STAR 82, conducted in October-November 1981, was the largest United States exercises ever conducted in the Southwest Asia Region. The exercises involved forces deployed in Egypt, Somalia, Sudan, and Oman, and were under the command and control of the Commander, Rapid Deployment Joint Task Force. The purpose of BRIGHT STAR 82 was to exercise the Rapid Deployment Joint Task Force headquarters command and control of a deployed joint task force, provide an interface between senior United States and host nation officials, familiarize the Rapid Deployment Joint Task Force with environmental and operational characteristics of the region, evaluate logistics and communications concepts, and provide a highly visible display of United States resolve and ability to protect vital interests in Southwest Asia. President Anwar el-Sadat was assassinated while reviewing an Army parade in Cairo, on 6 October 1981, by a group of Egyptian religious militants who opposed his policies.

Saudis' *AWACS*

The Pentagon acknowledged on 2 November 1981 that it had held discussions with Saudi officials about an integrated defense for the Middle East that would include prepositioning United States combat equipment there. The Pentagon also conceded that there was an understanding that Saudi Arabia would let American forces use Saudi facilities to defend the Persian Gulf from attack by the Soviet Union. Department of Defense spokesman Benjamin Wells denied that there was any formal agreement.

The sale of the airborne warning and control system planes set the stage for the development, with United States backing, of a regional air defense system for the entire Gulf region. Saudi Arabia was building airfield facilities beyond its current needs, which could sustain United States forces in intensive regional combat involving the Soviet Union.

American Oil Base

The Coastal Corporation, a Texas-based oil company, obtained in January 1982 a 25-year lease and exclusive control of the China Bay storage farm at Trincomalee, Sri Lanka. Built by Lord Mountbatten as a strategic refueling base for the Allied fleet in World War II, the farm had 99 oil storage tanks spread over 676 acres. Coastal planned to refurbish and develop the farm into a modernized oil terminal. Sri Lanka reserved the right to prohibit foreign naval vessels and customers using the tanks.

Final Resettlement Compensation

In March 1982, the British Government agreed to pay Mauritius four million pounds sterling as a full and final settlement to about 1,500 people displaced from Diego Garcia and other islands of the Chagos Archipelago. A trust fund was set up to ensure that the funds were properly distributed. An individual share was worth 2,555 pounds sterling; children received a half share. The Mauritius Government promised to build decent homes for the 900 Ilois who needed them.[57]

Seewoosagur Ramgoolam's Labor Party lost the general election in 1982. The new government passed a bill declaring Diego Garcia a part of Mauritius territory, and blocked American offers of jobs and provisioning contracts for Diego Garcia.

FY 1983 Program

Protection of Persian Gulf oil ranked second only to defending North America and the North Atlantic Treaty Organization countries in Department of Defense Guidance for the armed services. Congressman Bo Ginn chaired the Military Construction subcommittee hearing on 31 March 1982 concerning the Persian Gulf/ Indian Ocean construction request from the Department of Defense. The principal witness was David M. Ransom, Director, Near East, South Asia Region, in the office of the Assistant Secretary of Defense for International Security Affairs.

The fiscal year 1983 construction request in the Indian Ocean/Persian Gulf area and enroute facilities in the Atlantic totaled $474 million to support Rapid Deployment Force contingency operations and those facilities required to support peacetime naval presence. The request provided for additional contingency facilities in Egypt, Oman, Kenya, Somalia, Diego Garcia, and Lajes, Portugal. The proposed program for Egypt, when combined with facilities proposed in the $106 million fiscal year 1982 supplemental, and a contingency request of $7 million for Ras Banas, would provide basic support facilities in Egypt for initial staging capability.

Military Capabilities

Facilities were required in Oman for support of sea control and maritime operations in proximity to a major regional choke point, the Strait of Hormuz, and to support tactical air operations and rear area staging. The Somali facilities also supported sea control and maritime operations at another major regional choke point, Bab al Mandab, and fleet support for deployed United States Naval forces and access to Somalia. Navy P-3 operations were conducted in the vicinity of Somalia and other airfields in the littoral countries that provided refueling and crew rest. These were located at: Karachi, Pakistan; Masirah, Oman; Djibouti; Mahe, Seychelles; and Nairobi and Mombasa, Kenya. Similarly Kenyan facilities would provide fleet support for deployed Indian Ocean naval units, and support sea control operations. Diego Garcia, also supported naval units operations in the Indian Ocean, provided anchorage for prepositioning ships, supported communications, logistics, intelligence, and basing for strategic operations. In Egypt, Ras Banas would provide for staging, logistics activities, and fighter and bomber support. The fiscal year 1983 program also included upgrading facilities at Lajes Field, Azores. Lajes Field was not a NATO airfield, and therefor not eligible for NATO infrastructure funding.

Ras Banas

In Conference Report 97–400, on the fiscal year 1982 construction program, the conferees supported the need to continue efforts to develop a Rapid Deployment Joint Task Force facility at Ras Banas, Egypt. The conferees recommended that the design of this facility be accelerated and provided $14 million for that purpose. The conferees indicated that should the Secretary of Defense consider it necessary to establish construction mobilization activities prior to receipt of regular appropriations, he should consider the use of his contingency fund. The conferees indicated that the inclusion of the Ras Banas facilities in a fiscal year 1982 supplemental would be acceptable.

Mobilization Camp

In order to establish construction mobilization activities, Deputy Secretary of Defense Frank C. Carlucci notified congressional committees on 23 March 1982, that he approved $7.0 million from his contingency construction fund. The contingency construction was for the rehabilitation of buildings for a mobilization camp, utilities for the camp, and for mine clearing.

United States and Egyptian representatives met on 15 through 17 December 1981 to develop technical arrangements for the mine removal. The Government of Egypt agreed to provide the necessary supplies and equipment to remove the mines for a fixed fee of $700,000. United States technical representatives were to certify the procedure and assist. The mine clearing operation was completed in February 1982. The Egyptian Army lost three men and had six wounded accomplishing this task.

A second generation agreement with Egypt, called the Construction Technical Arrangement for Ras Banas, was in the final stages of review prior to completion of negotiations with the Egyptian Ministry of Defense. This arrangement concerned details of the relationship of the United States Government and its construction contractors with the Egyptian Government, and the operation and maintenance of facilities after construction. The construction estimate for Ras Banas was now $600 million. The American firm of Louis Berger International, Inc., of East Orange, New Jersey, had the design contract for Army and Air Force facilities at Ras Banas.

The dependence of the United States and the rest of the free world on Persian Gulf oil was still a major concern. Since the United States and the rest of the free world could not make up for the loss of Persian Gulf oil, the cost of contingency facilities to support national policy in Southwest Asia area were considered an insurance policy. However, at that time the Europeans were developing a gas pipeline from the Soviet Union that would leave the Europeans dependent on gas from the Soviet Union. The United States was unable to dissuade its Allies from proceeding with the project.

Host Nation Support

Germany agreed to establish a 93,000-man contingent in their Army Reserve to provide wartime Host Nation Support for United States forces. The United Kingdom, Belgium, Netherlands and Luxembourg also agreed to provide extensive Host Nation Support. The United States signed Line-of-Communications and Collocated Operating Base agreements with almost all the NATO countries that involved substantial Host Nation Support. The United States was also asking its European Allies to facilitate possible United States deployments to Southwest Asia and, as feasible, to contribute directly to enhancing security in Southwest Asia. Japanese Prime Minister Suzuki pledged increased Japanese Host Nation Support efforts when he met with President Reagan in May 1981.

Supplemental Appropriations for FY 1982

The fiscal year 1982 Supplemental Military Construction request totaled $198.7 million in appropriations and $52.1 million in new authorizations for appropriations. The difference was primarily funding for construction at Ras Banas, Egypt, which had been authorized, but not funded in fiscal year 1982. The major elements of the supplemental were:

| | $ in Millions | |
	Approp.	**Auth.**
Air Force:		
MacDill AFB, FL		
RDJTF/RECOM and Support		
Building Additions	17.000	17.000
Wright-Patterson AFB, OH		
Alter. Bldg. for Foreign		
Military Sales Center	(F.M.S.)	.395
Ras Banas, Egypt—RDF Facilities	64.400	(FY1982)
Army:		
Ras Banas, Egypt—RDF Facilities	34.000	(FY1982)
Family Housing		
Operations & Maintenance, and Leasing	*80.300*	*34.706*
	198.700	52.101

The additional appropriations were requested to begin construction of the Ras Banas facilities, to correct a shortfall in facilities to support current and emergent missions of the Rapid Deployment Joint Task Force, the United States Readiness Command, and Joint Deployment Agency facilities at MacDill Air Force Base, Florida; and to alleviate unacceptable living conditions confronting United States forward-deployed service people and their families, and for executing additional family housing leases in Korea.

Ras Banas

The prior Conference on Appropriations had stated that if the Department of Defense considered it necessary, it should seek funding for the Ras Banas facility as a fiscal year 1982 supplemental. The Army requested $34 million for the first phase of a construction program for Ras Banas that totaled $211.2 million, for water supply, sewage, and switched to cement block housing rather than tents. The Army made three changes to the scope of work; they deleted the high frequency communications towers as an Air Force responsibility, deferred dredging to the fiscal year 1983 program, and added a small craft maintenance shop.

The follow on program for fiscal year 1983 would provide the required port facilities and additional support elements to give a complete unit configuration. It also included ammunition and petroleum storage. The Air Force request for Ras Banas was for runway strengthening and lengthening to 13,000 feet, and taxiway, apron, and parking construction. The Air Force planned to use Harvest Bare or Harvest Eagle equipment, which were air conditioned tents or expandable building that would be moved in as mobility forces deployed into Ras Banas. The Air Force request was essentially the same as was authorized in fiscal year 1982.

TABLE 9
CONSTRUCTION PLAN FOR RAS BANAS
$ in Millions

	FY 1982	FY 1983	FY 1984	FY 1985	Total
Army	36.0	53.0	75.0	47.2	211.2
Air Force	70.4	125.6	58.2	57.3	311.5
Totals	106.4	178.6	133.2	104.5	522.7

Morocco

Secretary of State Alexander M. Haig, Jr., and King Hassan, II, in February, discussed the potential availability of transient facilities at the former United States Air Force B-47 base at Sidi Slimane, near Rabat, for use by United States forces. Further discussions were held at the April 1982 Joint Military Commission meeting with the goal of formalizing an access agreement. On his visit to the United States, King Hassan, II reached an agreement with President Reagan on 19 May 1982 on the United States use of the Moroccan air base. The country-to-country agreement with Morocco was signed on 27 May 1982.

A detailed site survey team visit was conducted in October 1982. The basic provisions included the use and transit by United States forces of agreed aerial ports in emergencies and for periodic training, and authorization for the United States to make the necessary facility improvements for their planned use. An implementing agreement of the same date stipulated that United States military authorities would notify Moroccan military authorities of anticipated arrivals of United States aircraft at least 24 hours prior to arrival at each aerial port.

The agreement had an initial term of six years, but could continue at the pleasure of both parties. Termination was based on a two-year notification. Permanent stationing of United States forces was not authorized. Morocco insisted that local contractors be allowed to participate so a joint venture approach was adopted for building the American facilities. President Reagan asked Congress for $100 million in military sales credits for Morocco, and removed all restrictions on the use of the military gear in the desert war with the Polisario Front guerrillas over the Spanish Sahara.

Continued Soviet Threat

The Soviets increased the number of men they committed in action in Afghanistan, and Soviet weapons were being used in Syria, Lebanon, in the Iraq-Iran War, and in Ethiopia.

Strategic Projection Force at Diego Garcia

Strengthening and widening the runway at Diego Garcia making it capable of handling all air elements of the Rapid Deployment Force, including B-52 bombers, would begin after completion of the parallel taxiway in January 1984. Funds were needed in fiscal year 1983 for procurement and shipping of construction materials for the runway work. The Air Force project proposed to overlay the first 1,000 feet of each end of the runway with concrete, and overlay the interior of runway with asphalt. The runways and overruns would be widened by 25 feet of pavement on each side. Existing aircraft arresting barriers and runway edge lighting would be relocated.

Saudi Arabian Joint Committee

Secretary of Defense Caspar W. Weinberger, during a visit to Saudi Arabia, was successful in establishing a Joint Committee for Military Projects. The United States and Saudis would meet annually to promote cooperation and coordination of military matters of mutual interest. The United States had no written agreement, or offer, to use Saudi facilities during a conflict.

Somalia Airlift

The United States airlifted military equipment, including radar and ground-to-air missiles, in August 1982 to Somalia to help Somalia fight against Ethiopian and Ethiopian-backed guerrillas.

Ras Banas

Initially, the House Appropriations Committee denied funding for Ras Banas because the United States had not received adequate assurances from Egypt about its availability to United States forces in an emergency. The Committee also denied funding for Lajes Field because long term use was not clear. The House and Senate Appropriations Committees conferees on 29 September 1982 approved $91 million for Ras Banas contingent on: (1) further written assurances on the use of Ras Banas from the Government of Egypt, (2) certification through specific documentation that negotiations have proceeded with NATO Allies and Japan that would insure either direct funding or indirect offset funding support for the Persian Gulf program, and (3) submission of a detailed letter from the Secretary of Defense to the Committees on Appropriations outlining his understanding of how, when, and for what purposes the Government of Egypt will allow the United States to use the Ras Banas facility. The conferees also recommended the scope of the building program not exceed $350 million.

On 23 December 1982, following the adjournment of the 97th Congress, Secretary Weinberger responded to the Chairmen of the Appropriations Committees, Senator Mark O. Hatfield and Representative Jamie L. Whitten. Secretary Weinberger wrote that the relevant point about Persian Gulf oil and its susceptibility to disruption was not its relative contribution to individual economies in Western Europe, Japan, and the United States. Rather, its importance was in terms of its contribution to the worldwide supply of oil, and the cumulative effect of oil cutoffs on the complex trade and economic interrelationships that existed.

The Secretary acknowledged that all United States Allies must pay their fair share to protect vital natural resources, and that the United States would press on this issue. The Secretary's letter forwarded a classified letter regarding the use of facilities in Egypt and a letter regarding written assurances. The Committees were also provided a copy of the letter from Deputy Prime Minister Abdul-Halim Abu Ghazala of Egypt who wrote, "Egypt is making definite preparations for the use of our facilities at Ras Banas by the United States Armed Forces." Secretary Weinberger said that he was directing that construction of the Ras Banas facilities move ahead as rapidly as possible.

Oman Maneuvers

Approximately 2,500 American troops were on maneuvers for five days in Oman in early December 1982 to test defense capabilities in event of a Soviet or other foreign attack on the Persian Gulf region.

Secret Egyptian Base

The United States Air Force established a secret contingency air base in an unpopulated part of Egypt, and had 100 airmen stationed there according to testimony of Major General Richard V. Secord, Deputy Assistant Secretary of Defense for Near Eastern and South Asian Affairs, before the House Appropriations Committee in February 1983.[58] The base, upgraded in 1982, was used for deployment of AWACS planes and for training missions to the Middle East, and could support in certain contingencies, up to two tactical fighter squadrons. Because the air base had been upgraded with $7 million in operational funds, the military construction committees were not informed of its existence. Military supplies totaling about $70 million were stored at the secret base.

Central Command

On 1 January 1983, the former Rapid Deployment Joint Task Force became a new unified command called the United States Central Command. Because Central Command was home based at MacDill Air Force Base in Tampa, Florida, it was referred to as the "rapidly deployable command." The new command was unique in that its headquarters and military forces were not located in theater. The Commander in Chief was Lt. Gen. Robert C. Kingston. The Central Command was responsible for military planning, exercises involving United States and regional forces, and administration of security assistance. Its mission was to deter aggression and to protect United States interests in Southwest Asia.

The United States ambassador remained the senior United States official in each country. All significant Central Command actions were to be coordinated with or approved by the ambassador. The area of responsibility included all states on the Arabian Peninsula south of the northern borders of Saudi Arabia and Kuwait; the countries of Iran, Iraq, Jordan, Afghanistan, and Pakistan on the Middle East landmass; Egypt, Sudan, Ethiopia, Djibouti, Somalia, and Kenya on the Horn of Africa; and the Red Sea and the Persian Gulf. Israel, located on the eastern Mediterranean, remained under the sphere of the European Command. Israel was also excluded so that the relationship of the new Central Command would not be poisoned with the other Arab states. There were 29 Soviet divisions circling the borders of the Central Command. A full deployment of the United States Central Command could involve about 300,000 personnel.

TABLE 10
CENTRAL COMMAND FORCE LIST

U.S. Central Command Headquarters (augmented)	11,000
U.S. Army Forces Central Command	131,000

    Headquarters, U.S. Army Forces Central
    Command (Third U.S. Army)
    XVIII Airborne Corps Headquarters
    82d Airborne Division
    101st Airborne Division (Air Assault)
    24th Infantry Division (Mechanized)
    6th Cavalry Brigade (Air Combat)
    1st Corps Support Command

U.S. Naval Forces Central Command

Headquarters U.S. Naval Forces Central Command	53,000

    3 Carrier Battle Groups
    1 Surface Action Group
    3 Amphibious Ready Groups
    5 Maritime Patrol Squadrons
    U.S. Middle East Force

U.S. Marine Corps Forces	70,000

    1 Marine Amphibious Force including:
    1 Marine Division (reinforced)
    1 Marine Aircraft Wing
    1 Force Service Support Group
1 Marine Amphibious Brigade, including:
    1 Marine Regiment (reinforced)
    1 Marine Aircraft Group (composite)
    1 Brigade Service Support Group

U.S. Air Force Central Command	33,000

    Headquarters, U.S. Central Command Air
    Forces (9th Air Force)
    7 Tactical Fighter Wings

4 Tactical Fighter Groups
1 Tactical Fighter Squadron
1 Airborne Warning and Control Wing
1 Tactical Reconnaissance Group
1 Electronic Combat Group
1 Special Operations Wing
Unconventional Warfare and Special Operations Forces   3,000

Total   ———
                                                                                    301,000

Persian Gulf Importance

Energy Secretary Donald Hodel, in testifying in February 1983, in support of cutbacks in strategic petroleum reserve deposits, told a Senate Committee that the Gulf's strategic value was less now because the potential for an oil embargo was less. A State Department spokesman, repairing damage to the Department of Defenses policy statements, later said "Our belief is that this region remains of greatest importance to the global strategic balance and to our national interests."

6

Completing RDF Construction

Diego Garcia

The Navy request for Diego Garcia totaled $34.5 million and was nearly the end of the Rapid Deployment Force construction expansion program with only $32 million left for the fiscal year 1985 program and nothing beyond. The total funded for Navy through fiscal year 1983 was $362.1 million.

The Navy testified that some ex-Diego Garcia residents had claimed that the Mauritius Government had not provided them with the assistance due them. The United States State Department said this problem was strictly the concern of Britain and Mauritius. Prime Minister Jugnauth of Mauritius was pressing Britain for Mauritius sovereignty over Diego Garcia. The Prime Minister said he would make this an issue at the seventh summit of the Nonaligned Movement in March 1984. Prime Minister Margaret Thatcher said that Mauritian sovereignty could be considered when the base was no longer a strategic imperative. Jugnauth banned United States warships from visiting Mauritius.

The Congress had earlier deferred the Air Force's planned airfield improvement. The $41.3 million requested in fiscal year 1984 was to upgrade the existing runway to support refueling operations for strategic forces from the Pacific to Southwest Asia in a contingency. By 1988, the Navy expected over 2,200 personnel to be assigned. The Navy still had no plans to make Diego Garcia an accompanied tour.

Ras Banas

The Army's appropriation request for Ras Banas totaled $41 million and included $14.4 million for port facilities and $13.9 million for land facilities. The port facilities included a pier for the off-loading of POL, rehabilitation of an ammunition pier, and dredging and navigation aids. Land facilities included an airdrop rigging facility, cantonment, and the first phase rehabilitation of an underground bunker. Also the Army would build communications, paving, and utilities. The Air Force requested $55.39 million to continue construction of airfield pavements, fuel storage and distribution systems, munitions storage facilities, and utility systems as a continuation of the $91 million program, which was completely designed, but on hold by the Appropriations Conferees.

Morocco

A new addition to the Persian Gulf construction program was the $28 million requested by the Air Force for enroute POL facilities, similar to those at Lajes Field in the Azores, to support C-5 Galaxy transports and C-141 Starlifter cargo heavy lift aircraft in Morocco at the former United States Air Force B-47 base at Sidi Slimane. These facilities would be used during rapid deployment airlift operations to the Persian Gulf and back again. The total cost of facilities at this base was estimated to be $85.8

million. Construction was to upgrade existing POL facilities to safe and operating conditions, and to construct refueling systems, storage facilities, and associated airfield pavement and power support.

Oman

The Air Force requested $39.6 million for Oman facilities at Masirah, Seeb Air Base, and Thumrait Air Base. Although there remained $75 million in the out year program, the Joint Chiefs of Staff completed their Southwest Asia facilities study based on the planned 1988 force levels in September 1982. The requirements in this study had not yet been approved by the Secretary of Defense. The completed facilities would be maintained by contract, and were estimated to be $3 million by 1987 when more of the facilities were completed. Upon completion of the fiscal year 1984 projects, Masirah would have the capability to support Navy P-3 Orion antisubmarine patrol operations, fleet resupply, Military Airlift Command operations, tactical staging and Air Force prepositioning.

Lajes Field

The fiscal year 1984 program included housing for unaccompanied personnel and 150 family housing units, neither of which were part of the Rapid Deployment Force requirements. The fiscal year 1982 projects totaling $34.4 million were on hold until the United States obtained an agreement from Portugal that would allow use of the facilities for their intended purposes.

Somalia

The fiscal year 1984 program had $.9 million for projects in Somalia. The projects approved in fiscal years 1982 and 1983 still had not been awarded because of a contract protest that the General Accounting Office had to resolve. Also after the fiscal year project was approved, the ship types that were to use the facility were changed thereby obviating the need to dredge the entrance channel and turning basin. The funds approved for the dredging were still required to offset other increases in the project.

Nonaligned Summit

Indira Gandhi was the chairperson of the seventh summit of 101 nonaligned nations that conferenced in Delhi in March 1983. The drafting committee of the conference spent three days arguing over the future of the Indian Ocean island of Diego Garcia and Britain's culpability in leasing it to the United States. The evacuees from Diego Garcia were called the "Palestinians of the Indian Ocean" by the foreign minister of Mauritius. The summit communiqué stated that the British role over Diego Garcia would be strongly attacked. In return, the moderates won the concession that the issue would not be linked with the "peace zone" demand in the communiqué.[59]

Ras Banas

The House Appropriations Subcommittee, on 9 June 1983, denied the request for $96.4 million for Ras Banas, Egypt, and rescinded the $91 million appropriated in fiscal year 1983. The Department of Defense had informed the Committee that plans to build a rear staging complex and other facilities at Ras Banas had fallen through. The

Committee directed the Department to submit a report explaining the circumstances. The Committee said it had for several years expressed the belief that a signed agreement was necessary. Had that been done in the case of Ras Banas, millions of dollars in United States expenditures for design and mine clearing could have been avoided. The Committee hoped that a written agreement could be obtained for the use of other access facilities that met both Egyptian and United States requirements. However, the Appropriations Conferees later suggested that if a comprehensive proposal could be prepared on Ras Banas, they could review it in an early fiscal year 1984 supplemental.

The House Appropriations Committee felt that the United States had assumed the leading role for maintaining stability of the Southwest Asia Region. It further noted that neither NATO nor Japan had taken any steps to support facility construction or develop other offsets. Additionally, the Committee noted that certain western European countries had concluded arrangements to build a natural gas pipeline from the Soviet Union.

Marine Disaster in Lebanon

In 1983, Israeli and Syrian troops remained in Lebanon, along with some Palestinian groups in the north. A multinational peace force, consisting of 2,000 soldiers from France, 1,400 soldiers from Italy, 90 soldiers from Britain, and 1,600 United States marines were stationed in Beirut in an attempt to maintain peace. These units came under repeated terrorist attacks. On Sunday, 23 October 1983, a suicide terrorist driving a truck loaded with explosives blew up the four story American Marine headquarters at the Beirut airport at 6:20 in the morning, killing 161 marines and sailors and wounding 75 more. Two minutes later, another bomb-laden terrorist truck slammed into a French paratroop barracks two miles away. At least 12 paratroopers were killed, 13 wounded, and 48 were initially reported missing. The new United States Ambassador, Reginald Bartholomew, who had just arrived the afternoon before the attack, was one of the first American officials to tour the devastated Marine headquarters. The suicide mission was similar to the assault on the American Embassy on 18 April 1983, which killed 63 people. By 1984, the multinational peacekeeping forces had withdrawn from Lebanon.

Enacted Indian Ocean/Persian Gulf FY 1984 Construction Program
$ in Millions

Description	Requested	Auth'd	Funded	Remarks
		Diego Garcia		
Navy Facilities Expan.	34.500	31.800	31.800	NAF for EM Club
AF RDF Facilities	41.300	41.300	41.300	Runway Upgrade
AF GEODSS Facilities	1 6.900	16.900	16.900	Not for RDF
		Egypt		
Army RDF Facilities	41.000	(Prior)	0	Plans Changed
AF RDF Facilities	55.390	(Prior)	0	Plans Changed
		Oman		
AF RDF Facilities Questioned RDF	39.600	28.600	28.600	
		Lajes		
Port. Housing	13.662	13.662	13.662	Not for RDF
		Somalia.		
	900	(Exigent)	900	
		Morocco		
Var. POL Support Fac.	*28.000*	*28.000*	*25.000*	
Totals	271.252	160.262	158.162	

Ras Banas Supplemental

On 2 November 1983, the Department of Defense requested $55 million in a fiscal year 1984 supplemental for Air Force facilities at Ras Banas. Late in 1983, the Mubarak Government said it did not want to have the United States develop Ras Banas. The Egyptians were planning to do that themselves unilaterally, but would make the facilities available to the United States in times of emergencies. The only exception to that Egyptian policy was the Air Force facilities included in the fiscal year 1984 supplemental request. President Reagan was convinced that the upgrading of the base was critical to United States interest and military strategy. He directed the Secretary of Defense Weinberger to do everything possible to undertake the planned construction as soon as possible. The $55 million would provide an austere rear staging area for air operations, and would be constructed in conjunction with the Egyptian funded improvement program. The United States portion included POL support facilities providing 252,000 barrels of storage and supply and distribution systems; water desalinization and distribution systems rated at 250,000 gallons per day; a 3,500-kilowatt power plant and distribution system; airfield lighting; two warehouses, and a fire station.

The Government of Egypt insisted that the actual construction work be accomplished by the Egyptian Government or its entity. The contract limited materials to be used in the construction to those manufactured in the United States or Egypt. Since desalinization units, generators, transformers, and rolled steel plates or stainless steel were not produced in Egypt, those items, totaling $40 million had to come from the United States. All the United States materials would be shipped on United States flag carriers. The Egyptian Ministry of Defense provided the Corps of Engineers a list of eight "nationalized" contractors.

The House Appropriations Committee agreed to fund $49 million for Ras Banas, however, they were considering a requirement that would make most of the subcontracts go to United States firms.

Flotilla Headquarters

The United States Central Command established, in November 1983, a forward headquarters aboard a Navy ship operating with the Middle East Force because no country in the Command's region was willing to allow its territory to be used for that purpose. About 20 officers and men were assigned.

Diego Garcia Contract Base Support

On 30 September 1983, the Navy awarded an operations and maintenance contract for Diego Garcia with four one-year options to Frank E. Basil, Burns and Roe of Washington, D.C. The cost of the operations and maintenance caretaker contract during the first year phase was $5,647,000. The Navy estimated that the total operations and maintenance for Diego Garcia would be $31.2 million for fiscal year 1983, $42.2 million in fiscal year 1984, and $39.5 million for fiscal year 1985. The contract was for base operating support including work needed for day-to-day operations of the island's facilities. It included such elements as food service, provision of utilities, fire protection, fuels and stevedoring. The cost of the operations and maintenance contract, while minimized by the employment of approximately 1,200 third country nationals, was secondary to inadequate military personnel available for both shore sites and afloat.

Earthquake

An earthquake struck Diego Garcia on 30 November 1983; the first earthquake since the United States facilities were commissioned on the island. Centered approximately 20 miles southwest of Diego Garcia, the earthquake was a large one, registering 7.6 on the Richter Scale. Despite concerns over sensitive electronic equipment and three story barracks buildings, there was minimal impact to operations. The quake did not cause any major structural damage and no injuries. Seismologists estimated that an earthquake of this magnitude could occur in this area only once every 300 years.

Fiscal Year 1985 Program

The United States strategy for Southwest Asia continued to center about preserving stability in the region. The United States had three main objectives; first, to support the territorial integrity of friendly countries, second, to assure United States allies access to oil, and third, to maintain freedom of navigation and the strategic sea-lanes of communication open. The Central Command developed a master program list of facilities that was approved and published on 25 February 1984, which was subsequent to a visit by the Surveys and Investigations Staff.

The construction requested for fiscal year 1985 for Southwest Asia continued the development of support facilities for contingency operations and readiness of naval units in the Indian Ocean. A total of $129 million was requested for additional facilities. Defense also requested the extension of the fiscal year 1983 authorization for Ras Banas to provide the United States share of a planned facility that now would be jointly financed and constructed.

Diego Garcia

The $6.8 million fiscal year request for Navy at Diego Garcia was for water wells, piping, treatment, and storage; lighted buoys along the lagoon channel to assist ships; and for support of the expanding capabilities of the CLASSIC WIZARD mission. The water system improvements was designed by Hope/VTN of Irvine, California. The $16.1 million for Air Force at Diego Garcia was for construction of the first of a two-phase program to provide conventional munitions storage and maintenance facilities; as well as billets for 58 Ground-Based Electro-Optical Deep Surveillance System (GEODSS) personnel. Diego Garcia was one of five sites located at approximately equal intervals around the world that made up the GEODSS. The GEODSS would provide a capability to detect, track, and identify manmade objects in deep space at near real-time on a routine basis. The GEODSS site was to be operated by 52 contract (officer equivalent) personnel and six Air Force officers.

Morocco

For Morocco the Air Force requested $5 million for four additional hydrant refueling points, additional parking apron, an access road, and shoulder stabilization to continue the facilities started in the fiscal year 1984 program. The Air Force still programmed additional fuel storage and a resupply system for delivery and rotation of fuel between the delivery port (Mohammedia Port) and Sidi Slimane.

Oman

The Air Force requested $42 million for rapid deployment force support facilities at Seeb Air Base, and Thumrait Air Base in Oman. This was the fifth of a proposed seven phase program for Oman facilities. $13 million was for hardened aircraft shelters at Seeb Air Base. In the event that hostilities erupted in the Arabian Gulf and the United States was requested to intervene, the United States Central Command forces would be afforded priority use of the shelters for contingency operations and for revetment of electronic warfare assets. The Air Force planned to store a deployable hospital in one of the warehouses at Seeb Air Base. Upon completion of the fiscal year 1985 projects, Thumrait Air Base could support American tactical air operations, Military Airlift Command operations and prepositioning of Air Force War Readiness Matériel assets.

The Army's classified program included $62 million for the first time for the construction of an intermediate staging base located adjacent to an Air Force staging facility in Oman. The intermediate staging base was to support two Army brigades and construction included airdrop rigging facilities, beddown of troops, communications facilities, and storage for essential supplies. These facilities were to support the reception and forward deployment of Army forces from the United States to the Central Command area in Southwest Asia. The purpose of the intermediate staging base was to preposition Army forces in theater to show resolve, transition from an administrative configuration to an organization for combat, and to rig selected units for parachute assault. Desirable characteristics of such a location were the availability and supportability over a long term, the accessibility to a marshaling airfield, the relative freedom from hostile attack, and prepositioned to support multiple contingencies.

Once the Army units drew the prepositioned equipment from the staging base, they would move away to establish a bivouac camp. The budget request, however, did not contain funding for the bivouac camp. The Army was planning two such staging bases, the other was at Ras Banas, Egypt, for flexibility of operations in the event that one or the other was not available in a particular contingency. Because of the

Egyptian Government's policy not to allow the United States to develop Ras Banas other than the Air Forces's request contained in the fiscal year 1984 supplemental, and the Congressional insistence on a written agreement, Army opted to defer further funding requests for Ras Banas until the Ras Banas situation became more encouraging.

Surveys and Investigations Staff Report

The Surveys and Investigations Staff completed a report in April 1984 that criticized the minimal capability provided by the present facilities built in Southwest Asia for the Rapid Deployment Force.

Iran-Iraq War

The Iran-Iraq War escalated to include several incidents involving commercial shipping in the Persian Gulf. President Reagan stated that the United States would not allow the Persian Gulf to be closed to shipping. Khomeini made threats about kamikaze attacks that prompted the Central Command to issue a notice to mariners and an advisory to airmen in the Persian Gulf, Strait of Hormuz area that required aircraft and ships to identify themselves and stay clear of American ships.

Presidents's Revisions

On 2 May 1984, President Reagan sent a communication to the Congress to make changes to the spending programs, revenues, and defense. This plan included a contingent proposal to reduce defense spending by $14.4 billion. Included in this was $1.5 billion reduction from military construction. Very few reductions were made to overseas programs. One of the overseas projects included in the reduction package was the lighted navigational range at Diego Garcia.

CENCOM Operations

Elements of the United States Central Command were involved in three significant operations in 1984. The bombing of the radio station in Omdurman, Sudan, in March 1984 prompted a request for help from Egypt and Sudan. The Central Command deployed AWACS surveillance and support aircraft. In June 1984, in response to Iranian attacks on shipping which resulted in the Saudi shoot down of an Iranian F-4 on 5 June 1984, Central Command provided KC-10 support on a daily basis for Royal Saudi Air Force F-15's. The next month, at Egypt's request, Central Command provided surface and helicopter mine countermeasures when a mining threat in the Gulf of Suez and the Red Sea endangered shipping through these waterways. At the completion of these deployments, most of the forces returned to their bases in the United States.

Gulf Force

The Gulf Cooperation Council announced in November 1984 that they established a force of 10,000 to 13,000 troops from units of the six countries to help each other repel outside attacks. Joint maneuvers were held in northern Saudi Arabia. The unified command was to be centered at the Council's headquarters in Riyadh.

Lajes Field, Azores

The new access agreement between Portugal and the United States, for use of facilities at Lajes Field, in the Azores, was signed on 13 December 1983 by Secretary of State George P. Shultz for the United States. The agreement called for $60 million in United States grants and $45 million in guaranteed loans for the Portuguese military, and $40 million in economic aid. The agreement included a pledge by the United States to increase and then to maintain aid to Portugal in return for use of the base. Aid jumped from $147.9 million in 1984 to $207.9 million in 1985. The new accord ran until February 1991.

Congressional Actions

The Senate Appropriations Committee deferred without prejudice $31.9 million for various facilities in Oman in support of the Rapid Deployment Force. The Committee agreed with the House on the questionable need for so-called facility accommodation support (prepositioned latrines, laundry facilities, and so forth) at a contingency facility. The Committee suggested that the other facilities— semihardened aircraft shelters and a taxiway/dispersal pavement project be considered for NATO funding or seek Host Nation Support since the Government of Oman will use the facilities except during a United States contingency operation.

The House Appropriations Subcommittee served notice to the Department of Defense that in light of the substantial United States investment to date, about $1.1 billion, and the absence of new burden-sharing initiatives by NATO countries and Japan, the Committee viewed the Persian Gulf facility program as essentially completed. The Committee said that the United States Central Command should make every effort to adapt its generic concept of operations to the facility network that already existed. Of the $131.9 million requested by Defense for the Persian Gulf/Indian Ocean, the Committee approved only $29.7 million that was requested for Diego Garcia, Morocco, and $2.3 million for Oman.

Fiscal Year 1986 Program

The fiscal year 1986 Defense Budget request included funds to place the second Maritime Prepositioned Squadron in Diego Garcia and a third in the Western Pacific. The budget request also included the acquisition of 16 C-5 and 12 KC-10 airlift, additional ships for the Ready Reserve Force, and the third set of Maritime Prepositioning ships for strategic mobility forces. The construction program included $70.5 million for the Indian Ocean/Persian Gulf area to complete the Rapid Deployment Force expansion program that began in 1981. Only the Air Force had construction projects in Southwest Asia. None were within the Central Command's region. There were two major reasons for this. First, there were difficulties in obtaining access agreements, and second, the 1984 House Appropriations Committee report viewed the Persian Gulf facility program as essentially complete. The Committee said that "the United States Central Command should make every effort to adapt its concept of operations to the facility network that already exits in the region."

The Central Command heeded the Committee's guidance and developed a four-tier approach to facility acquisition:

1. To seek facilities from host nations or host nations support;
2. To utilize leasing and service contracting to obtain facilities; such as the administrative facilities in Bahrain, and the warehousing in Port Sudan;

3. To utilize relocatables, theater of operations type construction; and lastly,

4. To seek military construction.

Absent from the fiscal year 1986 construction plans were Army staging facilities. Up to March 1986, there were no active initiatives to conclude written access agreements for Army staging or prepositioning facilities. High on the Army's list of preferred locations were Saudi Arabian air bases.

Naval Air Facility, Diego Garcia

The Navy's program for the Naval Air Facility at Diego Garcia included a fire station addition, a P-3 maintenance hangar, and a weapons complex. The maintenance hangar was needed to support a full antisubmarine warfare squadron. The three plane detachment was to be increased to a full nine plane squadron to better protect fleet operations in the Indian Ocean area. Prior to January 1984, various three plane detachments rotated to Diego Garcia every three months. This was disruptive to squadron operations and costly, therefore, Navy went to a full nine plane squadron on the island. The Navy had a small 17,820 square foot hangar on Diego Garcia, but it was too small to accommodate the P-3 aircraft that had a 100-foot wingspan and 34-foot high tail. The weapons complex was needed to support increased weapons operations, including the harpoon missile, depth charges, and torpedoes. The Navy had no other planned projects for the Naval Air Facility. The upgrading of the runway approved in the fiscal year 1984 program became operational in October 1985. (See Figure 17, a 1983 aerial view of the runway and operations area.)

Naval Support Facility, Diego Garcia

The Naval Support Facility had five projects: antenna support facilities, lighted navigational aids, a fleet support warehouse, a bachelor enlisted quarters, and a laundry building addition. Relocation of an cryptographic mission antenna system to Simpson Point was required due to the electromagnetic interference caused by increased encroachment of industrial equipment in the Public Works area and small boat repair shops. An additional warehouse was needed to prevent the loss of material not prepacked in weatherproof containers. The Navy needed 273 billets for officer personnel. They had eight adequate spaces. Officers were being housed in temporary huts and portable vans. The fiscal year project would provide for 58 officer billets. The balance would be programmed later. The Navy picked up the lighted navigational aids project dropped in the previous year. This project provided a lighted navigation range for ships entering the lagoon and approaching the pier and wharf. The laundry, which was sized for the austere communications facility when the island population was less than 1,000 persons, could not handle the laundry needs of an island population of 2,150. The 80 inches of rainfall a year, a high average temperature of 85 degrees Fahrenheit, and a high average humidity of 75-90 percent, prevented clothing washed in basins to dry properly. The Navy planned to enlarge the existing laundry and boiler plant.

FIGURE 17. 1983 view of Naval Air Facility runway and air operations area. U.S. Navy Photo

FIGURE 18. 1987 aerial view of the personnel and recreation area at the Naval Support Facility. U.S. Navy Photo

Naval Security Group Detachment

The Naval Security Group Detachment surveillance and processing mission was expanding. There was no space to house equipment and personnel. The Navy proposed additions to the operational building and standby generator building. More pyrotechnic storage space was required. This project, costing $3.7 million, completed all known construction needs of the Naval Security Group Detachment.

Air Base

The Navy had consolidated its remaining construction projects at Diego Garcia in the fiscal year 1986 program to take advantage of the economies associated with having the current on island joint venture contractor finish the major construction effort. The Air Force requested $5.3 million for the second and final phase of a munitions storage program at Diego Garcia. The project provided for ten covered revetted pads and six preengineered buildings.

TABLE 11

U.S. DIEGO GARCIA PERSONNEL STRENGTH

As of 30 September 1984

	Officers	Enlisted	Civilians	Total
Naval Air Facility	18	133	0	151
Naval Support Facility	297	1962	3396	5655
Naval Security Group Detachment	3	121	0	124
Air Force	1	12	0	13
Totals	319	2228	3396	5943

Footprint of Freedom

Simon Winchester, a British journalist, and Ruth Boydell, an Australian, visited Boddem Island in the Salomon Atoll in August 1984, a group of 10 small islands arranged around a five-mile lagoon, on a 30-foot schooner.[60] The schooner spent a week on the deserted island that formally was part of a copra plantation. There they found a May 1984 Royal Engineers survey marker that led to speculation concerning plans to build further installations on Solomon Atoll. The presence of the uninvited visitors was observed by P-3 Orion antisubmarine reconnaissance planes.

The schooner was not welcomed at Diego Garcia, and was only allowed to enter the harbor after explaining to British Indian Ocean Territory Customs and Immigration officers that they were out of water, low on fuel, and had some faulty navigation equipment. Winchester and Boydell spied the sign on the water tower that said "Welcome to the Footprint of Freedom." The "Footprint" was a reference to the resemblance of the shape of the island to a human footprint. The schooner stayed for a full day, allowing a journalist to visit the island for the first time since the buildup of forces began five years ago.

The journalist noted the 14 permanently anchored prepositioned freighters that contained military gear for a heavily mechanized Marine Amphibious Brigade, as well as water and petroleum for attached Army and Air Force units. The visitors sailed around the command ship *LaSalle* (AGF-3), with the Central Command headquarters aboard, had conversations with the crews of the old Holy Loch submarine tender *Proteus* (AS-19), and the Los Angeles class nuclear attack submarine *City of Corpus Christi* (SSN-705), and saw the three-mile runway being lengthened and strengthened on steel piling built into the lagoon.

Lajes Field, Portugal

The fiscal year 1986 construction program at Lajes Field included a construction project to support additional C-141 sorties, during periods of heavy use, from the United States to Southwest Asia. This project was for 28 POL storage tanks that would hold 512,000 barrels of fuel, and was estimated to cost $19.4 million. The Department of Defense planners estimated a need for 3.5 million barrels of fuel storage at Lajes;

they had 1.9 million barrels of adequate storage and .5 million barrels of substandard storage capacity. The remaining deficiency was planned for future construction programs.

TABLE 12
NEAR TERM PREPOSITIONED FORCE
As of January 1985

Vessel	Charter Type	Began	Ended	At
USNS *Mercury* (T-AKR 10)	Vehicle Cargo Ship	4/80	Acq'd	D.G.
USNS *Jupiter* (T-AKR 11)	Vehicle Cargo Ship	3/80	Acq'd	D.G.
M/V *Lyra* (T-AKR 112)	Vehicle Cargo Ship	5/81	5/86	D.G.
SS *American Trojan* (T-AE 1010)	Ammunition Ship	12/81	1/85	D.G.
SS *President Adams* (T-AK 2039)	Cargo Ship	83	-	D.G.
SS *American Spitfire* (T-AK 1003)	Cargo Ship	9/81	9/84	Guam
SS *Letitia Lykes* (T-AK 2043)	Cargo Ship	5/83	5/85	D.G.
SS *Mormacstar* (T-AWT 1207)	Water Tanker	5/83	-	D.G.
SS *Green Valley* (T-AKB 2049)	Barge Cargo Ship	10/84	-	D.G.
SS *American Veteran* (T-AKB 2046)	Barge Cargo Ship	2/84	-	D.G.
SS *Austral Rainbow* (T-AKB 1005)	Barge Cargo Ship	10/81	10/84	D.G.
SS *Green Island* (T-AKB 1015)	Barge Cargo Ship	9/82	-	D.G.
SS *Overseas Valdez* (T-AOT 1204)	Transport Oiler	8/82	8/87	D.G.
SS *Transcolorado* (T-AK 2005)	Cargo Ship	7/68	-	E.Med.
SS *Overseas Vivian* (T-AOT 1205)	Transport Oiler	11/82	11/87	D.G.
SS *Overseas Alice* (T-AOT 1203)	Transport Oiler	10/82	10/87	D.G.
M/V *Falcon Leader* (T-AOT)	Transport Oiler	2/85	-	D.G.

Morocco

The Air Force included $3.1 million for airfield improvements at Sidi Slimane Air Base. The construction proposed altering a maintenance hangar, apron lighting, and water storage. The facilities begun in 1984 were required to provide enroute support for United States forces deploying to Southwest Asia. The facilities at Sidi Slimane were a supplement and alternative to those provided at Lajes Field.

Regional Instability

The expanding influence of Islamic Fundamentalism from Iran had a major impact in the Southwest Asia region. Iran and Iraq continued the four and one half year old war, and heightened danger to shipping in the Persian Gulf. The Soviets presence in Syria, Libya, and South Yemen, and continued occupation of Afghanistan threatened the independence and territorial integrity of states in the region. The border struggle between Ethiopia and Somalia, the Ethiopian-Eritrean separatist movement that began in 1962 when Emperor Haile Selassie annexed Eritrea, and continued Sudanese internal problems caused unrest in the Horn of Africa.

Enacted Indian Ocean/Persian Gulf FY 1986 Construction Program
$ in Millions

Location	Item	Rqstd	Auth'd Funded
Diego Garcia Navy			
Expansion Fac	42.680	42.680	42.680
AF Munitions Storage Fac	5.300	5.300	5.300
Lajes, Port. MAC Facilities	4.000	4.000	4.000
	1.850	1.850	1.000
RDF Facilities	19.435	19.435	0
GEODSS Facilities	14.650	14.650	14.650
Morocco Facilities	3.100	3.100	3.100
Totals	91.015	91.015	70.730

BRIGHT STAR 85

More than 9,000 troops were maneuvering for six days in the Middle East in August 1985, including forces from the United States, Egypt, Jordan, Oman, and Somalia. This was the third major BRIGHT STAR exercise with Egypt. The exercise included amphibious landings on Egypt's Mediterranean coast, desert maneuvers, and a simulated B-52 bomber strike.

Achievements and Costs

Completion of the Rapid Deployment facilities approved for Diego Garcia, Kenya, Somalia, Oman, Portuguese Azores, and Morocco resulted in the United States military access to seven separate airfields (Ras Banas, Egypt; Seeb, Thumrait, and Masirah, Oman; Mombasa, Kenya; and Berbera and Mogadishu, Somalia) and three ports (Mombasa, Berbera, and Masirah) in the immediate Persian Gulf area, as well as providing for air and sea support from Diego Garcia; Sidi Slimane, Morocco; and Lajes Field in the Azores. From the inception of the Rapid Deployment Force facility expansion program in 1981 through 1986, a total of $1.2 billion was approved for construction in the Indian Ocean/Persian Gulf. The cost of planning and design (about $29.1 million for Diego Garcia projects), equipping and storing military supplies, maintaining the facilities (about $40 million a year just for Diego Garcia), and foreign aid demands by host nations made the total expenditures even greater.

Diego Garcia

TABLE 13
SOUTHWEST ASIA AND ENROUTE CAPABILITIES

Location	Supports Major Airlift	Supports Strategic Projection Ops (B-52)	Navy Fleet Support	Enroute SWA Support	Prepositioned Cargo or POL	Supports Tactical Operations	Supports P-3 Operations	Supports MAC Ops	Supports Rear Staging
Bahrain			X						
Diego Garcia									
Naval Air Fac.				X				X	
Naval Supp. Fac.			X	X					
Naval Sec. Grp.			X						
Air Force Base	X	X		X	X				
Djibouti			X					X	
Egypt									
Ras Banas	X				X	X		X	
Kenya (Mombasa)									
Moi International Apt			X						
Kilindini Harbor			X						
Morocco									
Sidi Slimane Afld	X			X					
Port Mohammedia	X			X					
Oman									
Khasab AB						X	X		
Masirah Island			X			X	X	X	X
Seeb Inter. Apt.						X	X		
Thumrait AB						X	X	X	
Portugal									
Lajes AB				X	X			X	X
Somalia									
Berbera Airfield			X				X		
Berbera Harbor			X						
Mogadishu Airfield			X				X		

Appendix

Appendix 1

1966 BRITISH INDIAN OCEAN TERRITORY AGREEMENT
COPIED FROM TIAS 6196; 18 UST 28

The British Secretary of State for Foreign Affairs to the American Ambassador

FOREIGN OFFICE,
LONDON S.W. 1.

From the Minister of State

30 DECEMBER 1966.

YOUR EXCELLENCY, I have the honour to acknowledge receipt of your Note No. 25 of the 30th of December, 1966, which reads as follows:

UNITED KINGDOM OF GREAT BRITAIN AND NORTHERN IRELAND
Availability Of Certain Indian Ocean Islands For Defense Purposes
Agreement Effected By Exchange Of Notes Signed At London
December 30, 1966; Entered Into Force December 30, 1966

The American Ambassador to the British Secretary of State for Foreign Affairs

30 December 1966

Sir, I have the honor to refer to recent discussion between representatives of the Government of the United States of America and the Government of the United Kingdom of Great Britain and Northern Ireland concerning the availability, for the defense purposes of both Governments as they may arise, of the islands of Diego Garcia and the remainder of the Chagos Archipelago, and the islands of Aldabra, Farquhar, and Desroaches constituting the British Indian Ocean Territory, hereinafter referred to as "the Territory." The United States Government has now authorized me to propose an Agreement in the following terms:

(1) The Territory shall remain under United Kingdom sovereignty.
(2) Subject to the provisions set out below the islands shall be available to meet the needs of both Governments for defense. In order to ensure that the respective United States and United Kingdom defense activities in the islands are correlated in an orderly fashion:
   (a) In the case of the initial United States requirement for use of a particular island the appropriate governmental authorities shall consult with respect to the time required by the United Kingdom authorities for taking those administrative measures that may be necessary to enable any such defense requirement to be met.
   (b) Before either Government proceeds to construct or install any facility in the Territory, both Governments shall first approve in principle the requirement for that facility, and the appropriate administrative authorities of the two Governments shall reach mutually satisfactory arrangements concerning specific area and technical requirements for respective defense purposes.
   (c) The procedure described in sub-paragraphs (a) and (b) shall not be applicable in emergency circumstances requiring temporary use of an island or part of an island

not in use at that time for defense purposes provided that measures to ensure the welfare of the inhabitants are taken to the satisfaction of the Commissioner of the Territory. Each Government shall notify the other promptly of any emergency requirements and consultation prior to such use by the United States Government shall be under taken as soon as possible.

(3) The United Kingdom Government reserves the right to permit the use by third countries of British-financed defense facilities, but shall where appropriate consult with the United States Government before granting such permission. Use by a third country of United States or jointly-financed facilities shall be subject to agreement between the United Kingdom Government and the United States Government.

(4) The required sites shall be made available to the United States authorities without charge.

(5) Each Government shall normally bear the cost of site preparation, construction, maintenance, and operation for any facilities developed to meet its own requirements. Within their capacities, such facilities shall be available for use by the forces of the other Government under service-level arrangements. However, there may be certain cases where joint financing should be considered, and in these cases the two Governments shall consult together.

(6) Commercial aircraft shall not be authorized to use military airfields in the Territory. However, the United Kingdom Government reserves the right to permit the use in exceptional circumstances of such airfields, following consultation with the authorities operating the airfields concerned, under such terms or conditions as may be defined by the two Governments.

(7) For its defense purposes on the islands, the United States Government may freely select United States contractors and

the sources of equipment, material, supplies, or personnel, except that—

    (a) the United States Government and United States contractors shall make use of workers from Mauritius and Seychelles to the maximum extent practicable, consistent with United States policies, requirements and schedules; and

    (b) the appropriate administrative authorities of the two Governments shall consult before contractors or workers from a third country are introduced.

(8) The exemption from charges in the nature of customs duties and other taxes in respect of goods, supplies and equipment brought to the Territory in connection with the purposes of this Agreement by or on behalf of the United States Government, United States contractors, members of the United States Forces, contractor personnel or dependents, and the exemption from taxation of certain persons serving or employed in the Territory in connection with those purposes, shall be such exemption as is set out in Annex I to this Note.

(9) The arrangements regarding the exercise of criminal jurisdiction and claims shall be those set out in Annex II to this Note.

(10) For the purpose of this Agreement:

    (a)"Contractor personnel" means employees of a United States contractor who are not ordinarily resident in the Territory and who are there solely for the purpose of this Agreement;

    (b)"Dependents" means the spouse and children under 21 years of age of a person in relation to whom it is used; and, if they are dependent upon him for their support, the parents and children over 21 years of age of that person;

    (c)"Members of the United States Forces" means (i) military members of the United States Forces on active duty; (ii) civilian personnel accompanying the United States Forces and in their employ who are not ordinarily resident in the Territory and who are there solely for the purpose of this Agreement; and (iii) dependents of the persons described in (i) and (ii) above;

(d)"United States authorities" means the authority or authorities from time to time authorized or designated by the United States Government for the purpose of exercising the powers in relation to which the expression is used;

(e)"United States contractor" means any person, body or corporation ordinarily resident in the United States of America, that, by virtue of a contract with the United States Government, is in the Territory for the purposes of this Agreement, and includes a sub-contractor;

(f)"United States Forces" means the lands, sea and air armed services of the United States, including the Coast Guard.

(11)The United States Government and the United Kingdom Government contemplate that the islands shall remain available to meet the possible defense needs of the two Governments for an indefinitely long period. Accordingly, after an initial period of 50 years this Agreement shall continue in force for a further period of twenty years unless, not more than two years before the end of the initial period, either Government shall have given notice of termination to the other, in which case this Agreement shall terminate two years from the date of such notice.

If the foregoing proposal is acceptable to the Government of the United Kingdom of Great Britain and Northern Ireland, I have the honor to propose that this Note and its Annexes, together with your reply to that effect, shall constitute an Agreement between the two Governments which shall enter into force on the date of your reply.

Accept, Sir, the renewed assurances of my highest consideration.

DAVID BRUCE,
American Ambassador

ANNEX I.—CUSTOM DUTIES AND TAXATION

1. CUSTOMS DUTIES AND OTHER TAXES ON GOODS

(1) No import, excise, consumption or other tax, duty or impost shall be charged on:

    (a) material, equipment, supplies, or goods for use in the establishment, maintenance, or operation of the facilities which are consigned to or destined for the United States authorities or a United States contractor;

    (b) goods for the use or consumption aboard United States public vessels or aircraft;

    (c) goods consigned to the United States authorities or to a United States contractor for the use or for sale to military members of the United States Forces, or to other members of the United States Forces, or to those contractor personnel and their dependents who are not engaged in any business or occupation in the Territory;

    (d) the personal belongings or household effects for the personal use of persons referred to in sub-paragraph (c) above, including motor vehicles, provided that these accompany the owner or are imported—(i) within a period beginning sixty days before and ending 120 days after the owner's arrival; or (ii) within a period of six months immediately following his arrival;

    (e) goods for consumption and goods (other than personal belongings and household effects) acquired after first arrival, including gifts, consigned to military members of the United States Forces, or to those other members of the United States Forces who are nationals of the United States and are not engaged in any business or occupation in the Territory, provided that such goods are: (i) of United States origin if the Commissioner so requires, and (ii) imported for the personal use of the recipient.

(2) No export tax shall be charged on the material on the material, equipment, supplies or goods mentioned in paragraph (1) in the event of reshipment from the Territory.

(3) Article 1 of this Annex shall apply notwithstanding that the material, equipment, supplies or goods pass through other parts of the Territory enroute to or from a site.

(4) The United States authorities shall do all in their power to prevent any abuse of customs privileges and shall take administrative measures, which shall be mutually agreed upon between the appropriate authorities of the United States and the Territory, to prevent the disposal, whether by resale or otherwise, of goods which are used or sold under paragraph (1)(c), or imported under paragraph (1)(d) or (1)(e), of Article 1 of this Annex, to persons not entitled to buy goods pursuant to paragraph (1)(c), or not entitled to free importation under paragraph (1)(d) or (1)(e). There shall be cooperation between the United States authorities and the Commissioner to this end, both in prevention and in investigation of cases of abuse.

2. MOTOR VEHICLE TAXES

No tax or fee shall be payable in respect of registration or licensing for use for the purpose of this Agreement in the Territory of motor vehicles belonging to the United States Government or United States contractors.

3. TAXATION

(1) No members of the United States Forces, or those contractor personnel and their dependents who are nationals of the United

States, serving or employed in the Territory in connection with the facilities shall be liable to pay income tax in the Territory except in respect of income derived from activities within the Territory other than such service or employment.

(2) No such person shall be liable to pay in the Territory any poll tax or similar tax on his person, or any tax on ownership or use of property which is situated outside the Territory or situated within the Territory solely by reason of such person's presence there in connection with activities under this Agreement.

(3) No United States contractor shall be liable to pay income tax in the Territory in respect of any income derived under a contract made in the United States in connection with the purposes of this Agreement, or any tax in the nature of license in respect of any service or work for the United States Government in connection with the purposes of this Agreement.

ANNEX II—JURISDICTION AND CLAIMS

1. (a) Subject to the provisions of sub-paragraphs (b) to (1) of this paragraph,

   (i) the military authorities of the United States shall have the right to exercise within the Territory all criminal and disciplinary jurisdiction conferred on them by United States law over all persons subject to the military law of the United States; and

   (ii) the authorities of the Territory shall have jurisdiction over the members of the United States Forces with respect to offenses committed within the Territory and punishable by the law in force there.

(b)

  (i) The military authorities of the United States shall have the right to exercise exclusive jurisdiction over persons subject to the military law of the United States with respect to offenses, including offenses relating to security, punishable by the law of the United States but not by the law in force in the Territory.

  (ii) The authorities of the Territory shall have the right to exercise exclusive jurisdiction over members of the United States Forces with respect to offenses, including offenses relating to security, punishable by the law in force in the Territory but not by the law of the United States.

  (iii) For the purposes of sub-paragraphs (b) and (c), an offense relating to official secrets or secrets relating to national defense.

(c) In cases where the right to exercise jurisdiction is concurrent the following rules shall apply;

  (i) The military authorities of the United States shall have the primary right to exercise jurisdiction over a member of the United States Forces in relation to (aa) offenses solely against the property or security of the United States or offenses solely against the person or property of another member of the United States Forces; and (bb) offenses arising out of any act or omission done in the performance of official duty.

  (ii) In the case of any other offense the authorities of the Territory shall have primary right to exercise jurisdiction.

  (iii) If the authorities having the primary right decide not to exercise jurisdiction, they shall notify the other authorities as soon as practicable. The United States authorities shall give sympathetic consideration to a request from the authorities of the Territory for a waiver of their primary right in cases where the authorities of the Territory consider such waiver to be particular importance. The authorities of the Territory will waive, upon request, their primary right to exercise jurisdiction under this paragraph, except where they in their discretion determine and notify the United States authorities that it is of particular importance that such jurisdiction be not waived.

(d) The foregoing provisions of this paragraph shall not imply any right for the military authorities of the United States to exercise jurisdiction over persons who belong to, or are ordinarily resident in, the Territory, or who are British subjects or Commonwealth citizens or British protected persons, unless they are military members of the United States Forces.

(e)

(i) To the extent authorized by law, the authorities of the Territory and the military authorities of the United States shall assist each other in the service of process and in the arrest of members of the United States Forces in the Territory and in handing them over to the authorities which are to exercise jurisdiction in accordance with provisions of this paragraph.

(ii) The authorities of the Territory shall notify promptly the military authorities of the United States of the arrest of any member of the United States Forces.

(iii) Unless otherwise agreed, the custody of an accused member of the United States Forces over whom the authorities of the Territory are to exercise jurisdiction shall, if he is in the hands of the United States authorities, remain with the United States authorities until he is charged. In cases where the United States authorities may have the responsibility for custody pending the completion of judicial proceedings, the United States authorities shall upon request, make such a person immediately available to the authorities of the Territory for the purposes of investigation and trial and shall give full consideration to any special views of such authorities as to the way in which custody should be maintained.

(f)

(i) to the extent authorized by law, the authorities of the Territory and of the United States shall assist each other in the carrying out of all necessary investigations into offenses, in providing for the attendance of witnesses and in the collection and production of evidence, including the seizure and, in proper cases, the handing over of objects connected with an offense. The handing over of such items may, however, be made subject to their return within the time specified by the authorities delivering them.

(ii) The authorities of the Territory and of the United States shall notify one another of the disposition of all cases in which there are concurrent rights to exercise jurisdiction.

(g) A death sentence shall not be carried out in the Territory by the military authorities of the United States.

(h) Where an accused has been tried in accordance with the provisions of this paragraph and has been acquitted or has been convicted and is serving, or has served, his sentence or has been pardoned, he may not be tried again for the same offense within the Territory. Nothing in this paragraph shall, however, prevent the military authorities of the United States from trying a military member of the United States Forces for any violation of rules of discipline arising from an act or omission which constituted an offense for which he was tried by the authorities of the Territory.

(i) Whenever a member of the United States Forces is prosecuted by the authorities of the Territory he shall be entitled

    (i) to a prompt and speedy trial;

    (ii) to be informed in advance of trial of the specific charge or charges made against him;

    (iii) to be confronted with the witnesses against him;

    (iv) to have compulsory process for obtaining witnesses in his favor if they are within the jurisdiction of the Territory;

    (v) to have legal representation of his own choice for his defense or to have free or assisted legal representation under conditions prevailing for the time being in the Territory;

    (vi) if he considers it necessary, to have the services of a competent interpreter; and

    (vii) to communicate with a representative of the United States and, when the rules of the court permit, to have such representative present at his trial which shall be public except when the court decrees otherwise in accordance with the law in the Territory.

(j) Where a member of the United States Forces is tried by the military authorities of the United States for an offense committed outside the areas used by the United States or involving a person, or the property of a person, other than a member of the United States Forces, the aggrieved party and representatives of the Territory and of the aggrieved party may attend the trial proceedings except where this would be inconsistent with the rules of the court.

(k) A certificate of the appropriate United States commanding officer that an offense arose out of an act of omission done in the performance of official duty shall be conclusive, but the

commanding officer shall give consideration to any represen-
tation made by the authorities of the Territory.

(l) Regularly constituted military units or formations of the United States Forces shall have the right to police the areas used by the United States. The military police of the United States Forces may take all appropriate measures to ensure the maintenance of order and security within these areas.

2 (a) The Government of the United States of America and the Government of the United Kingdom respectively waive all claims against the other of them—

(i) for damage to any property owned by it and used by its land, sea or air armed services if such damage—(aa) was caused by a member of the armed services or by an employee of a Department with responsibility for the armed services of either Government in the execution of his duties or (bb) arose from the use of any vehicle, vessel or aircraft owned by either Government and used by its armed services provided either that the vehicle, vessel or aircraft causing the damage was being used in connection with official duties, or the damage was caused to property being so used.

(ii) For injury or death suffered by any member of its armed services while such member was engaged in the perform-ance of his official duties.

(iii) For the purpose of this paragraph "owned" in the case of a vessel includes a vessel on bare boat charter, a ves-sel requisitioned on bare boat terms and a vessel seized in prize (except to the extent that the risk of loss or liability is borne by some person other than either Government).

(b)

(i) The united States Government shall, in consultation with the Government of the Territory, take all reasonable precautions against possible danger and damage resulting from operations under this Agreement.

(ii) The United States Government agrees to pay just and reasonable compensation, which shall be determined in accordance with the measure of damage prescribed by the law of the Territory, in settlement of civil claims (other than contractual claims) arising out of acts or omissions of members of the United States Forces done in the performance of official duty or out of any other act or omission or occurrence for which the United States Forces are legally responsible.

(iii) Any such claim presented to the United States Government shall be processed and settled in accordance with the applicable provision of United States law.

The Right Honorable GEORGE BROWN, M.P.
Secretary of State for Foreign Affairs, Foreign Office, Whitehall, London, S.W.1.

I have the honour to inform Your Excellency that the foregoing proposal is acceptable to the Government of the United Kingdom of Great Britain and Northern Ireland, who therefore agree that Your Excellency's Note, together with the Annexes thereto and this reply, shall constitute an Agreement between the two Governments which shall enter into force on this day's date.

I have the honour to be, with the highest consideration,
Your Excellency's obedient Servant,

                 CHALFONT,
            (For the Secretary of State).

His Excellency,
The Honourable DAVID K. E. BRUCE, C.B.E.

Appendix 2

DIEGO GARCIA AGREEMENT 1972
Copied from TIAS 7481; 23 UST 3087

UNITED KINGDOM OF GREAT BRITAIN
AND NORTHERN IRELAND
Naval Communications Facility on Diego Garcia

Agreement supplementing the agreement of December 30, 1966.
Effected by exchange of notes
Signed at London October 24, 1972;
Entered into force October 24, 1972.

———————

The British Secretary of State for Foreign and Commonwealth
Affairs to the American Charge d'Affaires ad interim
Note No HKT 10/1 Foreign and Commonwealth Office,
London, 24 October 1972
    Hon. Earl D Sohm,
    etc etc etc
    Embassy of the United States,
    Grovenor Square,
    London, W.1.

Sir,

I have the honor to refer to the Agreement constituted by Exchange of Notes dated 30 December 1966,[1] between the Government of the United Kingdom of Great Britain and Northern Ireland and the Government of the United States of America concerning the availability of the British Indian Ocean

Territory for defence purposes. Pursuant to paragraph 2 (b) of that Agreement, I now convey the approval in principle of the Government of the United Kingdom to the construction of a limited navalcommunications facility on Diego Garcia and propose an Agreement in the following terms:

(1) SCOPE OF THE FACILITY

(a) Subject to the following provisions of this Agreement, the Government of the United States shall have the right to construct, maintain and operate a limited naval communications facility on Diego Garcia. The facility shall consist of transmitting and receiving services, an anchorage, airfield, associated logistic support and supply and personnel accommodation. For this purpose immovable structures, installations and buildings may be constructed within the specific area shown in the plan annexed to Note. The specific area may be altered from time to time as may be agreed by the appropriate administrative authorities of the two Governments.

(b) During the term of this Agreement the Government of the United States may conduct on Diego Garcia such functions as are necessary for the construction, maintenance, operation and security of the facility.

---

1. TIAS 6196;18UST28.

For this purpose the Government of the United States shall have freedom of access to that part ofDiego Garcia outside the specific area referred to in sub-paragraph (a), but may erect or construct immovable structures, installations and buildings outside the specific area only with the prior agreement of the appropriate administrative authorities of the Government of the United Kingdom.

(c) Delimitation of the specific area shall, subject to the provisions of the BIOT Agreement, in no way restrict the Government of the United Kingdom from constructing and operating their own defence facility within that area, provided that no technical interference to existing operations will result from such construction and operation.

(2) PURPOSE

The facility shall provide a link in United States defence communications and shall furnish improved communication support in the Indian Ocean for ships and state aircraft owned or operated by or on behalf of either Government.

(3) ACCESS TO DIEGO GARCIA

(a) Access to Diego Garcia shall in general be restricted to members of the Forces of the United Kingdom and of the United States, the Commissioner and public officers in the service of the British Indian Ocean Territory, representatives of the Governments of the United Kingdom and of the United States and, subject to normal immigration requirements, contractor personnel. The Government of the United Kingdom reserves the right, after consultation with the appropriate United States administrative authorities, to grant access to members of scientific parties wishing to carry out research on

Diego Garcia and its environs, provided that such research does not unreasonably interfere with the activities of the facility. The

Commanding Officer shall afford appropriate assistance to members of these parties to the extent feasible and on a reimbursable basis. Access shall not be granted to any other person without prior consultation between the appropriate administrative authorities of the two Governments.

(b) Ships and state aircraft owned or operated by or on behalf of either Government may freely use the anchorage and airfield.

(c) Pursuant to the provisions of the second sentence of paragraph (3) of the BIOT Agreement, ships and state aircraft owned or operated by or on behalf of a third government, and the personnel of such ships and aircraft, may use only such of the services provided by the facility, and on such terms, as may be agreed in any particular case by the two Governments.

(4) PROTECTION AND SECURITY

Responsibility for protection and security of the facility shall be vested in the Commanding Officer, who shall maintain a close liaison with the Commissioner. The two Governments shall consult if there is any threat to the facility.

(5) SHIPPING, NAVIGATION AND AVIATION FACILITIES

The Government of the United States shall have the right to install, operate and maintain on Diego Garcia such navigational and communications aids as may be necessary for the safe transit of ships and aircraft into and out of Diego Garcia.

(6) RADIO FREQUENCIES AND TELECOMMUNICATIONS

(a) Subject to the prior concurrance of the Government of the United Kingdom, the Government of the United States may use any radio frequencies, powers and band widths for radio services (including radar) on Diego Garcia which are necessary for the operation of the facility. All radio communications shall comply at all times with the provisions of the International Telecommunications Convention.[2]

(b) The Government of the United States may establish such land lines on Diego Garcia as may be necessary for the facility.

(7) CONSERVATION

As far as possible the activities of the facility and its personnel shall not interfere with the flora and fauna of Diego Garcia. When their use is no longer required for the purposes of the facility, the two Governments shall consult about the condition of the three islets at the mouth of the lagoon with a view to restoring them to their original condition. However, neither Government shall be under any obligation to provide funds for such restoration.

(8) ANCHORAGE DUES AND AVIATION CHARGES

Collection of dues and charges for use of the anchorage and airfield at Diego Garcia which may be levied by the Commissioner shall be his responsibility. State aircraft and ships owned or operated by or on behalf of the Government of the United States shall be permitted to use the anchorage and airfield without the payment of any dues or charges.

(9) METEOROLOGY

The Government of the United States shall operate a meteorological facility on Diego Garcia and supply such available meteorological information as may be required by the Government of the United Kingdom and the Government of Mauritius to meet their national and international obligations.

(10) ROYAL NAVY ELEMENT

The Royal Navy element on Diego Garcia shall be under the command of a Royal Navy officer who shall be known as the

---

2. TIAS 6267; 18UST 575.

Officer-in-Charge of the Royal Navy element. He shall be the Representative on Diego Garcia of the Commissioner.

(11) FINANCE

The Government of the United States shall wholly bear the cost of constructing, operating and maintaining the facility. The Government of the United Kingdom shall be responsible for the pay, allowances and any other monetary gratuities of Royal Navy personnel, for the cost of their messing, and for supplies or services which are peculiar to or provided for the exclusive use of the Royal Navy or its personnel and which would not normally be provided by the Government of the United States for the use of its own personnel.

(12) FISHERIES, OIL AND MINERAL RESOURCES

The Government of the United Kingdom will not permit commercial fishing in the lagoon or oil mineral exploration or exploitation on Diego Garcia for the duration of this Agreement. Furthermore, the Government of the United Kingdom will not permit commercial fishing or oil or mineral exploration or exploitation in or under those areas of the waters, continental shelf and sea bed around Diego Garcia over which the United Kingdom has sovereignty or exercises sovereign rights, unless it is agreed that such activities would not harm or be inimical to the defence use of the island.

(13) HEALTH QUARANTINE AND SANITATION

The Commanding Officer and the Commissioner shall collaborate in the enforcement on Diego Garcia of necessary health, quarantine and sanitation provisions.

(14) NEWS BROADCAST STATION

The Government of the United States may establish and operate a closed circuit TV and a low power radio broadcast station to broadcast news, entertainment and educational programmes for personnel on Diego Garcia.

(15) PROPERTY

(a) Title to any movable property brought into Diego Garcia by or on behalf of the Government of the United States, or by a United States contractor, shall remain in the Government of the United States or the contractor, as the case may be. Such property of the Government of the United States, including official papers, shall be exempt from inspection, search and seizure. Such property of either Government of the United States or of a United States contractor may be freely removed from Diego Garcia, but shall not be disposed of within the British Indian Ocean Territory or Seychelles unless an offer, consistent with the laws of the United States then in effect, has been made to sell the property to the Commissioner and he has not accepted such offer within a period of 120 days after it was made or such longer period as may be reasonable in the circumstances. Any such property not removed or disposed of within a reasonable time after termination of this Agreement shall become the property of the Commissioner.

(b) The Government of the United States shall not be responsible for restoring land or other immovable property to its original condition, nor for making any payment in lieu of restoration.

(16) AVAILABILITY OF FUNDS

To the extent that the carrying out of any activity or the implementation of any part of this Agreement depends upon funds to be appropriated by the Congress of the United States, it shall be subject to the availability of such funds.

(17) RESTRICTION OF RIGHTS

The Government of the United States shall not exercise any of the above rights or powers, or permit the exercise thereof, except for the purposes herein specified.

(18) SUPPLEMENTARY ARRANGEMENTS

Supplementary arrangements between the appropriate administrative authorities of the two Governments may be made from time to time as required for the carrying out of the purposes of this Agreement.

(19) DEFINITIONS AND INTERPRETATION

(a) For the purposes of this Agreement

"BIOT Agreement" means the Agreement referred to in the first paragraph of this Note;

"Commanding Officer" means the United States Navy Officer in command of the facility;

"Commissioner" means the officer administering the Government of the British Indian Ocean Territory;

"Diego Garcia" means the atoll of Diego Garcia, the lagoon and the three islets at the mouth of the lagoon.

(b) The provisions of this Agreement shall supplement the BIOT Agreement and shall be construed in accordance with that Agreement. In the event of any conflict between the provisions of the BIOT Agreement and this Agreement the provisions of the BIOT Agreement shall prevail.

(20) DURATION AND TERMINATION

This Agreement shall continue in force for as long as the BIOT Agreement continues in force or untilsuch time as no part of Diego Garcia is any longer required for the purposes of the facility, which ever occurs first.

2. If the Government of the United States of America also approves in principle the construction of the facility subject to the above terms, I have the honour to propose that this Note and the plan annexed to it, together with your reply to that effect, shall constitute an Agreement between the two Governments which shall enter into force on the date of your reply and shall be known as the Diego Garcia Agreement 1972.

> I have the honour to be
> with high consideration
> Sir
> (For the Secretary of State)
> /S/
> Anthony Kershaw

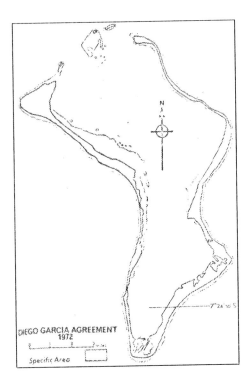

Copy of Diego Garcia Agreement 1976 Map

Appendix 3

DIEGO GARCIA AGREEMENT 1976
Copied from TIAS 8230; 27 UST 315

The British Minister of State for Foreign and Commonwealth
Affairs to the American Charge d'Affaires ad interim

Note No. DPP 063/530/2 Foreign and Commonwealth Office,
London
25 February 1976

Sir,

I have the honour to refer to the Agreement constituted by the
Exchange of Notes dated 30 December[3] 1966 between the Government of
the United Kingdom of Great Britain and Northern Ireland and the
Government of the United States of America concerning the availability
of the British Indian Ocean Territory for defence purposes and to the
Agreement constituted by the Exchange of Notes dated 24 October 1972[4]
between the two Governments concerning a limited United States naval
communications facility on Diego Garcia, British Indian Ocean Territory.
Pursuant to paragraph 2(b) of the former Agreement, I now convey the
approval in principle of the Government of the United Kingdom to the
development of the present limited naval communications facility on

---

3. TIAS 6196; 18 UST 28.
4. TIAS 7481; 23 UST 3087.

Diego Garcia into a support facility of the United States Navy and propose an Agreement in the following terms:

(1) *Scope of the facility*

(a) Subject to the following provisions of this Agreement, the Government of the United States shall have the right to develop the present limited naval communications facility on Diego Garcia as a support facility of the United States Navy and to maintain and operate it. The facility shall consist of an anchorage, airfield, support and supply elements and ancillary services, personnel accommodation, and transmitting and receiving services. Immovable structures, installations and buildings for the facility may, after consultation with the appropriate administrative authorities of the United Kingdom, be constructed within the specific area shown in the plan attached to this Note. The specific area may be altered from time to time as may be agreed by the appropriate administrative authorities of the two Governments.

(b) During the term of the Agreement the Government of the United States may conduct on Diego Garcia such functions as are necessary for the development, use, maintenance, operation and security of the facility. In the exercise of these functions the Government of the United States, members of the United States Forces and contractor personnel shall have freedom of access to that part of Diego Garcia outside the specific area referred to in sub-paragraph (a), but the Government of the United States may erect or construct immovable structures, installations and buildings outside the specific area only with the prior agreement of the appropriate administrative authorities of the Government of the United Kingdom.

(c) Delimitation of the specific area shall, subject to the provisions of the BIOT Agreement and after consultation with the appropriate

United States authorities with a view to avoiding interference with the existing use of the facility, in no way restrict the Government of the United Kingdom from constructing and operating at their own expense their own defence facilities within that area, or from using that part of Diego Garcia outside the specific area.

(2) *Purpose*

The facility shall provide an improved link in United States defence communications, and furnish support for ships and aircraft owned or operated by or on behalf of either Government.

(3) *Consultation*

Both Governments shall consult periodically on joint objectives, policies and activities in the area. As regards the use of the facility in normal circumstances, the Commanding Officer and the Officer in Charge of the United Kingdom Service element shall inform each other of intended movements of ships and aircraft. In other circumstances the use of the facility shall be a matter for the joint decision of the two Governments.

(4) *Access to Diego Garcia*

(a) Access to Diego Garcia shall in general be restricted to members of the Forces of the United Kingdom and of the United States, the Commissioner and public officers in the service of the British Indian Ocean Territory, representatives of the Governments of the United Kingdom and of the United States and, subject to normal immigration requirements, contractor personnel. The Government of the United Kingdom reserves the right, after consultation with the appropriate United States administrative authorities, to grant access to members of scientific parties wishing to carry out research on Diego Garcia and its environs, provided that such research does not unreasonably interfere with the activities of the facility. The Commanding Officer shall afford appropriate assistance to members of these parties to the extent feasible and on a reimbursable basis. Access shall not be granted to any other person without prior consultation between the appropriate administrative authorities of the two Governments.

(b) Ships and aircraft owned or operated by or on behalf of either Government may freely use the anchorage and airfield.

(c) Pursuant to the provisions of the second sentence of paragraph (3) of the BIOT Agreement, ships and aircraft owned or operated by or on behalf of a third government, and the personnel of such ships and aircraft, may use only such of the services provided by the facility, and on such terms, as may be agreed in any particular case by the two Governments.

(5) *Protection and security*

Responsibility for protection and security of the facility shall be vested in the Commanding Officer, who shall maintain a close liaison with the Commissioner. The two Governments shall consult if there is any threat to the facility.

(6) *Shipping, navigation and aviation facilities*

The Government of the United States shall have the right to install, operate and maintain on Diego Garcia such navigational and communications aids as may be necessary for the safe transit of ships and aircraft into and out of Diego Garcia.

(7) *Radio frequencies and telecommunications*

(a) Subject to the prior concurrence of the Government of the United Kingdom, the Government of the United States may use

any radio frequencies, powers and band widths for radio services (including radar) on
Diego Garcia which are necessary for the operation of the facility. All radio communications shall comply at all times with the provisions of the International Telecommunications Convention.[5]

(b) The Government of the United States may establish such land lines on Diego Garcia as may be necessary for the facility.

(8) *Conservation*

As far as possible the activities of the facility and its personnel shall not interfere with the flora and fauna of Diego Garcia. When their use is no longer required for the purposes of the facility, the two Governments shall consult about the condition of the three islets at the mouth of the lagoon with a view to restoring them to their original condition. However, neither Government shall be under any obligation to provide funds for such restoration.

(9) *Anchorage dues and aviation charges*

Collection of dues and charges for use of the anchorage and airfield at Diego Garcia which may be levied by the Commissioner shall be his responsibility. Aircraft and ships owned or operated by or on behalf of the Government of the United States shall be permitted to use the anchorage and airfield without the payment of any dues or charges.

(10) *Meteorology*

The Government of the United States shall operate a meteorological facility on Diego Garcia and supply such available meteorological information as may be required by the Government of the United Kingdom and the Government of Mauritius to meet their national and international obligations.

---

5. TIAS 6267; 18 UST 575.

(11) *United Kingdom Service element*

The United Kingdom Service element on Diego Garcia shall be under the Command of a Royal Navy Officer who shall be known as the Officer-in-Charge of the United Kingdom Service element.

(12) Finance

(a) The Government of the United States shall bear the cost of developing, operating and maintaining the facility. However, in relation to United Kingdom personnel attached to the facility, the Government of the United Kingdom shall be responsible for their pay, allowances and any other monetary gratuities, for the cost of their messing, and for supplies or services which are peculiar to or provided for the exclusive use of the United Kingdom Services or their personnel and which would not normally be provided by the Government of the United States for the use of its own personnel.

(b) Except in relation to the United Kingdom Service personnel attached to the facility, logistic support furnished at Diego Garcia by either Government, upon request, to the other Government, shall be on a reimbursable basis in accordance with the laws, regulations and instructions of the Government furnishingthe support.

(13) *Fisheries, oil and mineral resources*

The Government of the United Kingdom will not permit commercial fishing in the lagoon or oil or mineral exploration or exploitation on Diego Garcia for the duration of this Agreement. Furthermore, the Government of the United Kingdom will not permit commercial fishing or oil or mineral exploration or exploitation in or under those areas of the waters, continental shelf and sea-bed around Diego Garcia over which the United Kingdom has sovereignty or exercises sovereign rights, unless it is agreed that such activities would not harm or be inimical to the defence use of the island.

(14) *Health, quarantine and sanitation*

The Commanding Officer and the Commissioner shall collaborate in the enforcement on Diego Garcia of necessary health, quarantine and sanitation provisions.

(15) *News broadcast station*

The Government of the United States may establish and operate a closed circuit TV and a low power radio broadcast station to broadcast news, entertainment and educational programmes for personnel on Diego Garcia.

(16) *Property*

(a) Title to any removable property brought into Diego Garcia by or on behalf of the Government of the United States, or by a United States contractor, shall remain in the Government of the United States or the contractor, as the case may be. Such property of the Government of the United States, including official papers, shall be exempt from inspection, search and seizure. Such property of either the Government of the United States or of a United States contractor may be freely removed from Diego Garcia, but shall not be disposed of within the British Indian Ocean Territory or Seychelles unless an offer, consistent with the laws of the United States then in effect, has been made to sell the property to the Commissioner and he has not accepted such offer within a period of 120 days after it was made or such longer period as may be reasonable in the circumstances. Any such property not removed or disposed of within a reasonable time after termination of this Agreement shall become the property of the Commissioner. (b) The Government of the United States shall not be responsible for restoring land or other immovable Property to its original condition, nor for making any payment in lieu of restoration.

(17) *Availability of funds*

To the extent that the carrying out of any activity or the implementation of any part of this Agreement depends upon funds to be appropriated by the Congress of the United States, it shall be subject to the availability of such funds.

(18) *Representative of the Commissioner*

The Commissioner shall designate a person as his Representative on Diego Garcia.

(19) *Supplementary arrangements*

Supplementary arrangements between the appropriate administrative authorities of the two Governments may be made from time to time as required for the carrying out of the purpose of this Agreement.

(20) *Definitions and interpretation*

(a) For the purpose of this Agreement "BIOT Agreement" means the Exchange of Notes dated 30 December 1966, between the Government of the United Kingdom of Great Britain and Northern Ireland and the Government of the United States of America concerning the availability of the British Indian Ocean Territory for defence purposes;

"Commanding Officer" means the United States Navy Officer in command of the facility; "Commissioner" means the officer administering the Government of the British Indian Ocean Territory;

"Diego Garcia" means the atoll of Diego Garcia, the lagoon and the three islets at the mouth of the lagoon.

(b) Questions of interpretation arising from the application of this Agreement shall be the subject of consultation between the two Governments.

(c) The provisions of this Agreement shall supplement the BIOT Agreement and shall be construed in accordance with that Agreement. In the event of any conflict between the provisions of the BIOT Agreement and this Agreement the provisions of the BIOT Agreement shall prevail.

(21) *The Diego Garcia Agreement 1972*

This Agreement shall replace the Agreement constituted by the Exchange of Notes dated 24 October 1972 between the Government of the United Kingdom of Great Britain and Northern Ireland and the Government of the United States of America concerning a limited United States naval communications facility on Diego Garcia, British Indian Ocean Territory.

(22) *Duration and termination*

This Agreement shall continue in force as long as the BIOT Agreement continues in force or until such time as no part of Diego Garcia is any longer required for the purposes of the facility, whichever occurs first.

2. If the Government of the United States of America also approves in principle the development of the facility subject to the above terms, I have the honour to propose that this Note and the plan annexed to it, together with your reply to that effect, shall constitute an Agreement between the two Governments which shall enter into force on the date of your reply and shall be known as the Diego Garcia Agreement 1976.

I have the honour to be with high consideration
Sir
Your obedient Servant
Roy Hattersley

The Honourable Ronald I Spiers
Embassy of the United States of America
Grosvenor Square
London

W1A 1AH

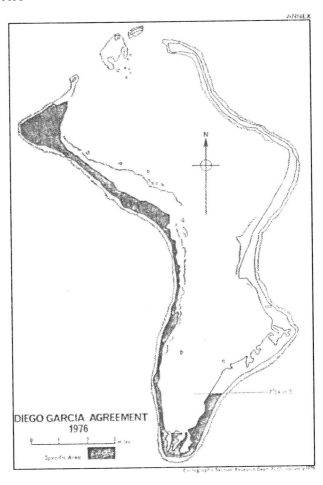

Copy of Diego Garcia Agreement 1976 Map

TITLE

SUPPLEMENTARY ARRANGEMENTS 1976 FOR DIEGO GARCIA FACILITY

PREAMBLE

Pursuant to paragraph 19 of the Diego Garcia Agreement 1976 between the Governmentof the United Kingdom of Great Britain and Northern Ireland and the Government of the United States of America concerning the United States Navy support facility on Diego Garcia, the Ministry of Defence (Navy) and the United States Navy (USN) have made the following supplementary arrangements:

PARAGRAPH 1

Personnel—The USN will establish a manning level for the facility. Representatives of both administrative authorities will jointly decide which positions shall be filled by UK Service personnel. All personnel assigned to Diego Garcia will serve an unaccompanied tour of duty.

PARAGRAPH 2

Military Command—The Officer-in-Charge of the UK Service element will, in matters relating to the operation of the facility, report to the Commanding Officer. The Commanding Officer and the Officer-in-Charge of the UK Service element will establish the manner in which orders and instructions will be complied with, which mannerwill be consistent with the concept of mutual respect for relative ranks. However, nothing in this paragraph is intended to require obedience to any command inconsistent with the obligation of their respective service laws nor to establish disciplinary power in either officer over members of the Armed Services of the other country.

PARAGRAPH 3

Support—Subject to Paragraph 4 below, military personnel of both Governments will be entitled to use; upon the same terms and conditions, such recreational, accommodation and messing facilities as are available or as are established for military personnel by either Government. UK Service personnel serving with this facility will be entitled to send and receive mail through the United States Fleet postal system. The USN will, upon request, transport UK Service personnel to and from the facility from such places as may be agreed from time to time by the USN and the Ministry of Defence of the United Kingdom (MOD). For the purpose of such transport UK Service personnel may be accompanied by personal baggage which does not exceed a gross weight of 120 pounds per man. The USN will give sympathetic consideration to requests for transportation of official UK Service visitors. The USN will, upon request, provide such supplies and services on an equivalent basis with USN personnel as may be required by UK Service personnel serving with the facility on Diego Garcia. When these supplies and services are peculiar to the UK Services the MOD will make them available to the USN at a place of places agreed to by the MOD and the USN at thetime.

PARAGRAPH 4

Finance—The financial arrangements have been laid down in paragraph 12 of the Diego Garcia Agreement 1976, which reads as follows:

"(a) The Government of the United States shall bear the cost of developing, operating and maintaining the facility. However, in relation to United Kingdom personnel attached to the facility, the Government of the United Kingdom shall be responsible for their pay, allowances and any other monetary gratuities, for the cost of their messing, and for supplies or services which are peculiar to or provided for the exclusive use of the United Kingdom Services or their personnel and which would not normally be provided by the Government of the United States for the use of its own personnel.

(b) Except in relation to the UK Service Personnel attached to the facility, logistic support furnished at Diego Garcia by either Government, upon request, to the other Government, shall be on a reimbursable basis in accordance with the laws, regulations and instructions of the Government furnishing the support."

PARAGRAPH 5

Radio Frequencies and Telecommunications—The following procedures for obtaining the prior concurrence of the Government of the United Kingdom to the use of any radio frequencies, powers and band widths for radio services (including radar) on Diego Garcia which are necessary for the operation of the facility, and for international notification, will be followed: a. Prior to the assignment, or modification of an assignment, of any radio frequency on Diego Garcia, concurrance for the same will be obtained from the United Kingdom through the established military co-ordination channel. This channel is between the Joint Frequency Panel (J/FP), USMCEB and the Defence Signal Staff, Signals 2 (DSS 2) Ministry of Defence, United Kingdom.

(b). Upon obtaining such concurrence the United Sates will transmit to the International Frequency Registration Board (IFRB) notification of the assignment in accordance with existing US/UK frequency co-ordination procedures.

PARAGRAPH 6.

Aids to Navigation and Approach Control—The United States may use and maintain existing electronic navigation and landing aids, such as airport surveillance radar, ground controlled approach (GCA), Tacan and instrument landing systems (ILS). If in the future it should be necessary to make significant changes to the present electronic navigation and landing aids or to expand them significantly, this may be done subject to agreement between the MOD and the USN.

PARAGRAPH 7.

Scientific Research—If the Government of the United Kingdom wishes to grant access to Diego Garcia to members of scientific parties wanting to carry out research on Diego Garcia and its environs written notice will be given to the United States Department of State or the US Embassy in London at least four weeks prior to the intended visit. This notice will contain the following information:

> a. identification of visiting party, including nationality and names of all members of the party;
> b. scientific purpose;
> c. date of arrival and expected duration;
> d. areas to be utilised
> e. activities to be conducted;
> f. equipment to be utilised;
> g. services requested from the facility.

Such notice and the response thereto will constitute the consultation referred to in sub-paragraph 3a of the Diego Garcia Agreement 1976. Scientific parties will, where necessary, be responsible for reimbursing the Government of the United States for any goods and services supplied to them by the USN.

PARAGRAPH 8

Local Administration—The following matters have been authorised by the Commissioner BIOT:

> a. *Drivers Licences*—United States or United Kingdom motor vehicle drivers licences will be accepted as valid for the operation of all motor vehicles on Diego Garcia.
> b. *Medical Services*—US medical personnel may perform medical services in Diego Garcia of the same type which such persons are authorised to perform at United States military medical facilities without prior examination or revalidation of their professional

certificate by the United Kingdom authorities, and such facilities will be made available to United Kingdom Service personnel. For the purposes of this paragraph, the term "US medical personnel" means the physicians, surgeons, specialists, dentists, nurses and other United States personnel in Diego Garcia who perform medical services, and other doctors of United States nationality or ordinarily resident in the United States employed or contracted in exceptional cases by the United States Forces.

c. *Recreational Fishing*—United States personnel and United Kingdom personnel are permitted reasonable recreational fishing on Diego Garcia and its environs without obtaining any licence or paying any fees. Such recreational fishing includes fishing from boats as well as from the shore.

PARAGRAPH 9

Alteration—These Supplementary Arrangements may be altered at any time by the mutual consent of the parties hereto.

PARAGRAPH 10

Interpretation—Unless the context otherwise requires, terms and expressions usedherein will have the meanings assigned to them in the Diego Garcia Agreement 1976. In the event of any conflict between the provisions of these Supplementary Arrangements and of the Diego Garcia Agreement 1976 the latter will prevail.

FOR THE ROYAL NAVY FOR THE UNITED STATES NAVY

/Signed/ /Signed/

R D LYGO   D H BAGLEY

VICE ADMIRAL   ADMIRAL

SIGNED IN DUPLICATE AT LONDON

THE TWENTYFIFTH DAY OF FEBRUARY 1976

RELATED NOTES

No.5

SIR:

I have the honor to refer to the Diego Garcia Agreement 1976, constituted by the Exchange of Notes of today's date between the Government of the United Kingdom of Great Britain and Northern Ireland and the Government of the United States of America, supplementing the British Indian Ocean Territory Agreement (BIOT Agreement), effected by an Exchange of Notes between the two Governments dated December 30, 1966.

In accordance with the recent discussions between representatives of our two Governments, I have the honor to inform you that the Government of the United States of America, subject to the availability of funds, plans to undertake the following additional construction on Diego Garcia for the United States Navy support facility to be developed there:

Item	Approximate Capacity or Size
Expanded dredging for fleet anchorage	4,000 acres
Fuel and general purpose pier	550 feet of berthing
Runway extension	4,000 linear feet
Aircraft parking apron	90,000 square yards
Hangar	18,000 square feet
Air operating building addition	2,900 square feet
Transit storage building	4,000 square feet
Aircraft arresting gear	———
Storage petroleum, oil and lubricants	640,000 barrels
Power plant expansion	2,400 kilowatts
Vehicle repair hardstand	1,200 square yards

Subsistence building addition	3,600 square feet
Cold storage addition	4,200 square feet
Armed forces radio and television station	1,200 square feet
General warehouse addition	13,200 square feet
Utilities	——
Ready issue ammunition magazine	2,000 square feet
Protective open storage area for munitions	6,000 square yards
Bachelor enlisted quarters	277 men
Bachelor officers quarters	32 men
Receiver building addition	1,300 square feet
Recreational facilities	(Scope to be determined)
Shed storage	7,100 square feet
Flammable storage	2,700 square feet
Navy exchange warehouse	5,400 square feet
Crash fire station	7,300 square feet
Structural fire station	3,000 square feet
Aircraft washrack	(Scope to be determined)
Aircraft ready issue refueler	(Scope to be determined)
Public works shops	16,600 square feet

The foregoing would be in addition to construction for the limited naval communications facility presently on Diego Garcia, regarding which information has previously been provided to United Kingdom authorities. In the event that further construction should be planned for the facility, it would, of course, be understood that such construction would be subject to the provisions of paragraph 2(b) of the BIOT Agreement as well as paragraph 1(a) or 1(b), as appropriate, of the Diego Garcia Agreement 1976.

Accept, sir, the renewed assurances of my highest regard.

RONALD I. SPIERS

The RT. HON. ROY HATTERSLEY, M.P.
   Minister of State for
      Foreign and Commonwealth Affairs
         Foreign and Commonwealth Office
            Downing Street,
               London, S.W.1
February 25, 1976

                              Foreign and Commonwealth Office
                              London SW1

                              25 February 1976

Sir,

I have the honour to acknowledge receipt of your letter of today's date concerning your Government's plans for construction in connection with the development of the present limited naval communication facility on Diego Garcia as a support facility of the United States Navy.

I note the additional construction planned by your Government and your statement concerning further construction. I confirm that your statement is in accordance with the understanding of my Government.

                  I have the honour to be with high consideration
                  Sir
                  Your obedient Servant
                  ROY HATTERSLEY

The Honourable Ronald I Spiers
Embassy of the United States of America
Grosvenor Square
London
W1A 1AH

Appendix 4

1976 DIEGO GARCIA AMENDED AGREEMENT
Copied from TIAS 8376; 27 UST 3448
UNITED KINGDOM OF GREAT BRITAIN AND
NORTHERN IRELAND
Availability of Certain Indian Ocean Islands
for Defense Purposes

Agreement amending the agreement of December 30, 1966.
Effected by exchange of note
Signed at London June 22 and 25, 1976;
Entered into force June 25, 1976;
Effective June 28, 1976.

The British Secretary of State for Foreign and Commonwealth
Affairs to the American Ambassador
FOREIGN AND COMMONWEALTH OFFICE
LONDON SW1A 1AH

No HKT 040/1   22 JUNE 1976
Her Excellency
The Honourable ANNE ARMSTRONG

YOUR EXCELLENCY
I have the honour to refer to recent discussions between representatives of the Government of the United Kingdom of Great Britain and

Northern Ireland and the Government of the United States of America concerning the Agreement constituted by the Exchange of Notes dated 30 December 1966[6] concerning the availability of the British Indian Ocean Territory islands for defence purposes (hereinafter referred to as "the Agreement") and to propose that the Agreement be amended by deleting the following words in the opening paragraph:", and the islands of Aldabra, Farquhar and Desroaches"

If the foregoing is acceptable to the Government of the United States of America, I have the honour to propose that this Note and Your Excellency's reply to that effect shall constitute an Agreement between the two Governments to amend the Agreement of 30 December 1966 with effect from 28 June 1976.

> I have the honour to be,
> with the highest consideration
> Your Excellency's obedient Servant,
> (for the Secretary of State)
> /Signed/
> (E N Larmour)

The American Ambassador to the British Secretary of State for
Foreign and Commonwealth Affairs
EMBASSY OF THE UNITED STATES OF AMERICA
LONDON
JUNE 25, 1976

DEAR SECRETARY:

I have the honor to acknowledge receipt of your Note no. HKT 040/1 of June 22 which reads as follows: "I have the honour to refer to recent

---

6. TIAS 6196; 18 UST 28

discussions between representatives of the Government of the United Kingdom of Great Britain and Northern Ireland and the Government of the United States of America concerning the Agreement constituted by the Exchange of Notes dated 30 December 1966 concerning the availability of the British Indian Ocean Territory islands for defence purposes (hereinafter referred to as "the Agreement") and to propose that the Agreement be amended by deleting the following words in the opening paragraph:—", and the islands of Aldabra, Farquhar and Desroaches" If the foregoing is acceptable to the Government of the United States of America, I have the honour to propose that this Note and Your Excellency's reply to that effect shall constitute an Agreement between the two Governments to amend the Agreement of 30 December 1966 with effect from 28 June 1976."

In reply I have the honor to inform you that the foregoing proposal is acceptable to the Government of the United States of America which therefore approves Your Excellency's suggestion that your Note and this reply shall constitute an Agreement between the two governments to amend the Agreement of 30 December 1966 with effect from 28 June 1976.

Accept, Sir, the assurances of my highest consideration.

ANNE ARMSTRONG

Rt. Hon. ANTHONY CROSLAND, MP
   Secretary of State for Foreign and
     Commonwealth Affairs
     Downing Street
     SW1

The American Ambassador to the British Secretary of State for
Foreign and Commonwealth Affairs
EMBASSY OF THE UNITED STATES OF AMERICA

LONDON
JUNE 25, 1976

DEAR SECRETARY:

I have the honor to refer to the Agreement between the United
Kingdom and Seychelles as of 29 June 1976 (Independence Day) which,
inter alia, makes provision for rights of access, entry, use and establishment on the part of states (referred to as "current users") which immediately before independence of Seychelles enjoyed rights of access,
entry, use or establishment with respect to Seychelles.

I am instructed by the Government of the United States, as one such
current user, to convey the acknowledgement of my Government of the
terms of the aforesaid Agreement, which make provision foror continue
rights of the United States.

Accept, Sir, the assurances of my highest consideration.

ANNE ARMSTRONG

Rt. Hon. ANTHONY CROSLAND, MP
Secretary of State for Foreign and
Commonwealth Affairs
Downing Street
SW1

Appendix 5

DIEGO GARCIA MILITARY CONSTRUCTION LEGISLATION
$ in Millions

FY	Requested From Congress			Enacted		
	Authorization	Appropriation	P.L.	Authorization	Appropriation	P.L.
1964	5.000 (N)	5.000		0.000	0.000	
1965	Navy PCP deferred because of gold flow considerations					
1967	Navy PCP deferred because diplomatic negotiations not concluded					
1968	Navy told to get British on board; cut estimate to $26 million					
1970	9.556 (N)	9.556	91-142	9.556	0.000	
1971		5.400 (N)	91-511	0.000	5.400	91-544
1972	4.794 (N)	8.950	92-145	4.794	8.950	92-160
1973	6.100 (N)	6.100	92-545	6.100	6.100	92-547
1974S	29.000 (N)	29.000	Deferred to FY 1975			
1975	3.300 (AF)	3.300	93-552	3.300	3.300*	93-636
	14.802 (N)	14.802	93-552	14.802	14.802*	93-636
1976	13.800 (N)	13.800	94-107	13.800	13.800	94-138
1978	7.300 (N)	7.300	95-82	7.300	7.300	95-101
1980	DecDef Contingency Auth.		96-125	8.600	8.600	
1980S	23.500 (N)	23.500			7.500	96-304
1981	17.977 (N)	17.977				
1981A	104.000 (N)	104.000	96-418	108.177	108.177	96-436
	23.700 (AF)	23.700	96-418	23.700	23.700	96-436

1982	80.130 (N)	80.130				
	78.794 (AF)	78.794				
1982A	122.750 (N)	122.750	97-99	122.750	122.750	97-106
	114.990 AF (AF)	114.990	97-99	114.990	114.990	97-106
1983	51.639 (N)	51.639	97-321	53.395	53.395	97-323
	36.550 (AF)	36.550	97-321	4.550	4.550	97-323
1984	34.500 (N)	34.500	98-115	31.800	31.800	98-116
	58.200 (AF)	58.200	98-115	58.200	58.200	98-116
1985	6.805 (N)	6.805	98-407	6.310	6.310	98-473
	16.100 (AF)	16.100	98-407	16.100	16.100	98-473
1986	42.680 (N)	42.680	99-167	42.680	42.680	99-173
	5.300 (AF)	5.300	99-167	5.300	5.300	99-173
1987	4.700 (AF)	4.700	99-661	4.700	4.700	

* Used available appropriations.

Appendix 6

OTHER INDIAN OCEAN/PERSIAN GULF MILITARY CON-
STRUCTION LEGISLATION
$ in Millions

	Requested From Congress		Enacted			
FY	Authorization	Appropriation	P.L	Auth.	Approp.	P.L.
1981	12.068 AF-Lajes	12.068	96-418	12.068	12.068	
1981A	21.361 A-Varlocs	21.361				
	35.000 N-Varlocs	35.000				
	27.800 AF-Lajes	27.800	96-418	20.000	20.000	
	85.700 AF-Oman	85.700				
	Special Cont. Fund		96-418	150.000	105.000	94-436
	AF-Oman			[85.500]	[85.500]	
	N-Kenya			[19.100]	[19.100]	
	N-Somalia			[.400]	[.400]	
1981S	N-Kenya	9.000		[9.000]	9.000	97-12
1982S	N-Kenya	26.500		[26.500]	26.500	97-106
1982	SecDef Cont.-Egypt			7.000	7.000	
	36.500 A-Egypt	36.500				
	73.000 AF-Egypt	73.000				
	17.600 N-Kenya	17.600				
	51.400 AF-Lajes	51.400				
	81.374 AF-Oman					

1982A	36.000 A-Egypt	36.000	97-99	36.000		
	70.400 AF-Egypt	70.400	97-99	70.400		
	26.000 N-Kenya	26.000	97-99	4.000	4.000	97-106
	49.570 AF-Lajes	49.570	97-99	46.570	46.570	97-106
	78.480 AF-Oman	78.480	97-99	78.480	78.480	97-106
	24.000 N-Somalia	24.000	97-99	24.000	24.000	97-106
1982S	(FY 1982) AF-Egypt	67.400				
	(FY 1982) A-Egypt	34.000				
1983	53.000 A-Egypt	53.000	97-321	50.400		
	125.600 AF-Egypt	125.600	97-321	121.700	91.000*	97-323
	15.000 AF-Egypt	15.000				
	SecDef Contingency			7.000	7.000	
	8.300 N-Kenya	8.300	97-321	8.300	8.300	97-323
	56.490 AF-Lajes	56.490				
	9.000 AF-Lajes	9.000				
	60.350 AF-Oman	60.350	97-321	60.350	60.350	97-323
	30.000 N-Somalia	30.000	97-321	30.000	30.000	97-323
	29.000 N-Cont	29.000				
1983S	(FY 1982) AF-Egypt	64.400				

| FY | Requested From Congress | | Enacted | | | |
	Authorization	Appropriat.	P.L.	Auth.	Approp	P.L.
1983S	(FY 1982) A-Egypt	34.000				
1984	Prior A-Egypt	41.000				
	Prior AF-Egypt	55.390				
	39.600 AF-Oman	39.600	98-115	28.600	28.600	98-116
	.900 N-Somalia	0.900				
	28.000 AF-Morocco	28.000	98-115	28.000	25.000	98-116
1984S	AF-Egypt	55.000			49.000	98-396
1985	42.000 AF-Oman	42.000	98-407	26.900	2.300	98.473
	62.000 A-Classified	62.000				
	2.050 AF-Morocco	5.050	98-407	2.050	5.050	98-473
	4.550 AF-Lajes	4.550	98-407	4.550	4.550	98-473
1986	39.935 AF-Portugal	39.935	99-167	39.935	19.650	99-173
	3.100 AF-Morocco	3.100	99-167	3.100	3.100	99-173
1987	2.550 N-Bahrain	2.550	99-661	2.550	2.550	
	25.400 AF-Morocco	25.400	99-661	25.400		
	6.900 AF-Oman	6.900	99-661	6.900		
	15.750 AF-Lajes	15.750	99-661	7.450		

* Rescinded

Endnotes

1. "Reminiscences of Admiral Roy L. Johnson," U.S. Naval Institute, p.336-7.

2. "U.S. Navy Seeking Indian Ocean Role," *New York Times*, 13 December 1963, p. 1.

3. Judith Miller, "U.S. Navy Still Pressing for Base in Indian Ocean," *Washington Post*, 19 May 1974, p. C2.

4. Senate Armed Services Committee Report, dated 21 October 1963, on the Fiscal Year 1964 Military Construction Authorization.

5. Robert H. Esterbrook, "U.S., Britain Consider Indian Ocean Bases," *Washington Post*, 29 August 1964, p. 1.

6. "Britain Buying Islands for Defense," *The Times*, 25 March 1967.

7. "Defence Minister Answers Plea to Save Atoll," The Times, 29 May 1967, p.5.

8. Ernest Weatherall, "Russia Seeks Bases For Indian Ocean Fleet," *The Sunday Star*, 5 April 1970, p. F14.

9. Robert C. Toth, "Indian Ocean Base Is Sought by U.S.," *Washington Post*, 20 November 1970.

10. Jim Hoagland, "Heath May Gain From New Indian Ocean Base," *Washington Post*, 17 December 1970, p. A15.

11. Judith Miller, "U.S. Navy Still Pressing For Base in Indian Ocean," *Washington Post*, 19 May 1974, p. C2.

12. Michael Getler, "Navy Extends Operations in Indian Ocean," *Washington Post*, 7 January 1972.

13. "U.S. Weighs Establishing Indian Ocean Naval Base," *New York Times*, 22 January 1974, p. 3.

14. Michael Getler and Dan Morgan, "U.S. Wants Indian Ocean Island Base," *Washington Post*, 26 January 1974.

15. Section 612 of Public Law 89-568, The Fiscal Year 1967 Military Construction Authorization Act, requires that the Secretary of Defense describe and report to the Armed Services Committees on certain public works projects for advanced planning, construction design and architectural services.

16. Congress, House, Armed Services Committee Hearings on Military Posture, Report No 93-43, p. 1071.

17. Michael Getler, "Indian Ocean Base Seen Unaffected," *Washington Post*, 7 March 1974, p. A2.

18. Congress, House, Armed Services Committee Report No. 93-40.

19. Martin Linton, "Diego Garcia—Crisis Isle," *Labor Weekly*, 22 March 1974.

20. Congress, House, Report No. 93-977 on the Second Supplemental Appropriations Bill, 1974, 4 April 1974.

21. Congress, Senate, Report No. 93-781.

22. Congress, Senate, Senator Symington on request for funds to expand U.S. facilities at Diego Garcia, *Congressional Record*, 1 August 1974, p. S 14092.

23. Congress, House, Committee on Appropriations Report No.93-1477 on the Military Construction Appropriation Bill 1975, 9 November 1974, pp. 16, 19.

24. "Indian Ocean Move, Moynihan Hits U.S. Base Policy, "*Washington Star-News*, 7 January 1975, p. D-Back page.

25. Jeremiah O'Leary, "U.S. Carrier Is Aiding In Mauritius Disaster," *Washington Star-News*, 12 February 1975.

26. "U.S. Warns of Soviet Missile Buildup Off IndianOcean," *Washington Star*, 11 June 1975, Section H.

27. Robert J. McCloskey, Assistant Secretary for Congressional Relations of the Department of State, in a letter dated 17 July 1975, to Senator Dewey F. Bartlett, wrote, "Before certifying to Congress that the expansion of facilities on Diego Garcia was essential to the national interest, the Administration re-evaluated the military and foreign policy implications of the Diego Garcia proposal, including the matter of arms limitations talks with the Soviet Union. On the basis of that review, it was decided not to approach the Soviets at this time."

28. According to a Brookings Institute report, the eventual deployment of an aircraft carrier task force in the Indian Ocean would cost between $5 billion and $8 billion in new ship construction. In addition, taxpayers would be saddled for years to come with an annual increase in Navy operating costs of $800 million.

29. David B. Ottaway, "Islanders Were Evicted for U.S. Base," *Washington Post*, 9 September 1975, p. A1.

30. *Washington Star*, 7 November 1975.

31. Congress, Conference Report on H.R. 10029, Military Construction Appropriations, 1976, 10 September 1975.

32. General Accounting Office Report B-184915, Financial and Legal Aspects of the Agreement on the Availability of Certain Indian Ocean Islands for Defense Purposes, 7 January 1976.

33. Department of State, "Availability of Certain Indian Ocean Islands for Defense Purposes," 25 June 1976, TIAS 8376, United States International Agreements, 27 UST 3448.

34. Department of State, "Tracking Station: Mahe Island," 29 June 1976, TIAS 8385, United States and Other International Agreements, 27 UST 3709.

35. See Section 112, Public Law 94-138, 28 November 1975.

36. Spencer Rich, "Ford Administration Role On Diego Garcia Is Assailed," *Washington Post*, 7 May 1976, p. A2.

37. "Twenty Soviet Ships Sighted On Indian Ocean Last June," *Washington Post*, 9 September 1976, p. A30.

38. *Congressional Record*, p. H 10991, 12 November 1975.

39. Henry S. Bradsher, "Indian Ocean: Can Militarization Be Reversed?", *Washington Star*, p. A3. 17 March 1977.

40. Henry S. Brasher, "Indian Ocean Fuel Stop Requested, "*Washington Star*, 2 April 1977, p. 8.

41. Lewis M. Simons, "Life Is 'Austere' for Sailors on Strategic Diego Garcia," *Washington Post*, 7 April 1977, p. A14.

42. "Diego Garcia Base Backed," *New York Times*, 14 April 1977, p. 6.

43. "Missile Cruiser, 3 Other U.S. Ships Enter Indian Ocean," *Washington Star*, 25 May 1977.

44. "Snag in the Indian Ocean Talks," *Washington Post*, 22 December 1977.

45. Captain James F. Kelly, Jr., "Naval Deployments in the Indian Ocean," *U.S. Naval Institute Proceedings*, May 1983, p. 179.

46. Don Oberdorfer, "The Evolution Of a Decision," *Washington Post*, 24 January 1980, p. A1.

47. "Use of 3 Gulf-Area Bases OKd," *Washington Star*, 12 February 1980.

48. George C. Wilson, "Marines to Form Rapid Reaction Force," *Washington Post*, 6 December 1979, p. A15.

49. Michael Getler, "U.S. Would Link Aid to Access to Bases," *Washington Post*, 28 February 1980, p. A24.

50. Department of State, TIAS 9791, United States Treaties and Other International Agreements, 32 UST.

51. Congress, Committee on Foreign Affairs Report, "United States Security Interests in the Persian Gulf," 16 March 1981".

52. Stuart Auerbach, "Brezhnev Urges Ban on Foreign Troops in Gulf," *Washington Post*, 11 December 1980, p. A1.

53. "Egypt Offers Bases For Limited U.S. Use," *Washington Post*, 8 January 1980, p. A14.

54. Denis Taylor, "Diego Garcia rejects cash offer by Britain", *The Times*, 3 July 1981, p. 6.

55. Congress, "Staff Report, U.S. Security Interests in the Persian Gulf," dated 16 March 1981.

56. General Accounting Office Report B-209865, "Further Improvements Needed in Navy's Oversight and Management Of Contracting For Facilities Construction On Diego Garcia," 23 May 1984.

57. Ian Jack, "The rising cry of the Noisy Ones", *The Times*, 1 May 1983, p. 8.

58. Walter Pincus and Fred Hiatt, "U.S. Has a Secret Base With 100 Men in Egypt", *Washington Post*, 23 June 1983, p. A2.

59. Mary Anne Weaver, "Britain and the Palestinians of the Indian Ocean", *The Times*, 13 March 1983, p. 22.

60. Simon Winchester, "Secret Voyage to the Footprint of Freedom", *The Sunday Times*, 2 September 1984, p. 10.

Annotated Bibliography

I participated in the planning of facilities for Diego Garcia within the Department of Defense and in classified presentations to congressional committees during the annual budget process. Some U.S. Government documents remain classified. All the references in this history were unclassified and are available for inspection. The primary sources for documents concerning the development of Diego Garcia into a United States military base are:

- Transcripts of the hearings before the House and Senate Armed Services and Appropriations Committee during the annual budget review process.

- Reports from the General Accounting Office.

- Interviews with Ambassador Robert W. Komer, Admiral Thomas H. Moorer, Stuart B. Barber, and Francis D. McGuire.

- Many articles from periodicals and the press.

- Photography from the Still Media Records Center in Washington, D.C.

Index

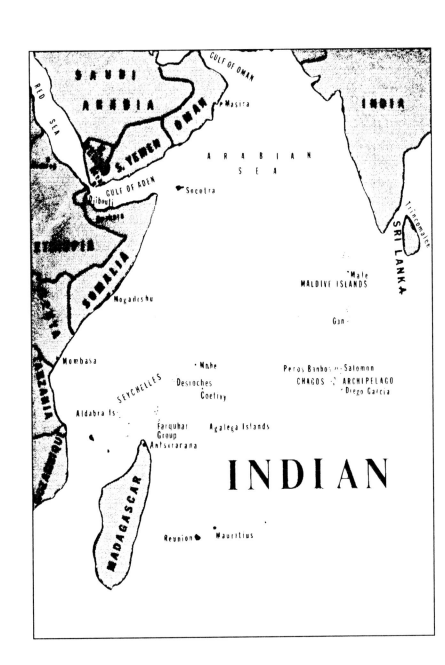

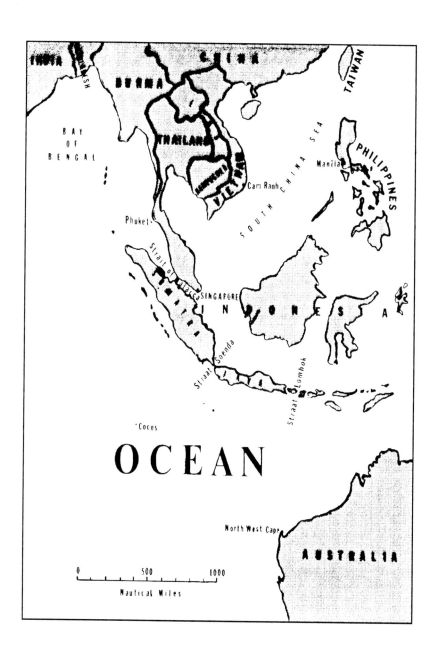

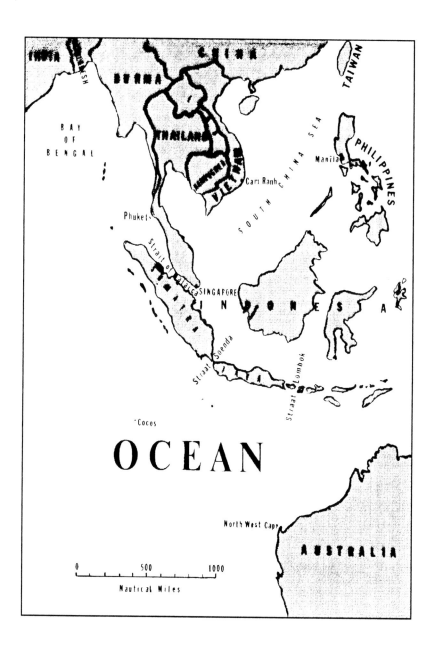

Printed in the United States
6844